The Making of Modern Intellectual Property Law

The British Experience, 1760–1911

One of the common themes in recent public debate has been the law's inability to accommodate the new ways of creating, distributing and replicating intellectual products that have developed in recent years. In this book the authors argue that in order to understand many of the problems currently confronting the law, it is necessary to understand its past.

Drawing on extensive archival research, Sherman and Bently provide a detailed account of the emergence of modern British intellectual property law. In doing so they explore two related themes. First, they explain why intellectual property law came to take its now familiar shape with sub-categories of patents, copyright, designs and trade marks. Arguing against those who see intellectual property law as occupying its natural position or as being shaped by some higher philosophical principles, the work sets out to show the complex and contingent nature of this area of law.

Secondly, as well as charting this emergence of intellectual property law as a discrete area of legal doctrine, the authors also set out to explain how it is that the law grants property status to intangibles and describe the ensuing problems. This work goes on to explore the rise and fall of creativity as an organising concept in intellectual property law, the creative nature of intellectual property law and the important role that the registration process plays in shaping intangible property.

BRAD SHERMAN, Law Department, Griffith University, Brisbane
LIONEL BENTLY, School of Law, King's College London

Cambridge Studies in Intellectual Property Rights

As its economic potential has rapidly expanded, intellectual property has become a subject of front rank legal importance. *Cambridge Studies in Intellectual Property Rights* is a series of monograph studies of major current issues in intellectual property. Each volume will contain a mixture of international, European, comparative and national law, making this a highly significant series for practitioners, judges and academic researchers in many countries.

Series Editor
Professor W. R. Cornish, University of Cambridge

Advisory Editors
Professor François Dessemontet, University of Lausanne
Professor Paul Goldstein, Stanford University
The Hon. Sir Robin Jacob, The High Court, England and Wales

The Making of Modern Intellectual Property Law

The British Experience, 1760–1911

Brad Sherman and Lionel Bently

CAMBRIDGE
UNIVERSITY PRESS

PUBLISHED BY THE PRESS SYNDICATE OF THE UNIVERSITY OF CAMBRIDGE
The Pitt Building, Trumpington Street, Cambridge, United Kingdom

CAMBRIDGE UNIVERSITY PRESS
The Edinburgh Building, Cambridge CB2 2RU, UK
40 West 20th Street, New York, NY 10011–4211, USA
477 Williamstown Road, Port Melbourne, VIC 3207, Australia
Ruiz de Alarcón 13, 28014 Madrid, Spain
Dock House, The Waterfront, Cape Town 8001, South Africa

http://www.cambridge.org

First published 1999
Reprinted 2000, 2002

Typeset in Plantin 10/12pt   [CE]

A catalogue record for this book is available from the British Library

ISBN 0 521 56363 1 hardback

Transferred to digital printing 2004

Contents

viii   Contents

Acknowledgments

In writing this book we received help from a number of people. We would like to thank in particular David Althus, Kier Ashton, Cate Banks, Robert Burrell, Jeremy Hopgood, and Katie O'Rourke for help with the research; Robert Burrell, Bill Cornish, Shaun McVeigh, Alain Pottage, Alain Strowel, Julian Thomas, Adam Tomkins, and Leanne Wiseman for reading and commenting on drafts; Virginia Catmur of Cambridge University Press for copy-editing the typescript; and King's College Research Strategy Fund and the Institute of Advanced Legal Studies External Research Fund for financial support.

Abbreviations

AC	*Law Reports: Appeal Cases*
All ER	*All England Law Reports*
Amb	*Ambler's Chancery Reports*
App Cas	*Law Reports: Appeal Cases*
Atk	*Atkyns' Chancery Reports*
Black W	*Sir William Blackstone's King's Bench Reports*
Bro PC	*Brown's Parliamentary Cases*
BT	Board of Trade
Bull NP	*Buller's Law of Nisi Prius*
Burr	Burrow's King's Bench Reports
CA	Court of Appeal
Carp Pat Cas	*Carpmael's Patent Cases*
CCD Mass	Circuit Court, District of Massachussetts
Ch	*Law Reports: Chancery*
Ch App	*Law Reports: Chancery Appeals*
Ch D	*Law Reports: Chancery Division*
Chit	*Chitty's King's Bench Reports*
CJ	*Commons Journal*
Co Rep	*Coke's King's Bench Reports*
Cowp	*Cowper's King's Bench Reports*
CPC	*Cooper's Chancery Patent Cases*
Dav Pat Cas	*Davies' Patent Cases*
De G J and S	*De Gex, Jones and Smith's Chancery Reports*
Eden	*Eden's Chancery Reports*
EIPR	*European Intellectual Property Review*
ER	*English Reports*
F	*Federal Reporter (US)*
F Cas	*Federal Cases*
FO	Foreign Office
FSR	*Fleet Street Intellectual Property Reports*
GATT	General Agreement on Tariffs and Trade
Giff	*Giffard's Chancery Reports*

HBL	*H. Blackstone's Common Pleas Reports*
HL	House of Lords
HLC	*House of Lords Cases*
HLJ	*House of Lords Journal*
HMSO	Her Majesty's Stationery Office
Holt	*Holt's King Bench Reports*
HPC	*Hayward's Patent Cases*
IIC	*International Review of Industrial Property and Copyright Law*
IPJ	*Intellectual Property Journal*
JPTOS	*Journal of the Patent and Trademark Office Society*
Jur Ns	*Jurist Reports, New Series*
K & J	*Kay and Johnson's Vice Chancellor's Reports*
LJ Ch	*Law Journal: Chancery*
LJCP	*Law Journal: Common Pleas*
LJJ	Lord Justices of Appeal
LQR	*Law Quarterly Review*
LR	*Law Reports*
LR Ch D	*Law Reports: Chancery Division*
LT	*Law Times*
LT NS	*Law Times (New Series)*
M & W	*Meeson and Welsby's Exchequer Reports*
Man & G	*Manning and Granger's Common Plea Reports*
Mer	*Merivale's Chancery Reports*
Mor Dict	*Morison's Dictionary of Decisions*
My & Cr	*Mylne and Craig's Chancery Reports*
New Rep	*New Reports*
Noy	*Noy's King Bench Reports*
PP	*Parliamentary Papers*
QB	*Law Reports: Queen's Bench Division*
RIDA	*Revue Internationale du Droit de l'Auteur*
RPC	*Report of Patent Cases*
Russ & M	*Russell and Mylne's Chancery Reports*
S Ct	*Supreme Court*
Salk	*Salkeld's King's Bench Reports*
Scott NR	*Scott's New Common Pleas Reports*
Sim	*Simons' Vice Chancellor's Reports*
Stark	*Starkie's Nisi Prius Reports*
Swans	*Swanston's Chancery Reports*
Taunt	*Taunton's Common Pleas*
TNAPSS	*Transactions of the National Association for the Promotion of Social Science*

TR	*Term Reports*
TRIPS	Agreement on Trade-Related Aspects of Intellectual Property Rights Including Trade in Counterfeit Goods
Web Pat Cas	*Webster's Patent Cases*
WLR	*Weekly Law Reports*
WR	*Weekly Reporter*
Y & CC	*Younge and Collyer's Chancery Cases*

Table of statutes and bills

Abbreviated titles and Command Paper numbers, where appropriate, are given in parentheses.

Table of cases

In footnotes to the text, cases are cited only by their ER references, where these exist. Details of other reports are given below.

Introduction

It seems, yet again, that intellectual property law is at a crisis point. Besieged by the creations and practices of the digital revolution, unsettled by the ethical dilemmas thrown up by the patenting of genetically modified plants and animals, and about to be caught out by organic computing, it seems, at least in the eyes of some, that contemporary intellectual property law faces a number of challenges that it is simply not equipped to deal with. While in many ways this can be seen as continuing the pathological concern with change that has long dominated legal analysis in this area, these arguments differ in that they are often premised on a belief that recent changes have created a series of problems for the law that are not only unique but also unanswerable. Within this general framework, there is also a sense in which the past is increasingly seen as being irrelevant, and that while the legal concepts, ideas and institutions that make up intellectual property law may once have been appropriate, they are now outdated and obsolete. John Perry Barlow, the American cyberspace activist, captured the tone of this style of argument when in speaking of what he regards as the 'immense conundrum' created by digitised property he said, '[i]ntellectual property law cannot be patched, retrofitted, or expanded to contain the gasses of digitized expression . . . We will need to develop an entirely new set of methods as befits this entirely new set of circumstances.'[1] In part this book is written against this way of thinking. More specifically, working from the basis that the past and the present are intimately linked, we believe that many aspects of modern intellectual property law can only be understood through the lens of the past. Moreover, while the law's confrontation with digitised property and recombinant DNA has created a number of real difficulties for it, much of what is taken as

---

[1] J. Barlow, 'Selling Wine without Bottles: The Economy of Mind on the Global Net' in (ed.) P. Ludlow, *High Noon on the Electronic Frontier: Conceptual Issues in Cyberspace* (Cambridge, Mass.: MIT Press, 1996), 10. He adds, the 'lawyers are proceeding as though the old laws can be somehow made to work, either by grotesque expansion or by force. They are wrong': *ibid.*

unique and novel about the interaction of intellectual property law and the new environment in which it finds itself can, especially when placed in an historical context, be seen as examples of the law working through an on-going series of problems that it has grappled with for many years. No matter how attractive the emancipatory appeal of a digitised, organic future may be, because the concepts which are under dispute and the language within which these arguments are posed are mediated by the past, even the most radical of accounts remain indebted to the tradition from which they are trying to escape. Paradoxically, the more the past is neglected, the more control it is able to wield over the future.

While thinking about intellectual property law in these terms opens up a number of possibilities, we have restricted ourselves to the exploration of two interrelated themes. The first concerns the nature of intangible property in law. More specifically we have concentrated on the problems which have confronted the law in granting property status to intangibles and, in turn, to the various techniques that the law has employed in its attempts to resolve these problems. Secondly, our aim has been to explain why it was that intellectual property law came to take on its now familiar form. In exploring these two themes we have largely limited ourselves to British law over the period from 1760 through to 1911: 1760 marking the height of the literary property debate; and 1911 the year in which copyright law in the United Kingdom was codified.

Before discussing these themes in more detail, a number of preliminary points need to be borne in mind. The first is that our overriding concern is with intellectual property *law*. Unlike many of the historical works in this area which are concerned with the relationship between intellectual property and other domains, such as the impact of patent law on the development of technology or the relationship between literary property and authorship, our primary focus is with intellectual property law. This should not be taken as if we are suggesting that the environment in which the law operates is not important or that we believe that legal judgment should be prioritised over other forms of law. Rather, it is to stress that our primary interest lies in what could be called the *doctrine* of intellectual property law, rather than in what, for example, economists or political philosophers may be able to tell us about intellectual property law.

The second point which needs to be made is that our arguments are based on a belief that during the middle period of the nineteenth century an important transformation took place in the law which granted property rights in mental labour (to use the language then employed to describe what we now call intellectual property law). More specifically we argue that while gradual, haphazard and in some ways still incomplete, by the 1850s or thereabouts modern intellectual property law had emerged as a separate and distinct area of law replete with its own logic and grammar. In order to highlight this transformation, we found it necessary to draw a distinction between what we have called 'pre-modern' and 'modern' intellectual property law. While we appreciate that this distinction is somewhat artificial, nonetheless we believe that it offers a useful basis from which to explore and understand intellectual property law. In so doing, we are not suggesting that modern law is in any sense better than pre-modern law nor that traces of pre-modern law cannot be found in present-day law. Nor are we suggesting that at some particular time during the nineteenth century there was a sudden and irreversible change that neatly marked the move from one period to the other. Rather, we have used these concepts as a way of describing what in many ways amount to very different ways of thinking about and dealing with intangible property. Given the important position that the concepts of pre-modern and modern law play in this work, it may be helpful at the outset to outline what we have taken to be some of the defining characteristics of each of these historical periods.

One of the most important points of contrast between modern and pre-modern law is in terms of the way the law is organised. While today the shape of the law is almost universally taken as a given – the general category of intellectual property law being divided into subsidiary categories of patents, designs, trade marks, copyright and related rights – under pre-modern law there was no clear consensus as to how the law ought to be arranged: no one way of thinking had yet come to dominate as *the* mode of organisation. Rather, there was a range of competing and, to our modern eyes, alien forms of organisation. It is also clear that, at least up until the 1850s, there was no law of copyright, patents, designs or trade marks, and certainly no intellectual property law. At best there was agreement that the law recognised and granted property rights in mental labour, although the nature of this legal category itself was uncertain.

Modern law also differs from pre-modern law in terms of the particular *form* that it took. More specifically, pre-modern law, which provided protection for things such as the printing of designs on calicos, muslins and linens, was subject specific and reactive. That is, it tended to respond to particular problems as and when they were presented to the law. In contrast, modern intellectual property law tends to be more abstract and forward looking. In particular, while the shape of pre-modern law was largely determined passively in response to the environment in which the law operated, in drafting modern legislation the law was not only concerned with the objects it was regulating, it was also interested in the shape that the law *itself* took when performing these tasks.

Another point of difference between the two regimes is in terms of the subject matter protected and the approach adopted by the law towards that subject matter. One of the notable features of pre-modern law was that it was concerned with the mental or creative labour that was embodied in the protected subject matter. Moreover, in so far as it influenced the shape that intellectual property law ultimately took and the way the duration and scope of the respective legal rights were determined, mental labour played a pivotal role in many aspects of intellectual property law. Despite the prominent role that creative labour played in pre-modern intellectual property law, as the law took on its modern guise it shifted its attention away from the labour that was embodied in the protected subject matter to concentrate more on the object in its own right. That is, instead of focusing, for example, on the labour that was embodied in a book, on what was considered to be the essence of the intangible property, modern intellectual property law was more concerned with the object as a closed and unitary entity; with the impact that the book had on the reading public, the economy and so on. This closure of intangible property was mirrored in the changes that took place in terms of the approach the law adopted when dealing with the protected subject matter. While pre-modern law utilised the language, concepts and questions of classical jurisprudence, modern intellectual property law employed the resources of political economy and utilitarianism. More specifically, while pre-modern law was characterised by self-styled metaphysical discussions about the nature of intangible property – such as how the essence of the protected subject matter was to be identified – with the closure of intangible property, modern intellectual property law abrogated all interest in this way of thinking about and dealing with the subject matter it protected.

Yet another important point which distinguishes the modern law from its pre-modern counterpart relates to the role that registration played in both regimes. While the registration of intangible property has long existed in intellectual property law, nonetheless there are important differences between the regimes used in pre-modern and modern law, notably in terms of the functions that it performed. In particular, while under pre-modern law proof was generally a matter of private control, in its modern guise, proof and the regulation of memory more generally became a matter of public concern. In addition, while in both its pre-modern and modern form registration played an important role in identifying intangible property, under the modern law, which increasingly relied upon a representation of the protected subject matter rather than on the object itself, registration took on another important role: namely that of managing and demarcating the limits of intangible property.

The problems with intangible property

Despite the central role played by the subject matter of intellectual property law, what we have tended to refer to as intangible property, there has been remarkably little attention given to this topic. One of the interesting points that emerged from our exploration of modern intellectual property law was the prominent role that intangible property played in a variety of domains. As well as highlighting the impact that the intangible had on intellectual property law, we have also given particular attention to the way in which the law grants property status to intangibles and to the problems that this generated. We begin our analysis of intangible property by focusing on the debate which took place in Britain in the middle part of the eighteenth century as to the status of perpetual common law literary property. Starting with the distinction which was drawn between labour of the mind and that of the body, we outline the problems that were identified by the opponents of literary property in the law granting property status to intangibles as well as some of the solutions proposed by the supporters of perpetual literary property. While by the end of the literary property debate the law felt comfortable, in a way it had never done before, in granting property status to intangibles, nonetheless problems of the type identified by the opponents of literary property continue to confront the law. Indeed many of the problems that Barlow identifies in relation to digitised property, which are very similar to those raised in relation to literary property in the eighteenth century, can be seen as forming part of a long process where the law has attempted to grant property status to intangibles.

While many of the problems that confront the law in its efforts to grant property status to intangibles are perennial, this is not to suggest that they have not changed over time nor that the way in which the law has responded has remained the same. It is noteworthy that the centralised publicly funded systems of registration that took shape under nineteenth-century intellectual property law became an important forum in which many of the problems generated by intangible property were played out. In particular, in so far as systems of registration required applicants to deposit representations of their creations rather than the creations themselves (as had often been the case previously), the task of identifying the owner and the boundaries of the property were resolved bureaucratically. Importantly these changes, which reinforced the closure of the property and the suppression of creativity in law, enabled the law to avoid the difficult task of having to identify the essence of the protected property.

The form of the law

As well as exploring the nature of intangible property in law, we also set out to explain the shape of intellectual property law as a legal category. In so doing we hoped to provide answers to the question: why was it that the law which granted property rights in mental labour came to be divided up into the now familiar categories of patents, copyright, designs and trade marks?

As we set out to explain the shape of intellectual property law, we argue against those who present intellectual property law as if it were a timeless entity that has always existed, albeit in a nascent and emerging form. Indeed we suggest that modern intellectual property law did not emerge as a discrete and separate area of law until the 1850s or thereabouts. Prior to this, the law was not only disorganised, open and fluid, there were also numerous competing ways in which the law which granted property rights in mental labour was organised. As such, there were many potential directions that the law could have taken. While the organisational structure of pre-modern law was characterised by its fluidity and uncertainty, by the 1850s or thereabouts the now familiar mode of categorisation had all but come to be accepted, in effect, as the only possible way in which the law could be organised.

In explaining the shape of intellectual property law, we have also argued against those who see the law as reflecting some natural ordering or as having adopted its proper philosophical position. More specifically our aim in writing this book has been to disentangle the conditions of intellectual property law's history, to de-naturalise it and to show that what are often taken as givens or as constructs of nature are, in fact, the products of a complex and changing set of circumstances, practices and habits.[2] We also hope to show that as a juridical category, intellectual property cannot be identified as a purposive technique governed by a teleology of function, principle or norm; nor can it, except at the most banal and trite level, be explained in terms of economic arguments, author's rights personality theory, or in terms of natural or positive law. We also hope to resist the endless temptation to mystify the story of law.

---

[2] As Barthes, said there is 'nothing natural anywhere, nothing but the historical' anywhere: R. Barthes, *Roland Barthes* (tr. R. Howard) (London: Macmillan, 1977), 139.

In this version of events, the philosophers, the International Conventions, the principles of law, as well as natural-law arguments are displaced from the centre of the narrative. Instead they are placed alongside things such as the act of negotiating bilateral treaties, the formation and exercise of rules designed to regulate the way patent specifications were drafted, and the stories intellectual property law tells about itself, to form an alloy of factors that go to explain the shape of intellectual property law.

Part 1

Towards a property in intangibles

We begin our exploration of intellectual property law with the debate over literary property that took place in Britain in the second half of the eighteenth century. This debate, which was 'costly, prodigious and protracted' and which was 'discussed everywhere and by everybody',[1] turned on the status and nature of common law literary property. More specifically, the debate was prompted by the fact that the Stationers' Company, whose power and control over the publication of books was being undermined, argued that, whatever the Statutes of the day may have said, at common law authors (and their assigns) enjoyed perpetual rights over their creations. While for some, such as Bentham, the discussions that this prompted were akin to an 'assembly of blind men disputing about colours',[2] we believe that they provide us with a unique opportunity to understand both the categorisation of intellectual property law as well as the way in which the law granted property status to intangibles.

While modern intellectual property law did not emerge as a separate and distinct area of law until midway through the nineteenth century, the literary property debate, or at least aspects thereof, can be seen as the law struggling with the conflicting demands of pre-modern and modern intellectual property law. More specifically it became apparent during the course of the debate that the law believed that mental labour, which was to be the exclusive and unifying concern of intellectual property law, was fundamentally different from manual labour. At the same time as the law came to privilege the creative labour of the mind

---

[1] See A. Birrell, *Seven Essays on the Law and History of Copyright in Books* (London: Cassel and Co., 1899), 121. It also 'exercised the talents of some of the our ablest advocates': *A Vindication of the Exclusive Rights of Authors to their own Works: A Subject now under Consideration before the Twelve Judges of England* (London: Griffiths, 1762), 1.

[2] 'The case of literary property, so thoroughly agitated not many years ago in Westminster Hall, presented a curious spectacle: multitudes of advocates and all the judges in and out of office talking about property in general, not one of them knowing what it was, nor how it was created; it was an assembly of blind men disputing about colours': J. Bentham, *Manual of Political Economy* (ed.) W. Stark (London: Allen and Unwin, 1952), 265 note.

over that of the body, we also see what in many ways was the first attempt to rationalise and order the various areas of law which granted property rights in relation to mental labour. Although the primary mode of reasoning was one of analogy between the subject-specific property rights that existed at the time, nonetheless this was the first occasion in which the shape of the law was openly and consciously discussed. In the first part of chapter 1 we utilise these arguments to explore the categories that were employed in pre-modern intellectual property law. In the second half of the chapter, we turn to focus on the question of the property status of the intangible in law. More specifically, we explore what the opponents of perpetual common law literary property considered to be fundamental and in many ways insurmountable problems that the law faced in granting property status to intangibles. There is a sense in which the proponents of literary property offered a number of plausible solutions to these objections, but we argue in chapter 2 that problems of the type that were discussed in the literary property debate remain a continuing issue for intellectual property law. While the nature of these questions changed over time (notably with the introduction of modern systems of registration) and differed according to the subject matter in question, nonetheless we suggest that they highlight the mentality of intangible property.

1   Property in mental labour

In February 1774, the House of Lords was called upon to determine whether in producing an unauthorised publication of Thompson's poem *The Seasons*, the Scottish bookseller, Alexander Donaldson, had infringed any rights that might have existed in the work. In deciding that Donaldson was free to publish *The Seasons*, the House of Lords not only found against perpetual common law literary property, it also effectively marked the end of the literary property debate. This was the dispute which was conducted in the tracts, pamphlets and newspapers of the day as well as in the English and Scottish courts, concerning the status of common law literary property.

The main impetus for the literary property debate arose from changes which took place at the end of the seventeenth century in the way the book trade was regulated.[1] Prior to this, the production and distribution of books had been regulated by way of controls exercised over printing presses and the types of works that were published.[2] Under this regime, which was designed to prevent the circulation of seditious, heretical, obscene and blasphemous materials, the Stationers' Company acquired a general monopoly over printing as well as over the printing of specific books. One of the consequences of the way these rights were allocated was that individual printers acquired what was in effect a perpetual monopoly over the publication of particular works.[3] With the lapse of

---

[1] See C. Blagden, *The Stationers' Company: A History, 1403-1959* (London: Allen and Unwin, 1960); J. Feather, *A History of British Publishing* (London: Croom Helm, 1988); L. Patterson, *Copyright in Historical Perspective* (Nashville, Tenn.: Vanderbilt University Press, 1968); M. Rose, *Authors and Owners: The Invention of Copyright* (Cambridge, Mass.: Harvard University Press, 1993), 9–30.

[2] See, e.g., An Act for Preventing the Frequent Abuses in Printing Seditious Treasonable and Unlicensed Bookes and Pamphlets and for Regulating of Printing and Printing Presses 13 & 14 Car. II c. 33 (1662).

[3] The Stationers' Charter (received from Mary in 1557) provided that no one in the realm should exercise the art of printing unless they were a freeman of the company or had been granted Royal permission. Significantly, the Ordinances made it an offence for stationers to put out a book before they had shown it to the wardens and entered it on a register.

the Licensing Acts in 1695, however, the Stationers began to lose the control that they had long exercised over the book trade. In response to this, they began a campaign to have their monopoly powers restored. After initial attempts to persuade Parliament to reinstate the Licensing Acts failed, the Stationers ultimately convinced the legislature to introduce the Act for the Encouragement of Learning, commonly known as the Statute of Anne (1710).[4] This provided authors and proprietors of 'copies' (or manuscripts) with the right to print and reprint copies of their works. In so far as the booksellers were able to convince authors to assign their rights to them, this had the effect of providing booksellers with an opportunity to reclaim some of the control they had previously exercised over the book trade. However successful this may have been, it provided the Stationers with a much more restricted form of control than they had been used to. In particular the right to print and reprint books which was recognised in the 1710 Statute of Anne only lasted for a limited period of time (fourteen years if the book was new; a further fourteen years if the author was alive at the end of that period; and twenty years for 'old books'). This meant that by the 1730s statutory rights over formerly profitable works had begun to lapse. Confronted with this situation, the Stationers began further action to restore the control they had once exercised over the book trade. Having failed to convince Parliament to extend the length of protection in 1735,[5] the Stationers began to argue that while the rights which had been granted under the Statute of Anne expired fourteen (or twenty-eight years) after registration, these rights merely supplemented the pre-existing, perpetual rights of authors which existed at common law. By acting as if these common law rights existed (the Stationers did this by continuing to assign rights in literary property after the statutory period had expired and by bringing actions in Chancery to enforce the supposed right),[6] the issue which they had raised began to be publicly debated.[7]

---

[4] An Act for the Encouragement of Learning 8 Anne c. 19 (1710).
[5] L. Patterson, *Copyright in Historical Perspective* (1968), 154 ff.
[6] On unpublished works see, e.g., *Webb v Rose* (1732) cited 96 ER 184; *Pope v Curl* (1741) 26 ER 608; *Queensberry v Shebbeare* (1758) 28 ER 924; *Eyre v Walker* (1735) cited 98 ER 213; *Walthoe v Walker* (1736) cited 96 ER 184; *Tonson v Walker* (1739) cited 96 ER 184; and *Tonson v Walker* (No. 2) (1752) 36 ER 1017.
[7] For a selection from the many accounts see H. Abrams, 'The Historic Foundation of American Copyright Law: Exploding the Myth of Common Law Copyright' (1983) 29 *Wayne Law Review* 1120; M. Rose, 'The Author as Proprietor: *Donaldson v Becket* and the Genealogy of Modern Authorship' in (eds.) B. Sherman and A. Strowel, *Of Authors and Origins: Essays on Copyright Law* (Oxford: Clarendon Press, 1994); T. Ross, 'Copyright and the Invention of Tradition' (1992) 26 *Eighteenth Century Studies* 1; J. Feather, *A History of British Publishing* (1988); L. Patterson, *Copyright in Historical Perspective* (1968); D. Saunders, *Authorship and Copyright* (London: Routledge, 1992).

The debate generated a large body of literature both in support of and against the legal recognition of perpetual common law literary property. In this debate a wide range of issues were discussed: from the metaphysical status of property and the differences between property in books and property in machines through to the relationship between Scottish and English common law and between statute and common law more generally. While a number of different questions arose in the course of these discussions, the central question in issue was whether authors, and through them booksellers, had a perpetual common law copy-right in their works or whether their rights were confined to the statutory period provided under the Statute of Anne.

At the same time as the status of common law copy-right was being discussed in the literature of the day, the courts were also called upon to consider the matter. Initially, a number of injunctions were granted by judges in Chancery which supported the common law right.[8] Given the separation between the Courts of Equity and those of the Common Law, however, this left unanswered the central question of whether or not a perpetual right existed at common law. After attempts to resolve this issue failed in Scotland[9] and in England,[10] the matter concerning literary property came to be considered by the King's Bench in the 1769 decision of *Millar v Taylor*.[11] This litigation arose from the fact that in 1729 Andrew Millar purchased the rights to Thompson's *The Seasons* for £242. After Robert Taylor, a bookseller from Berwick-upon-Tweed, published copies of the work in 1763, Millar sought relief. Given that by this time the statutory rights in *The Seasons* had elapsed (at the latest by 1757), in order for Millar to sustain this action it was necessary for him to establish that he had a common law right in the work. As such, the main issue in the case was whether at common law authors or their assigns retained a perpetual property right in their literary creations after publication, and the nature and effect that the Statute of Anne had on this common law right. After a wide-ranging debate, the Court of King's Bench, by a majority of three to one, ruled in favour of common law

---

[8] In *Tonson v Walker*, for example, Lord Hardwicke granted an injunction pending a hearing at which time he would consider whether such property existed. For an examination of the principles on which these injunctions were granted, see Lord Camden in *Donaldson v Becket* (1774) in Hansard: *The Parliamentary History of England from the Earliest Period to the Year 1803* (London: Longman, 1813), vol. 17 (1771–4) (hereinafter *Parliamentary History*) cols. 953–1003.

[9] *Millar v Kincaid* (1743) cited 98 ER 210; *Hinton v Donaldson* (1773) *The Decision of the Court of Session upon the Question of Literary Property in the cause of John Hinton against Alexander Donaldson* (Edinburgh: Boswell, 1774).

[10] *Tonson v Collins* (1760) 96 ER 169.

[11] (1769) 98 ER 201.

literary property,[12] with Lord Mansfield, Willes and Aston JJ finding for Millar and Yates J dissenting.[13]

Shortly after the decision of *Millar v Taylor* was handed down the status of common law literary property was reconsidered by the House of Lords in *Donaldson v Becket*.[14] As this case, which was handed down in February 1774, involved similar questions to those which had arisen in *Millar v Taylor* – namely as to whether there was a perpetual common law copy-right – and concerned the same work – Thompson's *The Seasons* – it can be seen as a *de facto* appeal of that decision.[15] Before deciding this question, the Lords sought the advice of the judges. While the advice given by the judges to the House of Lords as to the nature of common law copy-right was in support of the London publishers' arguments, when the full House of Lords came to decide the matter it voted twenty-two to eleven in Donaldson's favour, against the right of common law perpetual copy-right.[16] Interestingly, not only did the House of Lords reach the opposite conclusion to that of the King's Bench in *Millar v Taylor*, it also did so on the basis of a different style of reasoning.

Given that it seemed that the question which had preoccupied so many for so long was to be conclusively decided, it was unsurprising that *Donaldson v Becket* attracted great public attention. Moreover, given the judicial standing of the House of Lords, it is also unsurprising that when it was handed down *Donaldson v Becket* was taken as marking the

---

[12] On the possibly collusive nature of *Millar v Taylor* see R. Tompson, 'Scottish Judges and the Birth of British Copyright' (1992) *Juridical Review* 36.

[13] Yates had been counsel arguing against common law literary property in *Tonson v Collins* (1760) 96 ER 180. It was suggested later that 'the late Mr Justice Yates did not sufficiently divest himself of the advocate when he was determining as a judge': Attorney-General Thurlow commenting on Dunning's assertion in *Donaldson v Becket* (1774) 17 *Parliamentary History* col. 968. In *Hinton v Donaldson* (1773), the Scottish Court of Session declined to follow *Millar v Taylor* holding that even if such property existed in England, there was no such thing in Scotland. Although the Statute of Anne applied to both countries (being passed after the Union), England and Scotland were different jurisdictions with different common laws. Nevertheless, the English and Scottish decisions interacted: *Hinton v Donaldson* (1773) *Decisions of the Court of Session* (1774).

[14] (1774) 17 *Parliamentary History* col. 953.

[15] Donaldson published copies of *The Seasons*. Becket, who had acquired rights in *The Seasons* from Millar for £505, brought an action in Chancery for infringement of copyright. After Lord Chancellor Bathurst granted an injunction on the basis of *Millar v Taylor*, Donaldson appealed to the House of Lords.

[16] At the end of argument, the Lords sought advice from the judges on a number of questions. Most recognised the common law right (ten to one), and a smaller majority thought the right persisted even after publication (seven to four); however, the judges were divided on whether the Statute of Anne precluded authors from relying on the common law right. On the voting see J. Whicher, 'The Ghost of *Donaldson v Becket*' (1962) 9 *Bulletin of the Copyright Society of USA* 102.

end of what remains one of the most important periods in the history of intellectual property law. Indeed, one of the reasons why the battle of the booksellers is so interesting and why it has received so much attention in intellectual property scholarship is that it was not only the first but perhaps the only time in which so many issues were discussed at such length and in such detail. Moreover, because of the detailed and sophisticated nature of the arguments made and the fact that so many key legal ideas were subject to critical scrutiny, it also offers us a useful opportunity to explore various aspects of both pre-modern and modern intellectual property law. In particular it allows us to examine the two central themes of this work: viz., the categorisation of intellectual property law and the manner in which the law has granted property status to intangibles.

Labour of the mind

While there were many points of disagreement between the parties to the literary property debate, their discussions were conducted against a backdrop of shared ideas. One of the most important of these concerned the status of mental labour in law.[17] In particular, while precise details about the nature of mental labour remained contentious, it was widely agreed that mental labour – that which flows from the intellectual labours of the mind and the exertion of genius and thought – was fundamentally different from manual labour – the mere exertion of bodily strength and corporal application.[18] The separation of mental and manual labour, or as it was would come to be known creative and non-creative labour, was based on a range of factors: on the idea of the intrinsic value or dignity of the individual; on the growing belief that it was the mental faculty – the 'very Faculty which denominateth us Men'[19] – which distinguished

---

[17] In recent times it has become common to distinguish between mere mental labour and the expression of personality. During the eighteenth century, however, 'mental labour', which was used in a much broader sense, would have encompassed personality.

[18] The typical starting point was to divide property into immoveable and moveable property. Moveable property was further divided into natural property (which was acquired by occupancy) and artificial property (which was acquired through improvement). It was into this last form of property – artificial moveable property – that 'intellectual property' fell: W. Warburton, *A Letter from an Author to a Member of Parliament concerning Literary Property* (London: John and Paul Knapton, 1747), 7. As Blackstone said as counsel in *Millar v Taylor*, 'the labours of the mind and productions of the brain are as justly intitled to the benefit and emoluments that may arise from them, as the labours of the body are; and the literary compositions being the produce of the author's own labour and abilities, he has a moral and equitable right to the profits they produce': Quoted by Yates J, *Millar v Taylor* (1769) 98 ER 231.

[19] W. Warburton, *A Letter from an Author* (1747), 2.

'man' from the beasts;[20] and on the basis of economic arguments.[21] Moreover, informed by a growing belief in the genius of creation, the law not only came to differentiate between mental and manual labour, it also came to *privilege* the labour of the mind over that of the body.[22]

At the same time as the law came to distinguish labour of the mind from that of the body, mental labour came to be seen as providing the link between the various areas of law which granted property rights in intangibles. That is, it became clear over the course of the literary property debate that the thread which united such disparate areas as the 1742 Act for Securing to John Byrom, Master of Arts, the Sole Right of Publishing for a Certain Term of Years the Art and Method of Short-hand, Invented by him[23] and the 1735 Engravers' Act[24] was that they recognised or granted property rights in mental labour. Although it was not until the early part of the nineteenth century that the language of creativity was used with any degree of consistency, another way of presenting this common denominator was that what the various areas of law had in common was a shared concern with creativity. Importantly this concern with creativity extended not only to 'artistic' areas (such as literary property) but to *all* forms of intellectual property then in existence.

One of the consequences of thinking about the nature and limits of the law, and, more specifically, about what it was that united and separated the various areas of law which recognised property rights in mental labour, was that participants in the literary property debate began to think about the structure of the law in a way which they had

---

[20] *Ibid.*, 2. See also *Tonson v Collins* (1760) 96 ER 180.

[21] For Adam Smith distinctions drawn between skilled and common labour, or mental and manual labour, could be attributed to the amount of education 'invested' in each labourer and the relevant scarcity of the type of labour in question. A. Smith, *The Wealth of Nations* (1776) (ed. Edwin Cannan) (London: Grant Richards, 1904), 103.

[22] See, e.g., J. Reynolds, *Discourses on Art* (Discourse VIII) (ed. R. Wark) (New Haven: Yale University Press, 1959), 117. Commentators spoke of individuals as having genius, not being a genius. On the notion of genius and creativity see P. Kaufman, 'Heralds of Original Genus' in *Essays in Memory of Barrett Wendell* (Cambridge, Mass.: Harvard University Press, 1926); L. Pearsall Smith, 'Four Romantic Words' in *Words and Idioms: Studies on the English Language* (London: Constable and Co., 1925); R. Wittkower, 'Imitation, Eclecticism and Genius' in (ed.) E. Wasserman, *Aspects of the Eighteenth Century* (Baltimore, Md.: Johns Hopkins Press, 1965), 143–63; E. Panofsky, *Idea: A Concept in Art Theory* (tr. J. Peake) (Columbia, S.C.: University of South California Press, 1968); H. Dieckmann, 'Diderot's Conception of Genius' (1941) 11 *Journal of the History of Ideas* 151.

[23] See J. Hancox, *The Queens Chameleon: The Life of John Byrom* (London: Jonathan Cape, 1994), ch. 10.

[24] An Act for the Encouragement of the Arts of Designing, Engravings and Etchings Historical and Other Prints, by Vesting the Properties thereof in Inventors and Engravers during the Time therein Mentioned 8 Geo. II c. 13

never done before. For example, in comparing the property in inventions with that granted in books and engravings, commentators began to shift their focus of attention away from the industry-specific laws to consider the more abstract issue of the way in which the law was and should be organised. In so doing, they began to debate what was in effect the structure, sequence and organisation of the law. This is not to suggest, however, that by the time of the literary property debate modern intellectual property law existed as a separate and distinct area of law with its own logic and sub-categories. Indeed, as will become clear, such a law did not emerge until the middle period of the nineteenth century.

Although intellectual property law did not emerge as a discrete area of law until the middle of the nineteenth century and prior to this there was no consensus as to the way the law ought to be organised, this is not to deny that pre-modern law had its own patterning or syntax. While we return to focus on the *form* that the law took in more detail later, it may be helpful to outline briefly two notable features of the way pre-modern law was organised. The first is that, in contrast to modern law, which is characterised by abstract general categories which have the potential to apply to new subject matter, the law which granted property in mental labour at the time of the literary property debate and which continued through to the middle of the nineteenth century was a reactive and subject-specific law which tended to respond to particular (sometimes minor) problems.[25] For example, while modern law tends to be framed using more generalised concepts, pre-modern law provided subject-specific protection for sculptures of human and animal figures,[26] designs

---

[25] On the idea of backward-looking, reactive law see L. Davison and T. Keirn, 'The Reactive State: English Governance and Society 1688–1750' in (eds.) L. Davison, T. Hitchcock and R. Shoemaker, *Stilling the Grumbling Hive: The Response to Social and Economic Problems in England, 1688–1750* (Stroud, Glos. and New York: Alan Sutton and St Martins Press, 1992), xi–liv; J. Brewer, *Three Sinews of Power: War, Money and the English State, 1688–1783* (London: Century Hutchinson, 1988), esp. ch. 8. Cf. J. Innes, 'Parliament and the Shaping of Eighteenth-century English Social Policy' (1990) 5th series 40 *Transactions of the Royal Historical Society* 63–92 (a critique of the traditional view of the eighteenth-century House of Commons as an inefficient and unsystematic legislative body).

[26] An Act for Encouraging the Art of Making New Models and Casts of Busts, and other Things therein Mentioned, 38 Geo. III c. 71 (1798). The petition which prompted the 1798 Sculpture Copyright Act prayed 'that Leave may be given to bring in a Bill to secure their Authors the Copy Right of all new Models in Sculpture of the Human Figure and Animals, for a Time to be limited' to a period of fourteen years to the maker of new models or casts of humans or animals. Other examples of this reactive, quasi-private law include the 1831 petition for the protection of patterns on lace (J. Millward in 1836 *Report of the Select Committee on Arts and their Connexion with Manufactures* (Q. 171) (18)) and Joseph Merry's petition for the protection of new and original patterns for ribbons (1829) (84 CJ, index entry for 'ribbon trade'). Merry also wrote

for cottons, linens, muslins and calicos, and also granted exclusive privileges to individuals to perform certain activities (such as the grant given to William Cookworthy, chemist, for 'the sole use and exercise of a discovery of certain materials for making of Porcelain' or to James Watt, engineer, 'for the sole use and property in steam or fire engines').

At the same time as the law was becoming comfortable with mental labour as an abstract and open-ended category applicable (at least potentially) to all forms of creative labour, moves took place which would function to limit its scope. That is, just as we see the opening up of a general space for mental labour we also witness changes that would help to set the limits of the general category and, in turn, play a role in shaping the categories of modern intellectual property. Typically, these moves were a by-product of attempts to have new forms of subject matter protected by the law.[27] Rather than focusing upon the general category of mental labour, attention was placed on a specific area of mental labour: on those forms of mental labour which had already been granted property protection. This was because when a case was made for extending property protection to a new subject matter, it was usually done by drawing an analogy with pre-existing modes of protection.[28] More specifically, this was done by showing that the new subject matter shared similar features with the subject matter that had already been given protection. As such, the task of those arguing for protection was to find a common link between the forms of mental labour which had already been given property status and the particular case in hand. In these circumstances it thus became important not only to be able to identify how and where the boundaries of the pre-existing forms of protection were drawn, but also to be in a position to extrapolate from the pre-existing regimes in which property rights were granted. While still fluid and open, these links were to play an important role in shaping the form that the categories of intellectual property law were to take as they emerged in the course of the nineteenth century.

---

two letters to the Board of Trade praying for protection for the invention of machinery for ribbon velvet (filed 16 July 1829; 35 *Minutes of the Board of Trade*, Letter No. 33, 266). See also 1829 *Report of the Commissioners Appointed to Inquire into the Present State of the Law and Practice Relating to Granting of Patents for Inventions* 89–90.

[27] Such tactics can be seen in Hogarth's application for protection of engravers in 1735, in Kilburn's petition for calico printers in 1787 and Garrard's petition for the protection of sculptures of animals in 1798: each of which drew analogies with existing protection, but confined the scope of the proposed legislation to their specific grievances.

[28] On this see F. Hargrave, *An Argument in Defence of Literary Property* (London: Otridge, 1774), 8.

The problem with property

Of all the issues raised during the literary property debate, the most interesting discussion was reserved for the question of whether or not and, if so, in what circumstances the subject matter of a book – the ideas, sentiments, words, letters and style by which it was composed – could be conceived as a distinct species of property. This was because in answering questions which were 'seemingly entrenched in the profoundest subtlety of legal metaphysics'[29] the arguments moved from a narrow technical debate about the length of copy-right protection to a more general discussion about the ontological status of literary property. As the playwright, reviewer for the *Gentleman's Magazine*, satirist and self-styled inventor William Kenrick said, it 'is to little purpose to determine whether property be *temporary* or *perpetual*, unless the *nature* of that property be also precisely determined'.[30]

Although both the advocates and the opponents of perpetual literary property agreed that a distinction could and should be drawn between the labour of the mind and that of the body, there was disagreement over the possibility of recognising mental labour as a form of property. In particular, those opposed to perpetual literary property argued that this fantastic imaginary property was not and could not be recognised as a species of property by English common law.[31] These arguments were summed up in Yates J's dissenting judgment in *Millar* v *Taylor* when he said that while it was possible for a physical manuscript to be treated as a form of property, to 'extend this argument, beyond the manuscript, to the very ideas themselves was ... very difficult, or rather quite wild'.[32]

---

[29] *Ibid.*, 10.

[30] W. Kenrick, *An Address to the Artists and Manufacturers of Great Britain: Respecting an Application to Parliament for the Further Encouragement of New Discoveries and Inventions in the Useful Arts* (London: Domville, 1774), 45–6. 'The lawyers in general have not less perplexed the question respecting the origin of property than they have puzzled about the nature of it': *ibid.*, 4.

[31] *An Enquiry into the Nature and Origin of Literary Property* (London: Printed for William Flexney, 1762), 7. 'The ordinary subjects of property are well known, and easily conceived ... But property, when applied to ideas, or literary and intellectual compositions, is perfectly new and surprising ... by far the most comprehensive denomination of it would be a property in nonsense': Lord Gardenston, *Hinton* v *Donaldson* (1773), 25. Although the Statute of Anne had specifically referred to the existence of such a property (albeit limited in time), nevertheless, many contemporaries did not believe that the statute was concerned with property 'in the strict sense of the word': *Memorial for the Booksellers of Edinburgh and Glasgow Relating to the Process against them by some of the London Booksellers* (1774); reprint *The Literary Property Debate* (ed. S. Parks) (New York: Garland, 1974), 8. Cf. Lord Monboddo who found the argument that literary property was not property surprising, since it had been recognised as such by the Statute of Anne: *Hinton* v *Donaldson*, (1773), 9.

[32] *Millar* v *Taylor* (1769) 98 ER 230.

More specifically, Yates J denied the claim that products of the mind could be treated as a distinct species of property, arguing that mental labour did not exhibit what he and many others regarded as the crucial characteristics of property.[33]

A number of reasons were given as to why mental labour could not be treated as a form of property, yet in one way or another all the problems can be traced to its non-physical nature: to the incorporeal or, as we would now say, the intangible nature of literary property.[34] Unlike the forms of incorporeal property that the law had already accepted, such as the goodwill of an Inn, a nostrum, a particular seat in a theatre, as well as offices, titles, and annuities,[35] literary property had no direct or obvious connection with any physical object. Given, as Yates J said, that it was a well known and established maxim 'which arose from the necessary nature of all property' that 'nothing can be an object of property, which has not a corporeal substance',[36] it is unsurprising that the incorporeal nature of literary property created a number of difficulties for those arguing for a common law literary property.

While the idea of a property which could be stolen through a pane of glass and carried off by the eye without being found on a person offended the empiricist sensibilities of the law, the non-physical nature of mental labour created a number of more specific problems. Although closely related, these arguments fell into three broad heads. These were: firstly, the circumstances in which property could be legitimately acquired; secondly, the question of whether it was possible to identify literary property; and thirdly, concerns over the economic and cultural consequences of recognising a perpetual textual monopoly.

Justifying literary property

The first problem that the opponents of literary property saw in treating mental labour as a form of property relates to one of the most oft noted and at the same time perhaps most uninteresting aspects of the literary

---

[33] *Ibid.*, 229.

[34] As Hargrave said, the fact that literary property 'had no corporeal substance for its support' was the 'principal argument against the claim of Literary Property': F. Hargrave, *An Argument in Defence of Literary Property* (1774), 9–10.

[35] For an examination of some of these issues see *An Enquiry* (1762), 27–8.

[36] *Millar* v *Taylor* (1769) 98 ER 232. See also *Memorial for the Booksellers of Edinburgh and Glasgow*, 8; *Considerations on the Nature and Origin of Literary Property* (Edinburgh: Alexander Donaldson, 1767), 25. Lord Kames said property and corporeality are 'relative terms which cannot be disjoined, and *Property*, in a strict Sense, can no more be conceived without a *corpus*, than a Parent can be conceived without a Child': Lord Kames, *Midwinter* v *Hamilton* in *Remarkable Decisions of the Court of Session (1730–1752)* (Edinburgh: A. Kincaid and J. Bell, 1766), 157.

property debate: namely to the question of the way in which title in property arises.[37] According to contemporary understandings, there were a limited number of ways in which property could be acquired. As Blackstone wrote in his *Commentaries*, title to property could arise by Descent, Purchase, Escheat, Occupancy, Prescription, Forfeiture and Alienation.[38] Echoing the *Institutes* of Justinian, it was also agreed that the primary way in which a person could acquire title to objects *res nullius* – things which did not have or had never had an owner – was via 'occupatio' or occupancy; that is, simply by taking possession or occupying them.[39] Given this understanding of property, it is unsurprising that the question of the way in which title to literary property could be acquired, if at all, initially turned on the issue of whether the Roman law doctrine of occupancy, which was said to underlie the foundation of title to property, could be applied to the production of books.

The problem that confronted those who supported common law literary property was that while property 'was founded upon occupancy',[40] it was argued that intellectual ideas could not be possessed or occupied. This was because while 'some act of appropriation must be exerted to take the thing out of the state of being common ... All writers agree,' that no act of occupancy can be asserted on a bare idea of the mind.'[41] In short, as intellectual ideas could not be occupied they could not be considered as a form of property.[42]

The proponents of literary property responded to this argument in two different ways. First, while agreeing that title to unclaimed property arose by occupying or taking possession of that property, they argued against the way this had been applied to literary property. That is, while they accepted the basic premise of the argument that occupancy was the principle by which title to property could be acquired, they disagreed

---

[37] As Maine said, 'theory has made [the modes of acquisition] its favourite food': H. Maine, *Ancient Law* (London: Dent, 1917), 144. 'Occupancy is pre-eminently interesting on the scope of the service it has been made to perform for speculative jurisprudence, in furnishing a supposed justification of the origin of private property': *ibid.*, 147.

[38] W. Blackstone, *Commentaries on the Laws of England* (London: A. Strahan, 1809), Book II, chs. 13–19.

[39] Drawing upon the writings of Puffendorf and Grotius, these arguments were referring to the Roman law doctrine whereby one might establish an estate simply by taking possession of unclaimed land. See W. Blackstone, *Commentaries* (1809), Book II, ch. 26, 400.

[40] *Millar v Taylor* (1769) 98 ER 230.

[41] Ibid. On the need for a physical presence (or a proxy) in the occupancy argument see L. Becker, *Property Rights: Philosophic Foundations* (London: Routledge, 1977), 24–31.

[42] 'What numerous inconveniences would arise, if every man could at his pleasure, create a new species of property, to the support of which he might demand the aid of the law': *An Enquiry* (1762), 21.

with the conclusion that mental labour could not be occupied. In particular, the proponents of literary property suggested that '*occupancy* in the proper sense of the word, includes the principal *source* of literary property. The title by *occupancy* commences by the taking possession of a vacant subject; and the labour employed in the cultivation of it, confirms the title. Literary property falls precisely within this idea of occupancy'.[43] While Francis Hargrave, barrister for Thomas Becket in the early stages of his litigation against Donaldson and author of the influential *Argument in Defence of Literary Property*, went so far as to assert that the author's title was stronger than simple occupancy would suggest, in the face of the incorporeal nature of mental labour these arguments were difficult to sustain. In particular, they offered no acceptable response to the retort: how could you occupy something which had no physical existence?

The second response elicited by the Stationers and their supporters to the argument that ideas of the mind could not be seen as a species of property because they could not be occupied was to attempt to shift the basis of the argument. They did this by suggesting that occupancy was not the only means by which title to property could be acquired. In a move which has resonance in contemporary property debates, the proponents' response was, in effect, to argue for a non-unified notion of property as well as for a concept of property which was appropriate for the subject matter in hand.[44] The problem with arguments based on occupancy, it was said, was that while occupancy was a doctrine applicable to land and wild animals, it had no relevance in the case of incorporeal subject matter.[45] It was also argued that the writers who were relied upon for the account not only of occupancy but also of property more generally (such as Grotius and Puffendorf) modelled their image of property exclusively on land.[46] They were, to coin a modern simile, land lawyers masquerading as property lawyers.

These arguments were reinforced by the suggestion that while the

---

[43] F. Hargrave, *An Argument in Defence of Literary Property* (1774), 36 (and ff). See also W. Enfield, *Observations on Literary Property* (London: Johnson, 1774), 18.

[44] Cf. J. Ginsburg's call for recognition of a dual understanding of copyright, one based on expression of personality, the other on mere mental labour, in 'Creation and Commercial Value: Copyright Protection for Works of Information' (1990) 90 *Columbia Law Review* 1865.

[45] Wilkes J, *Millar* v *Taylor* (1769) 98 ER 218. On this see W. Kenrick, *An Address* (1774), 4; Solicitor-General Wedderburn, *Donaldson* v *Becket* (1774) 17 *Parliamentary History* col. 964.

[46] F. Hargrave, *An Argument in Defence of Literary Property* (1774), 12. 'And it is not to be wondered at that they who are chiefly conversant with title deeds of lands, should have some difficulty in conceiving of a settled property in the shadowy and insubstantial world of ideas': W. Enfield, *Observations on Literary Property* (1774), 18–19.

notions of property which were utilised in the arguments against literary property may once have been relevant, they were no longer appropriate for the enlightened times in which they now lived.[47] In short, it was said that the problem with those who argued against literary property was that they held overly narrow and conservative views of property. As a commentator at the time said, '[t]he idea of property has hitherto been too confined – even by Grotius – these writers [against literary property] have lost sight of the present state of the world, where new "rights" of the most valuable kind have been established'.[48] What was needed was a model of property which was more in tune with the prevailing social, economic, technological and cultural circumstances in which they lived.

The rejection of occupancy as the exclusive basis upon which original acquisition could be justified gave rise to the question: if occupancy was not the appropriate mode of acquisition, what was? The answer given, both in the pamphlets and in the Courts, was to shift the focus of attention away from occupancy towards labour; to invoke Locke's possessive individualism (or a version thereof). This was the idea that 'every Man has a *Property* in his own *Person*. This no Body has any Right to but himself. The *Labour* of his Body, and the *Work* of his Hands, we may say are properly his'.[49] What occurred in effect was that instead of relying upon occupancy as the foundation or original mode of acquisition, those who favoured perpetual common law literary property focused upon labour as the source of the property right. Another perhaps more accurate way of describing this is less as an outright rejection of occupancy as a reinterpretation of its role: occupancy was

[47] Yates J recognised the novelty of the argument when he said '[t]he occupancy of a thought would be a new kind of occupancy indeed': *Millar* v *Taylor* (1769) 98 ER 230. For a discussion of the 'enlightened times' in which the debate was conducted see D. Rae, *Information for Mess. John Hinton and Attorney against Mess. Alexander Donaldson and Others* (2 Jan. 1773), *Lord Coalston Reporter*, 9 – 10.

[48] *Information for John Mackenzie of Delvin, Writer of the Signet, and others, Trustees appointed by Mrs Anne Smith, Widow of Mr Thomas Ruddiman, Late Keeper of the Advocates Library, Pursuers against John Robertson, Printer in Edinburgh, Defender* (30 Nov. 1771), *Lord Monboddo Reporter*, 7. As Pocock explained, 'property was no longer defined within an unchanging structure of norms but was understood to exist within a historical process': J. Pocock, *Virtue, Commerce and History* (Cambridge: Cambridge University Press, 1985), 115.

[49] J. Locke, *Two Treatises of Government* (1690) (ed. P. Laslett) (Cambridge: Cambridge University Press, 1967), sect. 27. While Locke was sometimes explicitly used (as in *Millar* v *Taylor* (1769) 98 ER 201; *Tonson* v *Collins* (1760) 96 ER 180 citing Locke's *Two Treatises of Government*, Part 2, ch. 5; W. Blackstone, *Commentaries* (1809), Book II, ch. 26, 405), more often the form of argument reflected or resembled Locke's argument. See, e.g., F. Hargrave, *An Argument in Defence of Literary Property* (1774), 21 ff. For an argument as to the ubiquity and longevity of this mode of explanation (and one which takes it beyond political philosophy) see S. Oyama, *The Ontogeny of Information: Developmental Systems and Evolution* (Cambridge: Cambridge University Press, 1985), 10.

recast so as to be seen as a specific instance of a more general claim. That is, occupancy was subsumed within and became an example of the idea of labour as the basis for legitimising the appropriation of private property.[50]

The identification of literary property

The second argument raised against the idea of perpetual common law property arose from the belief that literary property, so called, did not exhibit what were commonly regarded as the characteristics necessary for it to be considered as a species of property. While the arguments against literary property based on occupancy were equally at home in political philosophy as in law, this second set of problems, which focused on ontological questions about the existence and identity of property, were very much *legal* questions: they concentrated on the problems that the law was likely to have in dealing with and accommodating this particular form of intangible property.

Those who opposed the Stationers' claims suggested that the immaterial nature of literary property meant that it failed to exhibit a number of the hallmarks which were commonly associated with and treated as prerequisites for an object being treated as a form of property. The opponents of literary property argued that it was important that any property recognised by the law be identifiable; as literary property failed to exhibit the 'ear-marks or tokens' of any particular proprietor this meant that in many cases the owner of the property could not be ascertained.[51] The intangible nature of literary property also meant that it was difficult to determine whether or not the interest in the property had been harmed.[52] Joseph Yates summed up these arguments when he said the whole existence of literary property

---

[50] 'There are then two sources of property, occupancy and labour, which may either subsist separately or be found united': W. Enfield, *Observations on Literary Property* (1774), 18.

[51] '[T]here are no indicia, or marks of appropriation to ascertain the owner of this species of property. What are the marks? It is not in manual occupation; it is not in visible possession, which Lord Kaym's History of Property lays down as an essential condition of property. How is an author to be distinguished?': *Tonson v Collins* (1760) 96 ER 185. Alan Ryan makes the point more clearly when he says, 'we should not wish to lose our beds the moment we rose from them or our clothes the moment we took them off. Hence, as was said by, among other writers, Blackstone, Rousseau, and Kant, we need some mark of an intention to continue as an owner, for example, continuing rather than continuous use, if we are to talk of property': A. Ryan, *Property and Political Theory* (Oxford: Basil Blackwell, 1984), 34.

[52] This led some to argue, for example, that translations did infringe copyright in the original work because 'the derivative right neither diminishes nor subtracts from the original ... therefore there is no injury done': *An Enquiry* (1762), 5.

is in the mind alone; incapable of any other modes of acquisition or enjoyment, than by mental possession or apprehension; safe and invulnerable from their own immateriality: no trespass can reach them; no tort affect them; no fraud or violence diminish or damage them. Yet these are the phantoms which the author would grasp and confine to himself: and these are what the defendant is charged with having robbed the plaintiff of.[53]

Another problem that confronted those arguing in favour of common law literary property related to the fact that as property operated to demarcate a zone of exclusion, it was necessary to show that there was something which was capable of being 'visibly and distinctly enjoyed';[54] that there was something which has 'boundaries to define it, and some marks to distinguish it'.[55] Focusing on these issues, the opponents of literary property argued that this ideal and imaginary property was 'so abstruse and chimerical in its nature' that it was 'beyond the comprehension of man's understanding and hardly capable of being defined'.[56] As such, it could not be considered as an object of law. More specifically, they argued that the problem with literary property was that as it merely consisted of mental ideas, there were no outward distinguishable proprietary marks by which it could be identified. It also meant that there was no obvious way by which the boundaries of the property could be determined.[57] The particular nature of literary property meant that the law was unable to answer the question: 'Where does this fanciful property begin, or end, or continue?'.[58] In all, the opponents of literary

---

[53] *Millar* v *Taylor* (1769) 98 ER 233.

[54] *Ibid.*, 232. There were no such problems with the statutory rights under the Statute of Anne because of the requirement of registration. In relation to the issue of identifying the intangible property, it was said that the legislature by the Statute of Anne enabled the literary property to be identified 'by directing an entry of the book in the registry of the Stationers' Company. But in a claim like the present, independent of the Act, this defect still remains: it wants one necessary quality to make it legal property': *Tonson* v *Collins* (1760) 96 ER 185.

[55] *Millar* v *Taylor* (1769) 98 ER 232.

[56] Attorney-General Thurlow, *Donaldson* v *Becket* (1774) 17 *Parliamentary History* col. 969. See also *Millar* v *Taylor* (1769) 98 ER 219.

[57] Yates J, *Millar* v *Taylor* (1769) 98 ER 234. The uncertain nature of the intangible property right mean that the establishment of a perpetual monopoly would be attended by 'endless confusion and litigation among authors and booksellers themselves'. Moreover, it was said that 'however desirable it might be to authors, that the perpetual possession of their literary compositions should be secured to them by law; it would be so difficult to define and ascertain the offence of invading copyright': W. Enfield, *Observations on Literary Property* (1774), 38.

[58] Lord Camden, *Donaldson* v *Becket* (1774) 17 *Parliamentary History* col. 997. This argument is one that continues to re-appear. For example it was recently said in relation to literary copyright that if 'words are property, they are an odd form of property. At any instant they are finite in number and yet can be freely and infinitely invented or duplicated. They cannot be marked with the insignia of ownership': L. Stearns, 'Copy Wrong: Plagiarism, Process, Property, and the Law' (1992) 80 *California Law Review* 536.

property argued that with no way of ascertaining whether the legal interest had been harmed, no means of identifying either the owner of the work or the work itself, and no means of drawing boundaries around the property to distinguish one person's rights from another's, intellectual ideas could not legitimately be considered as a species of property.

While the arguments based on occupancy were rejected for their implicit conservatism, the problems that were raised as to the nature of literary property as a species of property were not so easily ignored. This was made more pressing by the fact that even if the method by which title to property arose could be extended to include intangibles, there was no desire to alter what were seen as the fundamental traits of property. As all parties shared a similar image of the nature of property, it was clear that literary property would only be accepted as a form of property if it was able to take on (or could be made to appear to take on) these requisite characteristics.[59] In this situation, the task that confronted the proponents of literary property was to give 'limbs and features to this airy phantom',[60] that is, to provide the marks that would enable literary property to be identified and distinguished and, in so doing, transform the nothing into a something.[61]

A number of different techniques were proposed which would enable the mental labour of the author to be treated as a form of property. The suggestion that literary property could not be considered as a form of property because it was not possible to harm the owner by appropriating their ideas was answered by focusing on the future financial benefits – the profits – that were likely to accrue to the owner or to the appropriator if the property was taken.[62] As Hargrave said, if someone was to sell pirated copies the right was *wounded* and *affected* because of the fact that 'the profits, which would otherwise arise from the exercise of the right, are *diminished*; and the intruding on this particular right is as much a trespass, a tort, a fraud, a violence, a damage, as an invasion of any other incorporeal property can be'.[63]

While the focus on profit may have been useful in rendering a certain facet of literary property visible (and in so doing show that it was possible for it to be harmed), it offered little assistance in identifying the

[59] See *A Vindication* (1762).
[60] *An Enquiry* (1762), 2.
[61] In a different context see B. Edelman, *Ownership of the Image* (tr. E. Kingdom) (London: Routledge and Kegan Paul, 1979), 40.
[62] *Tonson* v *Collins* (1760) 96 ER 181. See also *A Vindication* (1762), 7. In *Millar* v *Taylor* (1769) 98 ER 201 Lord Mansfield said that according to natural justice it was not agreeable that strangers be allowed to reap the beneficial pecuniary produce of another person's work.
[63] F. Hargrave, *An Argument in Defence of Literary Property* (1774), 19.

property itself. As such the proponents of literary property were forced to consider the suggestion that literary property lacked the appropriate means by which it could be identified. One response which was proposed to counter this objection was to rely upon the fact that the author's name was fixed upon the title-page of a book.[64] However clever this answer may have been, it generated an equally astute response. 'Is the title page a mark of appropriation? No; that is often lost or omitted, and yet a purchaser of the book has as good a title to it, without a title page, as with it.' As such it 'cannot therefore be distinguished'.[65]

Faced with the obvious inadequacies of these approaches and with the fact that they only identified the owner of the work and not the work itself, the proponents of literary property were forced to develop other techniques that would enable them both to identify the protected subject matter and at the same time to draw boundaries around literary property. The initial strategy adopted to achieve this end was to focus upon the physical manifestation of the mental labour as it was captured or represented in the printed word.[66] As Aston J said in *Millar v Taylor*, although 'the sentiments and doctrine may be called ideal, yet when the same are communicated to the sight and understanding of every man by the *medium of printing*, the work becomes a distinguishable subject of property'. In short the fact that the labour of the author was represented by visible and known characters expressed on paper provided the marks and bounds to identify the property and in so doing 'to fix the possession and separate enjoyment of the right of printing'.[67] Moreover, it enabled the proponents of literary property to argue that it could be identified, distinguished and appropriated[68] and that, as such, it exhibited the requisite characteristics for it to be treated as a form of property.[69] As a result they were able to argue that although literary property was

---

[64] *Information for John Robertson, Printer in Edinburgh (Defender) against John Mackenzie of Delvin* (10 Dec. 1771), *Lord Monboddo Reporter*, 22. In an advisory opinion in *Donaldson v Becket* Ashurst J noted that 'a book with an author's name to it was the hawk, with the bells about its neck': (1774) 17 *Parliamentary History* col. 977. Cf. R. Chartier, 'Figures of the Author' in B. Sherman and A. Strowel, *Of Authors and Origins* (Oxford: Clarendon Press, 1994), 7.

[65] *Tonson v Collins* (1760) 96 ER 185.

[66] On the dominance of the veil of print see E. Eisenstein, *The Printing Press as an Agent of Change* (New York: Cambridge University Press, 1979), 10 ff.

[67] F. Hargrave, *An Argument in Defence of Literary Property* (1774), 15 and 18.

[68] *Donaldson v Becket* (1774) 17 *Parliamentary History* col. 981.

[69] In short it offered the *indicia certa* or foundation for it to be called a personal, incorporeal property. Aston J, *Millar v Taylor* (1769) 98 ER 221–2. From this basis the proponents of literary property were able to argue that although 'the sentiment or doctrine, considered abstractly, is incorporeal and ideal' as a result of the fact that it was 'impressed in visible characters on the paper, the manual copy is corporeal subject': *A Vindication* (1762), 17.

'abstract and ideal, novel and refined, it is yet intelligible, and may as easily be made to exist forever as for a term of years'.[70] However effective this fiction may have been in enabling the limits of the property to be ascertained, it only provided a temporary solution. Before focusing on the problems that arose in using print as a means of identifying intangible property, it is first necessary to consider the third argument which was raised against common law literary property; that through publication the owner abandoned any proprietary interests therein, effectively giving the work to the public.[71]

Literary property as gift?

The third objection which was brought against perpetual common law literary property was that once a work had been published authors should not be able to control the sentiments contained in the work.[72] As Yates J said, the act of publication, which was 'virtually and necessarily a gift to the public', meant that the work 'immediately and unavoidably becomes common'. In so doing it 'lays the author open to public scrutiny as much as when an owner of a piece of land lays it open into a highway'.[73]

While there were a number of reasons given as to why upon publication the very matter and contents of books should be irrevocably given to the public they all turned on a similar theme. This was that when assessing the status of literary property, the law had to take into account

[70] De Grey LCJ, *Donaldson v Becket* (1774) 17 *Parliamentary History* col. 988.

[71] There is some sense in which the advent of print itself created the problems that it was used to resolve. As Ong has argued, '[p]rint was a major factor in the development of the sense of personal privacy that marks modern society. By removing words from the world of sound where they first had their origin in active human interchange and relegating them definitively to visual space, and by otherwise exploiting visual space for their management of knowledge, print encouraged human beings to think of their interior consciousness and unconscious resources as more and more thing-like, impersonal and religiously neutral. Print encouraged the mind to sense that its possessions were held in some sort of inert mental space': W. Ong, *Orality and Literacy: The Technologizing of the Word* (London: Methuen and Co., 1988), 120. See also M. Ross, 'Authority and Authenticity: Scribbling Authors and the Genius of Print in Eighteenth-Century England' (1992) *Cardozo Arts and Entertainment Law Journal* 495.

[72] As Macaulay said, 'the last and most important question' is, 'is the rendering of literary property common, advantageous or disadvantageous to the state of literature in this country? The question, I think, is easily answered, that it will not only be disadvantageous, but ruinous to the state of literature. If literary property becomes common, we can have but two kinds of authors, men in opulence, and men in dependence': C. Macaulay, *A Modest Plea for the Property of Copy Right* (London: Printed by R. Cruttwell in Bath for E. and C. Dilly, 1774), 37.

[73] *Millar v Taylor* (1769) 98 ER 234. See also F. Hargrave, *An Argument in Defence of Literary Property* (1774), 15–16; *Tonson v Collins* (1760) 96 ER 185; *Information for John Robertson* (1771), 11.

the fact that books did not exist in isolation but were part of a complex network of communications which, for example, connected writer to reader and writer to writer.[74] Although the opponents of literary property accepted that prior to publication authors had complete control over their mental labour, they argued that it would be 'unreasonable, chimerical, impracticable and opposite to every idea of public utility' to give authors the same rights after publication as they enjoyed before it.[75] This sprang from the fear that perpetual common law literary property would impinge upon the rights both of other authors and the reading public more generally.[76] In particular it was said that while '[p]ublic Utility requires that Productions of the Mind should be diffused as widely as possible',[77] one of the consequences of allowing copy-right in published works would have been that the intellectual resources available to the public would have been diminished. To bind science and knowledge in the 'cobweb chains' of property protection[78] would have restricted the development of new works, translations and quotations[79] as well as the circulation of books. While the 'Learning of the present age' was considered as a vast superstructure to 'which the Geniuses of past times have contributed their proportion of wit and industry',[80] the effect of perpetual common law literary property would have been to restrict the use made of (and the accumulation of) the literary tradition,[81] and, as such, would have inhibited and constricted the advancement of learning and knowledge.[82] In short, it was argued that perpetual literary property was likely to be ruinous to the state of literature and, as such, should not be allowed.[83] In combination these

[74] Cf. D. Goodman, 'Epistolary Property: Michel de Servan and the plight of letters on the eve of the French Revolution' in (eds.) J. Brewer and S. Staves, *Early Modern Conceptions of Property* (London: Routledge, 1995), 348–9.

[75] F. Hargrave, *An Argument in Defence of Literary Property* (1774), 3.

[76] These arguments drew upon changing conceptions of the 'public' as well as upon the notion of the reading public more specifically: T. Ross, 'Copyright and the Invention of Tradition' (1992), 9.

[77] *The Cases of Appellants and Respondents in the Cause of Literary Property Before the House of Lords* (London: Printed for J. Bew, 1774), 6.

[78] Lord Camden, *Donaldson v Becket* (1774) 17 *Parliamentary History* cols. 992–1002.

[79] Lord Gardenston, *Hinton v Donaldson* (1773), 25.

[80] *An Enquiry* (1762), 4.

[81] Lord Kames, *Hinton v Donaldson* (1773), 19.

[82] *Information for John Robertson* (1771), 11. 'If there be anything in the world common to all mankind, science and learning are in their nature *publici juris*, and they ought to be as free and general as air or water. They forget their Creator, as well as their fellow creatures ... We entered society to enlighten each other's minds ... they must not be niggards to the world, or hoard up for themselves the common stock': Lord Camden, *Donaldson v Becket* (1774) 17 *Parliamentary History* col. 999.

[83] It was also feared that giving perpetual property right to authors would give them 'not only a right to publish, but a right to suppress too': Lord Chancellor, *Osborne v Donaldson* (1765) 28 ER 924.

factors enabled the opponents of literary property to argue that although perpetual literary property might have been of potential benefit to authors and publishers, as these benefits were outweighed by the harm that literary property would cause more generally there should be no property rights in the work post publication. In short, 'the private interest of individuals must necessarily give way to that of the public'.[84]

The initial response by the proponents of literary property was to agree with the general thrust of these arguments. In particular, they accepted that 'if an author was to claim the sole right of *using* the *knowledge* contained in his works … it would be both unfit and impossible to comply with a demand so absurd, so illiberally selfish … in which such an unlimited appropriation of the fruits of a man's industry would be equally unreasonable and ridiculous'.[85] Although the proponents agreed that it would be unfair to allow authors or publishers to control the knowledge contained in their works, they *denied* that this objection had any relevance to their arguments. This was because the proponents of literary property had a different understanding of the nature of what was protected from their opponents. That is, although the opponents and proponents agreed that it was undesirable to allow property protection of ideas and knowledge, they differed in terms of the way they viewed the scope of the right.

While the opponents' arguments were based 'on the supposition that the exclusive right claimed for an author is to the *ideas* and *knowledge* communicated in a literary composition',[86] the 'claim of literary Property' underlying the proponents' case was said not to have been 'of this ridiculous and unreasonable kind'. Moreover, 'to represent it as such, however it may serve the purposes of declamation, or of wit and humour, is a fallacy too gross to be successfully disguised'.[87] That is, while the opponents of literary property assumed that the right enabled the author to control the knowledge, doctrine and ideas embodied in the text, the arguments made by the proponents of literary property were based on a different view of the scope of the subject matter protected.[88] As Hargrave said, the title to benefit which the proponents claimed on behalf of the author 'depends on a proposition of a more limited kind'.[89] In particular, they argued that they were not claiming a monopoly in

---

[84] W. Kenrick, *An Address* (1774), 33.
[85] F. Hargrave, *An Argument in Defence of Literary Property* (1774), 22.
[86] *Ibid.*, 15–16.   [87] *Ibid.*, 22.
[88] *Information for John Robertson* (1771), 8. Lord Coalston noted that the pursuers claimed a perpetual property 'in the stile and ideas of [an author's] work': *Hinton v Donaldson* (1773), 27.
[89] F. Hargrave, *An Argument in Defence of Literary Property* (1774), 22.

ideas, sentiment or doctrine, but in something of a more restricted nature.

The first technique adopted by the proponents of literary property to differentiate their view of literary property from that held by their opponents was to argue that the scope of the intangible property was limited to the right to print and re-print the work.[90] In particular, they suggested that 'nothing more is meant by the term Literary Property, than such an interest in a written composition, as entitles the Author, and those claiming under him, to the sole and exclusive right of multiplying printed copies for sale'.[91] By limiting the scope of protection in this manner it was possible to argue that upon publication the ideas and knowledge contained in the work were left in common and, as such, were free to be used by all. Moreover, because the property claimed by the Stationers only enabled authors to restrain others from reprinting the identical work in its own original form, readers of a book could make whatever use they wished of the ideas and knowledge contained in the text.[92] All they were prohibited from doing was printing or reprinting the work. It was thus possible to argue that because the property was restricted to the surface of the text, it was inaccurate to suggest that an author had property in ideas, or that a claim was being made to the knowledge which lay behind the text.[93]

However helpful print may have been in avoiding the various objections brought against a right post publication, it severely weakened the proponents' own position. This was also the case with the use of print as a means of identifying the protected subject matter which we highlighted earlier. The reason for this was that while relying on the visible manifestation of the author's mental labour may have made the law's task of identifying the protected subject matter relatively straightforward, to have limited the protection provided to facsimile copies would

---

[90] This was based on the 'incontrovertible principle' that the author had the right 'to the sole printing and selling of his own works': *ibid.*, 22. 'I use the word Copy in the technical sense in which that name or term has been used for ages, to signify an incorporeal right to the sole printing and publishing of something intellectual, communicated by letters': Lord Mansfield, *Millar v Taylor* (1769) 98 ER 251.

[91] F. Hargrave, *An Argument in Defence of Literary Property* (1774), 4.

[92] D. Rae, *Information for John Hinton* (1773), 18–19. 'The freedom which is allowed, of borrowing thought, or making quotations, and even translations from preceding works, pleads strongly in favour of literary property; because it removes any pretence of hardship to the public, while others are restrained only from reprinting the identical work of an author in its own original form and figure': *ibid.*

[93] 'As to the ideas conveyed, every author, when he publishes, necessarily gives the full use of them to the world at large. To communicate and sell knowledge to the public, and at the same moment to stipulate that none but the author or his booksellers shall make use of it, is an idea, which Avarice herself has not yet suggested': F. Hargrave, *An Argument in Defence of Literary Property* (1774), 16–17.

have largely undermined the proponents' own interests. The problem with limiting literary property to a right to print and re-print was that although this would have covered many forms of piracy – such as the re-printing and selling of works which were identical in sentiment, method or expression[94] – it was unable to provide any protection in situations where the forms of copying involved a movement away from the text.[95] In particular, it would not have covered situations where pirated publications assumed the form of abridgments, compilations or translations.[96]

As soon as it was accepted that the scope of the right should extend beyond the surface of the text, which the proponents realised that it must do, the limits of a print-based approach in identifying the protected subject matter became apparent. Hargrave captured the nature of these problems when he said that if it was accepted that the subject matter should extend beyond literal copying (that is, beyond the surface of the text) print would no longer provide 'the manner and facility for tracing the difference between one literary work and another'.[97] It offered minimal guidance, for example, in determining whether a work purportedly translated from Latin to English infringed the copyright in the original work.[98]

Confronted with these difficulties, the proponents of literary property were forced to move away from the restricted right to print and re-print towards an examination of the nature and scope of the subject matter protected; beyond the printed page to the essence of the work itself. In so doing they were confronted with a two-fold task. First they had to

[94] W. Enfield, *Observations on Literary Property* (1774), 11. In any case, print provided little assistance beyond literary property and ornamental design. For criticisms of restricting protection to the arts dependent on the press, see W. Kenrick, *An Address* (1774), 26.

[95] It was still disputed as to whether many of these uses constituted piracy.

[96] The exact scope of the right given under the Statute of Anne had been the subject of some discussion as regards abridgments. For example when Cave abridged Trapp's sermons on *Nature, Folly, Sin and Danger*, Samuel Johnson spoke in his support. Johnson argued that existing practices indicated that the right conferred on an author was limited and did not extend to abridgments, and that this accorded with reason. There was a public interest stronger than the authors' right, an interest in confuting false notions, curbing long-windedness and summarising important ideas into condensed form. Johnson had recognised that 'every book, when it falls into the hands of the reader, is liable to be examined, confuted, censured, translated, and abridged . . . That all these liberties are allowed, and cannot be prohibited without manifest disadvantage to the public, may be easily proved': 'Considerations [by the late Dr Johnson] on the Case of Dr Trapp's sermons, Abridged by Mr Cave' (July 1787) 57 *Gentleman's Magazine* 555.

[97] F. Hargrave, *An Argument in Defence of Literary Property* (1774), 7–8.

[98] It was little help in circumstances where 'a work, the chief merit of which consists in the ideas independently of the expression, is pirated by copying of thoughts, and cloathing them in different words': W. Enfield, *Observations on Literary Property* (1774), 41–2.

provide a definition of literary property which somehow differentiated between that which was covered by the property right and that which remained free to be used by all. At the same time, when specifying what the private interest was, they needed to provide a definition or a way of identifying the protected property which would be flexible enough to move from one format to another, to trace the property as it moved into new domains. That is, it was necessary to provide a definition of literary property that had the clarity to enable the law to distinguish between that which was privately owned and that which was in the public domain, while at the same time retaining the flexibility to be able to protect the proprietor from simple evasions.

The way in which these two demands were navigated by the proponents of literary property was to argue that authors (and their assigns) were not claiming protection for the ideas, sentiment and doctrine which could be found in the work. Nor was the property limited to the printed word. Rather, what an author claimed protection for was the particular way the words were combined; that is, for the form or cast of language in which thoughts were represented or expressed[99] – in short, for the way ideas were reduced to writing.[100]

What occurred with this argument was that the book began to take on a more complex form. In one sense the book was made up of ideas, knowledge and sentiment. In another, it contained the physical marks or traces on the printed page. In addition, the work also embodied a third element, which was the exclusive domain of literary property. This was the style or mode of expression the author used to express their sentiments – the 'series of thoughts and expressions produced by the continued exertion of the powers of the mind'.[101] More specifically, by representing the book in this way, the proponents of literary property

[99] D. Rae, *Information for John Hinton* (1771), 9; W. Enfield, *Observations on Literary Property* (1774), 11–12. As Blackstone said, the identity of the composition 'consists entirely in the *sentiment* and the *language*': W. Blackstone, *Commentaries* (1809), Book II, ch. 26, 405. *Language* was defined at the time as 'Style; manner of expression'; whereas an author has the 'choice of his own words': S. Johnson, *A Dictionary of the English Language* (1755) (London: Times Books, 1983). 'The subject of property is the order of the words in the author's composition; not the words themselves, they being analogous to the elements of matter, which are not appropriated unless combined, nor the ideas expressed by those words, they existing in the mind alone, which is not capable of appropriation': *Jefferys v Boosey* (1854) 10 ER 702. See *Information for John Mackenzie* (1771), 8.

[100] 'The train of thoughts and sentiments which a man forms in his mind, though compounded of ideas which might have before existed in other minds, and expressed in words which have before existed in other minds, and expressed in words which have before been used, is nevertheless truly and properly his own': W. Enfield, *Observations on Literary Property* (1774), 19.

[101] *Ibid.*, 10–11.

were able to argue that a book was divided into a public realm (of doctrine, knowledge and ideas) which upon publication was free to be used by all and a private domain (of style, manner or expression) which, even on publication, remained the property of the author or their assigns. By arguing that literary property was restricted to the expression of the author, rather than to any ideas or knowledge that a work might contain, and by suggesting that the book was 'public in one sense, and private in another',[102] this meant that upon publication readers could make whatever use they wished of the ideas and knowledge embodied in the text: all they would be prohibited from doing was using the unique style or expression of the author.[103]

Moreover, because literary property was limited to the expression an author used in crafting the work, rather than the knowledge or ideas that the book may have contained, the proponents of literary property were also able to deny that recognition of perpetual literary property would detrimentally affect the progress and improvement of literature and genius.[104] As a result, they were able to argue that far 'from having a tendency to restrain others from the exercise of their faculties', literary property 'contributes to enlarge them; as it affords encouragement for others to compose works on which others may employ their intellectual talents, and thereby multiply their perceptions'.[105] In short, by representing the protected subject matter in this more limited way the proponents were able to distinguish their view of literary property from the more expansive, monopolistic views of which they were accused by their opponents.[106]

The fact that literary property was restricted to the style or mode of expression used by an author simultaneously offered a solution to the two problems confronting the proponents of literary property. First,

---

[102] Lord Camden, *Donaldson v Becket* (1774) 17 *Parliamentary History* col. 998.

[103] The proponents of literary property, by limiting property to the expression of the author, were thereby also able to avoid the problem of independent creation, of different persons claiming simultaneously to have created the same idea.

[104] 'The freedom which is allowed, of borrowing thoughts, or making translations from preceding works, pleads strongly in favour of literary property; because it removes any pretence of hardship to the public, while others are restrained only from reprinting an identical work of an author in its own original form and figure': D. Rae, *Information for John Hinton* (1773), 18–19. 'For he who obtaineth my copy may appropriate my stock of ideas, and, by opposing my sentiments, may give birth to a new doctrine': *A Vindication* (1762), 13. This argument was also expressed through the architectural metaphor that a person might build on another's foundations as long as they raised a different superstructure: *ibid.*, 14.

[105] *Ibid.*, 24.

[106] These developments can be seen as an early example of the idea–expression dichotomy. Cf. R. Jones, 'The Myth of the Idea/Expression Dichotomy in Copyright Law' (1990) *Pace Law Review* 551, who argues that the idea/expression dichotomy did not develop until the 1900s.

because the property only protected the unique expression of the author, and not the ideas or knowledge that were to be found in the work, the proponents of literary property were able to defend themselves against the accusation that literary property amounted to an illiberal, unjust monopoly that would be contrary to public utility.[107] At the same time, expression was open-ended and plastic enough for it to transcend different formats. As such, it provided a common denominator which would, so the argument went, enable the law to trace the work as it moved from one format to another.[108]

In arguing that literary property was limited to the expression used in crafting a work, the proponents of literary property were able to provide plausible responses to the objections which had been raised about the law granting property protection to intangibles. While the status of these responses and the way we should think about the literary property debate more generally remains contentious, nonetheless they provide us with a useful opportunity to explore certain issues about the nature of intangible property in law. It is to this task that we now turn.

Creator as individual

One important feature highlighted by the literary property debate concerns the role played by the individual in thinking about intangible property. Indeed, one of the most common claims made about eighteenth-century intellectual property law is that during this period the individual came to be seen as the source or origin of creation. More specifically, it is often suggested that in law the author came to be seen as the originator of the literary text rather than as a mere reproducer of tradition. It is argued, in effect, that the law came to embody a form of epistemological or aesthetic individualism.[109] Prior to this, the mind of the author had been seen as a reflector of the external world and the resulting work was itself comparable to a mirror presenting a selected and ordered image of life. The change that took place was that the mind of the author, which was motivated by organic qualities of genius, taste, judgment and imagination, came to be seen as something which was not

---

[107] F. Hargrave, *An Argument in Defence of Literary Property* (1774), 28.

[108] In this sense we are able to shed some light on the question Derrida raised of why and how, in the positive notion of rights that was established between the seventeenth and eighteenth centuries, the view of authors' rights only took into account form and content, why it excluded considerations of content, thematics, and meaning: J. Derrida, 'Psyche: Inventions of the Other' in (eds.) Lindsay Waters and Wlad Godzich, *Reading de Man Reading* (Minneapolis: University of Minnesota Press, 1989), 27.

[109] On which see S. Lukes, *Individualism* (Oxford: Basil Blackwell, 1985), 45–51.

only interposed between the world of sense and the literary work but also as something which was the cause for the conspicuous differences between art and reality.[110] What we witness with the adoption of an individualistic model of creation, so the argument goes, is a move away from God or Nature as the source of creation towards the individual; albeit that the individual, like Locke's labourer, worked with the tools provided by God.

Even a cursory glance at the writings of this period, which are strewn with references to genius, imagination, and the like, reveals that there can be little doubt that over the course of the eighteenth century the individual-as-creator took on a more prominent role in law than had hitherto been the case.[111] As we have already seen, one of the central issues discussed during the literary property debate was whether authors (not authors and proprietors as in the 1710 Statute of Anne) had a perpetual right to control the reproduction of their writings. While the idea of the author was used, or as Rose argued, virtually invented to further the ends of the London booksellers in the literary property debate,[112] it also marks an important change in the way in which intangible property was treated by the law. At the same time as the formal site in which the book trade was regulated shifted from the Stationers' Company and the guilds to the public courts, the *fulcrum* of regulation moved to focus upon the individual. This can be seen, for example, in the fact that during the eighteenth century the individual became the focal point around which many legal concepts and rules which dealt with intangible property were organised. The growing dependency on the individual was reflected not only in the arguments employed in the literary property debate, but also in the language used in the legislation which set out to regulate intellectual property. While the 1720 Statute of Anne, which provided authors with the right to

---

[110] M. Abrams, *The Mirror and the Lamp* (New York: Oxford University Press, 1953), 156.

[111] '[T]he coming about ... of the new must be due to an operation of the human subject. Invention always belongs to man as inventing subject. This is a defining feature of very great stability, a semantic quasi-invariant that we must take rigorously into account. For whatever may be the history or the polysemy of the concept of invention ... never, it seems to me, has anyone assumed the authority to speak of invention without implying in the term the technical initiative of the being called man': J. Derrida, 'Psyche: Inventions of the Other' (1989), 43–44. 'The status of invention in general, like that of a particular invention, presupposes the public recognition of an origin ... The latter has to be assignable to a *human subject*, individually or collectively, who is responsible for the discovery or the production of something new that is henceforth available to everyone': *ibid.*, 41.

[112] M. Rose, 'The Author as Proprietor' (1994), 31. See also R. Chartier, 'Figures of the Author' (1994), 7. See more generally A. Robinson, 'The Evolution of Copyright, 1476–1776' (1991) *Cambrian Law Review*, 67.

copy, is one of the earliest instances of this, a more interesting example is to be found in relation to the Calico Printers' Acts of 1787 and 1794 (which provided limited protection to fabric designs).[113] In the discussions preceding these Acts, the focus of attention was upon the product on which the print or design was stamped – the fabric, dress and so on. Unlike the literary property debate, which focused on the author-as-creator, there was no mention of individual designers in the discussions preceding the Calico Printers' Acts that we have found. Nonetheless, when these claims made their way into statutory language, they were cast in terms of the individual engraver or designer.

While there can be little doubt that during the eighteenth century the individual-as-creator took on a prominent position in law, we must careful of the conclusions we draw from this. For example, we need to pause for thought before we take this one step further and suggest that this period also saw the law adopt the idea of the author as 'an individual who is *solely* ... responsible for the production of a unique work'.[114] Likewise, we should take care about the suggestion that the law came to 'share a view of authors producing copy without assistance, expending mental labour and intellectual capital (their ideas) in creating goods of the mind which belong to them alone'.[115] This is because unlike the situation with credit or money, where the physical object was all but divorced from its incorporeal context, literary property never reached this degree of separation. Similarly, while in many areas the individual took on a more prominent role than he or she had previously enjoyed the author was not, at least in law, separated from the text, as is sometimes suggested.[116] What is striking about much of what was written about intellectual property throughout the eighteenth and nineteenth centuries is how conscious commentators were of the interpersonal nature of creation, of the debt and connection which existed between authors,[117] of the fact that creators existed within networks of

---

[113] An Act for the Encouragement of the Arts of Designing and Printing Linens, Cottons, Calicos and Muslins by Vesting the Properties thereof in the Designers, Printers and Proprietors for a Limited Time 27 Geo. III ch. 38 (1787). This Act conferred on the inventors and designers of new and original patterns for printing on calicos, muslins, cottons and linens the exclusive right to do so for two months.

[114] M. Woodmansee, 'The Genius and the Copyright: Economic and Legal Conditions of the Emergence of the "Author"' (1984) 17 *Eighteenth-Century Studies*, 426 (emphasis added). It should be noted that Woodmansee uses this view of the author as a point of critique.

[115] L. Zionkowski, 'Aesthetics, Copyright and the Goods of the Mind' (1992) 15 *British Journal for Eighteenth Century Studies* 167.

[116] See, e.g., S. Stewart, *Crimes of Writing: Problems in the Containment of Representation* (New York: Oxford University Press, 1991), 15.

[117] For example, it was said in argument against recognising perpetual literary property that 'if this idea, of property in compositions of the mind, is at all gone into, it is

communication, and that they drew upon and at the same time contributed to the traditions which they inhabited: in short, of the intertextuality of creation.[118]

While there is little doubt as to the increased role played by the individual in pre-modern intellectual property law, we should not focus on this at the expense of other, perhaps more fruitful, avenues. This is especially important given the legacy of romanticism, which tends to over-emphasise the role played by the individual-as-creator in the law. If we resist such totalising explanations, a number of different possibilities become apparent. One approach which is suggested by our reading of the literary property debate is the need to recognise that the individual exists within a series of complex networks that links tradition, ideas, authors, readers and so on. Such recognition enables us to appreciate the collaborative and interdependent nature of creation.[119] Moreover, if we are to understand intangible property, it is the framework of creation, rather than one particular element of it (such as the author or inventor), that needs to be highlighted: a topic we explore in more detail in the next chapter. This is not to deny the important role played by the legal subject in intellectual property law, so much as to relocate the individual-as-creator within this broader process.

Another notable feature of the literary property debate is that it exemplifies two different ways of thinking about and dealing with intangible property. Importantly, each of these corresponds with and typifies the modes of argument used in pre-modern and modern law respectively. The different ways of thinking about the intangible is apparent if we compare the mode of argument used in *Millar* v

---

difficult to see where to stop'. Recognising the prevalence of borrowing or 'repeating', it was said, 'the author of this paper may be prosecuted, for having taken many of his arguments from the works of others; yet he could not otherwise have done justice to his client': *Information for John Robertson* (1771), 18. A striking example of this can be found in Sir Joshua Reynolds' address to the Royal Academy of Art which emphasised the critical importance of copying and imitation in an artist's education. See, especially, Discourse VI, delivered in the same year as the House of Lords judgment in *Donaldson* v *Becket*: J. Reynolds, *Discourses on Art* (1959).

[118] In what could have been taken from a modern work on literary theory, Shortt wrote in 1871 that 'Every book in literature, science and art borrows and must necessarily borrow and use much which was well known and used before. No man creates a new language for himself, at least if he be a wise man, in writing a book': J. Shortt, *The Law Relating to the Works of Literature and Art* (London: Horace Cox, 1871), 80.

[119] As Gordon argues, the 'price to be paid for the compulsive power of the absolute dominion trope has been a heavy one, a maddeningly persistent tendency to suppress and to deny the collective and collaborative elements, the necessity of mutual dependence, inherent in social endeavour': R. Gordon, 'Paradoxical Property' in (eds.) J. Brewer and S. Staves, *Early Modern Conceptions of Property* (London: Routledge, 1995), 108.

Taylor,[120] which reflects the pre-modern approach, with the more modern approach employed by the House of Lords in *Donaldson* v *Becket*.[121] While the issue discussed in both cases was the same (whether there was a perpetual common law copy-right), the mode of argument used in each differed greatly. In answering, rather than ignoring this question, the court in *Millar* v *Taylor* focused upon the nature and basis of literary property protection. The *a priori* and reflexive nature of this decision is in stark contrast to the subsequent decision of *Donaldson* v *Becket*. While the House of Lords addressed similar questions to those which had arisen in *Millar* v *Taylor*, rather than considering the nature of literary property or how it differed from technical property, in *Donaldson* v *Becket* the Lords, with their liberal concern with exchange and circulation, focused upon the *consequences* that the grant of a perpetual monopoly to the London Stationers' Company would have upon the book trade.[122] That is, there was a subtle change in the mode of argument away from what could be called *a priori* style examinations to a *consequential* or *forward-thinking* mode of reasoning. Rather than asking questions about the ontological status of literary property, attention turned to focus on the impact that the granting of such property would have. What we witness, in effect, is the beginning of an epistemic shift within intellectual property law whereby reason, experience and wisdom were displaced by the consequential positivities that have come to characterise modern law. While it was not until the later part of the nineteenth century that these consequential arguments took on the pervasive role they now play, the debate provides a useful point of contrast between the *a priori* and the consequential modes of argument.

The move from an ontological examination into the nature of literary property to an examination of the consequences that the granting or not granting of a property right would have is reflected in Lord Camden's judgment in *Donaldson* v *Becket*. After dismissing the *a priori* style of argument used not only in *Millar* v *Taylor* but also in the bulk of the tracts, pamphlets and judicial decisions as a 'heterogeneous heap of rubbish',[123] Lord Camden focused on the consequences that were likely to flow from the granting of a perpetual monopoly. While decisions as to whether copyright was perpetual or not had previously been made on the basis of whether literary property, so called, could be properly regarded as a species of property, for Lord Camden the fact that the grant of perpetual copy-right would have meant that all the 'learning

---

[120] (1769) 98 ER 201.
[121] (1774) 17 *Parliamentary History* col. 953.
[122] See T. Ross, 'Copyright and the Invention of Tradition' (1992).
[123] (1774) 17 *Parliamentary History* col. 993.

will be locked up in the hands of the Tonsons and the Lintons of the age, till the public become as much their slaves, as their own hackney compilers are',[124] was sufficient reason for him to reject the Stationers' claims.

As well as exemplifying different ways of thinking about property in intangibles, the literary property debate is also noteworthy in that the literary property which was recognised in the 1710 Statute of Anne was indirectly confirmed and reinforced. Once there had been doubts as to whether it was an institution which should be supported and encouraged by the law, but over the course of the debate the legal status of literary property was placed beyond doubt (or as good as). While the legislation which preceded the literary property debate – the Statute of Anne, the Engravers' Act of 1735 – and the decisions that grew up around these played a role in the normalisation of literary property, the mere fact that literary property was discussed so widely and in so much detail had the effect that its normative status was effectively rendered incontestable.[125] Although the normative status of many forms of intangible property, notably patents, remained uncertain, the move towards normative closure of literary property had an important impact on legal practices. In particular the agreement as to the worth of literary property made it easier to argue by analogy for the extension of the scope of protection to new formats.

More importantly, the debate also witnessed a growing and wide-spread acceptance that mental labour *could* give rise to a distinct species of private property:[126] that is, it saw a form of conceptual closure. While

---

[124] *Ibid.*, col. 1000. It was said that under the pretence of serving the cause of literature, the booksellers hatched the notion of perpetual privilege in order to get the fruits of genius into their hands forever.

[125] Mark Rose, who has perhaps done more than anyone else to re-popularise this period of intellectual property law, suggests that the literary property debate saw 'the twin birth, the simultaneous emergence of, the proprietary author and the literary work': M. Rose, 'The Author as Proprietor' (1994), 39. Elsewhere, Rose suggests that by 1774 'all the essential elements of modern Anglo-American copyright law were in place. Most important, of course, was the notion of the author as the creator and ultimate source of property': M. Rose, *Authors and Owners* (1993), 132.

[126] See S. Sherman, 'Printing the Mind: The Economics of Authorship in *Areopagitica*' (1993) 60 *English Literary History* 325. 'The House of Lords had not merely defined the law. Lawyers had spent twenty years trying to decide exactly what copyright was ... Despite all the distrust of the idea of incorporeal property, such property was now deemed to exist': J. Feather, 'The Publishers and the Pirates: British Copyright Law in Theory and Practice, 1710–1775' (1987) 22 *Publishing History*, 25. Rose argues that *Pope and Curll* and the debates that surrounded it marked the moment when 'the concept of literary property as a wholly immaterial property in a text might be said to have been born': M. Rose, 'The Author in Court: *Pope v Curll* (1741)' (1992) 10 *Cardozo Arts and Entertainment Law Review* 493. See also M. Rose, *Authors and Owners* (1993), 132.

forms of intangible property such as reputation, marital felicity, good-will and firm name, property in copy and property in invention had been recognised in law prior to this, it was not until after the literary property debate that the modern notion of the intangible as a property right existing in a 'thing', with no direct connection to the realm of the physical, came to be accepted, with few questions or doubts. Despite the fact that there had once been doubts about whether it was possible to grant property status to intangibles, to that which could be stolen through a window and could not be seen, touched or smelled, by the end of the literary property debate it was widely accepted that the intangible could be considered as a form of property. While Yates J's judgment in *Millar* v *Taylor* shows that in 1769 the idea of intangible property had not gained widespread acceptance in the law,[127] by the time Parliament came to debate the question of legal protection for designs applied on calico in 1787, there were no questions raised about the possibility of property rights in intangibles. Indeed, in the discussions leading up to the Calico Printers' Act in the 1780s, not only was the worth of copy-right protection taken as a given by all parties involved, it was also accepted that the law was able to grant property status to intangibles.

While by the latter part of the eighteenth century the intangible had been widely accepted as a legitimate subject matter for property protection, it is wrong to assume that the law had somehow managed to develop a set of techniques which enabled it to deal with intangible property with relative ease; that the problems the opponents of common law literary property had identified in granting property status to the intangible had somehow been overcome. That is, while the law was willing to accommodate the intangible as a species of property, it is imprudent to take this one step further, as many do, and suggest that the literary property debate somehow solved the problems that the law might have had in accommodating the intangible as a species of property.

The reason for this is that while the proponents of literary property were able to produce a number of arguments which countered the objections raised by those who argued against common law literary property, this does not mean that the difficulties that the law might have experienced in its dealing with intangible property were thereby answered.[128] Although the debate format may suggest otherwise, it is

---

[127] For example, Baron Perrott found the idea 'exceedingly ill founded and absurd': *Donaldson* v *Becket* (1774) 17 *Parliamentary History* col. 981. Literary property was also said for 'all intents and purposes to be indefinable': Attorney-General Thurlow, counsel for Donaldson, *ibid.*, col. 969.

[128] Rose suggests that the problems brought against literary property were resolved by recourse to Romantic theory: M. Rose, 'The Author as Proprietor' (1994), 52–3.

inaccurate to assume that the problems that were raised about the law's ability to endow property status on intangibles were resolved. Before we are able to reach such a conclusion, we need to consider the impact that the literary property debate had on intellectual property law, which upon reflection may not be as decisive as is often assumed.

In part the tendency to suggest that the literary property debate enabled the law to overcome the problems the opponents of literary property raised about the ability of the law to recognise the intangible as a form of property stems from the fact that the series of events which took place in the eighteenth century not only came to be treated as a thing replete with its own name, it also came to be regarded as a debate: with beginning, middle and end. One of the problems of seeing the literary property debate as that – a debate – is that we not only expect it to have provided answers to the questions posed, but also that it should have resolved any problems that the law might have experienced in granting property status to intangibles. Seeing the question of literary property as a debate, which carries with it certain expectations, has a number of other consequences. In explaining intellectual property law it leads us, for example, to prioritise intellectual discussions, to give them a causal status that they may not deserve. It also leads us to read the literature in a particular fashion. It led one commentator, for example, to speak of *Donaldson* v *Becket* as posing a paradox. This was that 'the House of Lords managed to "settle" one of the most hotly debated legal questions of the eighteenth century, but it manifestly failed to provide any rationale for its decision'.[129] The paradox posed by *Donaldson* v *Becket* was that it failed to decide the question of literary property according to the rules of the debate or, more accurately, according to the rules that are retrospectively applied to it.

In contrast to this way of thinking, we wish to argue that far from resolving the problems the law experienced in its dealings with the intangible, the literary property debate is merely an example of the law working through a set of problems that arose and continue to arise in its dealings with intellectual property. Armed with this viewpoint, in the next chapter we look in more detail at the way in which the law deals with and accommodates the intangible as a species of property. Because of the perennial nature of these problems, in our discussions of the nature of intangible property in law we will digress somewhat from the historical narrative which we have been following so far.

---

[129] R. Coombe, 'Challenging Paternity: Histories of Copyright' (1994) 6 *Yale Journal of Law and the Humanities* 407.

2   The mentality of intangible property

If we open any present-day textbook on intellectual property law, one of the first things we notice about intangible property is that it is usually spoken of as and associated with objects or things. Moreover the subject matter of intellectual property law is usually thought of by intellectual property lawyers as being non-creative, unitary and closed. Typically, the tendency to think of the intangible in this fashion is not confined to contemporary intellectual property law, but is also at work when the subject is viewed historically. If we suspend our modern preoccupation with the intangible as a non-creative, closed object and let pre-modern law speak for itself, a different and somewhat perplexing picture of intangible property begins to emerge. It is our aim in this chapter to explore the nature of the intangible as it reveals itself in pre-modern intellectual property law. We will begin to do this by showing that one of the overriding concerns of pre-modern intellectual property law was with creativity. Indeed it could be argued that creativity was, at least in certain guises, the primary focus of the law.[1] In turn, we argue that to understand the way in which law grants property status to the intangible, it is necessary to appreciate that the legal conception of intangible property embodies a number of conflicting demands that pull the law in different directions. Importantly while creativity may have been displaced with the move from pre-modern to modern law, many of the tensions which coexist within the legal notion of intangible property continue to play an important role in shaping present-day law.

---

[1] It is often said of modern British intellectual property law, with its pragmatic and positive heritage, that it is not and has never been concerned with creativity (and other equally alien notions such as personality) and that it is more concerned with the sweat of the brow rather than the brain. Recent events such as the US Supreme Court decision of *Feist Publications* v *Rural Telephone* (1991) 111 SCt 1282, as well as efforts to protect data bases, have reopened the question of the role of creativity in intellectual property law; particularly in relation to copyright.

Creativity and intellectual property law

Although it was not until the early part of the nineteenth century that the language of creativity was used with any degree of consistency, the common denominator which united patent law, literary property and indeed all areas of law which granted property rights in mental labour was a shared concern with creativity. While in the eighteenth century most of the discussions concerning mental (or creative) labour focused on literary property, the concern with creativity extended far beyond this to include *all* forms of intellectual property then in existence.[2] As Thomas Webster was to write in his 1853 treatise on designs and patents, products 'of the mind or intellectual labour when embodied in a practical form, whether in books, music, paintings, designs, or inventions in the arts and manufactures' have the 'peculiar claim derived from the nature of the subject – namely, that the subject matter of such property did not exist like land, the air, or wild-animals . . . such property is, in the strictest sense of the term, *a creation*'.[3] It was also recognised that property in mental labour was not limited to the rights then in existence, but extended, at least potentially, to include intangibles of all types.

In addition to being unified by a common concern with creative labour, another important feature of pre-modern intellectual property law was that the various areas of law also came to embody and share a particular image of what it meant to create. Again, it is important to note that the model of creativity employed by the law was not limited to literary property nor was it restricted to the late eighteenth century. If we look, for example, at the embryonic patent law – an area not usually renowned for its concern with things creative – we see that in a series of decisions and commentaries which began to appear at the end of the eighteenth century the law gradually developed a picture of what it meant to invent or create a machine or a chemical process.[4] The starting point for this analysis was a belief in the existence of an *a priori*

[2] For example, William Kenrick argued that 'if linen-printers, paper-stainers etc. are entitled in equity and in law to an exclusive copy-right in their labours, no good reason can possibly be given why artificers of all kinds should not be equally entitled to such an exclusive privilege of fabricating any manufacture, whose novelty of form, or use and design are peculiar to themselves': W. Kenrick, *An Address* (1774), 27.

[3] T. Webster, *On Property in Designs and Inventions in the Arts and Manufactures* (London: Chapman and Hall, 1853), 7 (emphasis added). As Inlow said, one of the consequences of the move away from patents for importation was that 'invention, no longer being introduction thus becomes in America, creation. And with creation we come to the heart of the problem of invention': E. Burke Inlow, *The Patent Grant* (Baltimore, Md.: The John Hopkins Press, 1950), 137.

[4] It should however be noted that patents were still available for the introduction of new trades. On this see *Darcy v Allin* (1602) 74 ER 1131; *Edgeberry v Stephens* (n.d.) 90 ER 1162. The belief that patents could only be granted to creators of inventions was also

domain, a reservoir from which inventions were drawn. While the name given to this territory varied from 'tradition', 'nature', 'laws of science', 'ideas', and 'principles',[5] in all cases it was said to provide the 'first ground and rule for arts and sciences, or in other words the elements and rudiments of them'.[6] This domain, which consisted of 'facts existing from the commencement of the present creation' which had been 'created by the great Author',[7] included such things as gravitation, heat, chemistry, electricity, the property of matter, the elasticity of steam, the relations of pressure and density, the longitude at sea and the rotation of the earth. Just as ideas were deemed to be beyond the scope of literary property protection these principles, which were said to be universal in their essence, fell outside the remit of what was patentable.[8]

In the same way as literary property law distinguished between ideas and their expression, patentable inventions were juxtaposed against non-patentable discoveries. As Webster said, a 'discoverer is one thing and an inventor is another. The discoverer is one who discloses something which exists in nature, for instance, coal fields, or a property of matter, or a natural principle: such discovery never was and never ought to be the subject of a patent ... The Subjects of discovery are indeed sown broadcast; they exist in nature.' However, 'much effort may have gone into the discovery of a principle ... no one could be said to have invented these'.[9] While it was not possible to invent a law of nature or a general rules of physics, they could be discovered. As with all things which lay in nature, these principles awaited 'only the mind of the

---

eventually used to argue, successfully, against the granting of patents for the mere publication, introduction or importation of an invention.

[5] The term 'principle' was used in a number of senses. Rooke J observed that 'the term principle is equivocal – it might be used to refer to radical elementary truths of a science – such as the natural properties of steam, its expansiveness and condensability': *Boulton and Watt v Bull* (1795)126 ER 651. It was later said of 'this law-phantom' – principle – that 'the witchcraft used by lawyers consists in mingling three different meanings together and by the aid of certain professional solemnities, producing a mystical word, capable of harlequinizing an idea into many various forms': 'Unreasonableness of Judge-made Law in Setting aside Patents' (1835) 22 *The Westminster Review* 459.

[6] Buller J, *Boulton and Watt v Bull* (1795) 126 ER 662. See also J. Collier, *An Essay on the Law of Patents* (London: A. Wilson, 1803), 78; J. Davies, *A Collection of the Most Important Cases Respecting Patents of Inventions* (London: W. Reed, 1816), 415; J. Norman, *A Treatise on the Law and Practice Relating to Letters Patent for Invention* (London: Butterworths, 1853), 9; R. Frost, *Patent Law and Practice* (London: Stevens and Haynes, 1891), 35.

[7] T. Webster, *On Property in Designs* (1853), 7.

[8] 'A principle was a mere idea, and therefore could not be a fit subject for a patent': R. Godson, 'Law of Patents' (19 Feb. 1833) 15 *Hansard* col. 977.

[9] T. Webster, *On Property in Designs* (1853), 5–6.

philosopher of adequate powers and perseverance to discover and articulate the fact'.[10]

What then was required in order to move from the realm of discovery to that of invention? The simple answer was that it was necessary to show that abstract principles had been reduced to practice, that Nature had been individualised or activated. Highlighting the dynamic and creative nature of the inventive process, Justice Buller said in *Boulton and Watt v Bull* (1795), which involved Watt's patent for a steam condenser, that patents 'were granted for some production from these elements and not for the elements themselves'.[11] While philosophical or abstract principles could not on their own be patented, their embodiment in a material or practical form could.[12] In these circumstances it was clear that in law it was the artificial or created nature of the final product, its distance from Nature, which ensured that an object became an invention rather than a mere discovery.[13]

If we shift away from patents to look at pre-modern intellectual property law more generally, we see that one of the factors that the various areas of law which granted property rights in mental labour had in common was not only a concern with creative labour but also a similar image of what it meant to create: they adopted, if you like, a shared model of creativity. In particular, it is clear that while God may have provided the starting blocks for the creative process, it was the contribution made by the author, engraver, designer or inventor who individualised the subject matter they worked with which the law protected.[14] Put differently, what intellectual property law protected

---

[10] *Ibid.*

[11] Buller J, *Boulton and Watt v Bull* (1795) 126 ER 662. 'A principle cannot of itself, apart from a practical application, produce any vendible article or manufacture': *ibid.* Lord Chief Justice Eyre said, 'Undoubtedly there can be no patent for a mere principle, but for a principle so far embodied and connected with corporeal substances as to be in a condition to act, and to produce effects in any art, trade, mystery or manual occupation, I think there may be a patent': *ibid.*, 667.

[12] T. Webster, in (ed.) H. Dircks, *Statistics of Inventions Illustrating a Patent Law* (London: E. and F. Spon, 1869), 45. As Derrida reminds us, the notion of the invention 'does not have the theological meaning of a veritable creation of existence *ex nihilo*': J. Derrida, 'Psyche: Inventions of the Other' (1989), 43.

[13] T. Webster, *On Property in Designs* (1853), 5–6.

[14] The fact that patents were only granted for creations rather than revelations of pre-existing ideas or principles meant that it could not be suggested that the law was providing monopoly protection. So long as these property rights were only granted for creations – which by definition necessarily involved the introduction of something new – the law could not be accused of restricting existing ideas. As such it was possible to argue that patents were 'the very opposite of a monopoly; for a patent to be valid, must be for a new invention, consequently, no persons, by such a grant, are restrained from any freedom they had before': W. Carpmael, 'Introductory Observations of the Law of Patents for Inventions' (1835) 3 *Repertory of Patent Inventions* 68–9. See also T. Webster, in (ed.) H. Dircks, *Statistics of Inventions* (1869), 47.

was the creative or human element embodied in the resulting product.[15] While the way the model was used was to change over time, revealed itself more often than not in a partial and oblique manner, and was (as we shall see) difficult to apply to trade marks, it was adopted as *the* paradigm of creation in all areas of pre-modern intellectual property law. As we shall see, the logic of creation also played an important role in helping to distinguish the different categories of intellectual property law.

Intangible property as action

While in pre-modern law it was common, as it is now, to speak of intellectual property law in terms of its relationship with particular tangible objects – literary property was concerned with books and patents with machines – at the same time an important distinction exists between the way pre-modern and modern intellectual property law think about what is protected. While in modern intellectual property law the protected subject matter is thought of almost exclusively in terms of its relationship to particular physical objects (similar to the way intellectual property law more generally is seen), in pre-modern intellectual property law a distinction was drawn between the way each area of law was seen (for example, literary property) and the way the *subject matter* or intangible property was perceived. In its pre-modern form, the intangible (as distinct from the areas of law which granted property rights in mental labour) was thought of not as a thing but more as something which was done: or, as it was described at the time, a form of action or performance.[16] As Slater wrote in 1884, 'the owner of every

---

[15] 'The origin of property is in production. As to works of imagination and reasoning, if not of memory, the author may be said to create, and in all departments of the mind, new books are the products of the labour skill and capital of the author. The subject of property is the order of the words in the author's composition': Erle J, *Jefferys v Boosey* (1854) 10 ER 702. 'A person to be entitled to the character of an inventor must himself have conceived the idea embodied in his improvement. It must be the product of his own mind and genius and not of another's': Nelson J, *Pitts v Bull* (1851) 2 Black W 237. The idea that the invention must necessarily flow from the mind of an individual creator meant that a corporation could not be considered as a patentee.

[16] The image of the book more as action or communication than as a thing is reflected in a number of the tracts on the literary property debate which describe a book as a 'performance': For example, see *Memorial for the Booksellers of Edinburgh and Glasgow. The Decision of the Court of Session Upon the Question of Literary Property in the Cause John Hinton Against Alexander Donaldson per Lord Auchinleck* (1774); reprint *The Literary Property Debate* (ed. S. Parks) (New York: Garland, 1974), 3. See more generally M. Rose, 'The Author in Court: *Pope v Curll*' (1992) 10 *Cardozo Arts and Entertainment Law Review* 492. Sir Joshua Reynolds at this time described painting as a performance. J. Reynolds, *Discourses on Art* (1959), Discourse V, 81 and 87 and Discourse VI, 110–11.

intellectual production has in the fruits of his labour, has for its essence not merely the paper and print of the author, nor the marble block of the sculptor, nor yet again the canvas of the painter; but the *performance* – considered as an incorporeal creation embodied in material form'.[17] Henry Cunynghame made the case even clearer when he said, '[j]ust as by the words "painting" or "drawing" or "sculpture" we may mean either the practice of the art, or the objects made by the means of it, so also to the word manufacturing we may give either an abstract or concrete meaning'.[18] While the modern law has tended to think about intangible property as a concrete and static object, in the eighteenth and much of the nineteenth century the intangible was defined in more abstract and dynamic terms.

To our modern eyes, which are used to seeing the intangible as an object, the idea of the intangible as a form of action may be difficult for us to comprehend. Nonetheless it is clear that in pre-modern intellectual property law the intangible was perceived very differently from how it is now. Importantly, this image not only shaped the way the intangible was viewed, but also influenced decisions as to what formed part of the legitimate subject matter of intellectual property law. For example, given that it was widely agreed that (pre-modern) patent law protected the *art* by which something was produced rather than the product itself,[19] some commentators had difficulty in accepting that there could be such a thing as a patent for a product. Indeed Robert Frost found the concept to be so non-sensical that he excluded it from his 1891 treatise on patent law with the comment: 'it would appear that a product, apart from the art by the exercise of

---

[17] J. Slater, *The Law Relating to Copyright and Trade Marks Treated more Particularly with Reference to Infringement* (London: Stevens and Sons, 1884), 2.

[18] H. Cunynghame, *English Patent Practice* (London: William Clowes and Sons, 1894), 40. The concepts of 'work', 'creation' and 'invention' always carry with them a reference to practice and object, action and theory.

[19] 'A patent . . . is properly a right to an art or trade, a process, method or operation, and the forms of the machines and vessels are described by the patentee not as the invention, but to show "the manner in which it is to be performed". An equivalent apparatus might be substituted without altering the principle of the invention, but it might be a different form or configuration': T. Turner, *On Copyright in Design in Art and Manufacture* (London: Elsworth, 1849), v–vi. See also H. Cunynghame, *English Patent Practice* (1894), 45. 'The meaning given to "manufacture" by our best authors and lexicographers will be found to be "something made by art" or "the process of making anything by art"': W. Carpmael, *The Law of Patents for Inventions Familiarly Explained for the use of Inventors and Patentees* (6th edn) (London: Stephens, 1860), 13. 'It is this *art* . . . which is the exclusive property of the patentee, and which he . . . and no one else, is entitled to use during the continuance of the privilege': R. Frost, *Patent Law and Practice* (1891), 24–5. For the etymology of 'art' in this context see E. Johnson, 'The Mercantilist Concept of "Art" and "Ingenious Labour"' (1931) 6 *Economic History* 234.

hich is produced, cannot be the subject matter of letters patent':[20] a situation which is in marked contrast to the position in modern law where the product-patent is treated as the definitive patent and it is the process patent which occupies the more ambiguous position.[21]

Although in pre-modern intellectual property law the intangible was seen as a form of action, the law was faced with a problem: when talking about the subject matter which was protected as intellectual property, the law spoke of the intangible in dynamic terms, as something that was done; yet when it came to deal with and process the intangible, the law was unable to represent the intangible in a way which reflected its active or dynamic nature. One reason for this was that the law lacked the language with which to reproduce the performative nature of the intangible. This was because, as Bastide says, in 'the case of action, one can show only the result, the trace'.[22] Given that action or performance can only be displayed in terms of its forms and composition,[23] this meant that no matter how much the law wished to present itself as protecting the performative aspect of creation, it was unable to do so. This was reinforced by the fact that the law regularly spoke of intellectual property in terms of the tangible objects it regulated: the Statute of Anne dealt with books; patents were granted for playing cards and so on.[24] The law thus found itself in a paradoxical position in that although the intangible was seen primarily in dynamic terms, the law could never properly account for the performative nature of intangible property; it was always condemned to second-guess, to describe and deal with something else. As a consequence of being forced to represent these dynamic concepts in

---

[20] R. Frost, *Patent Law and Practice* (1891), 49. As Frost argued, the fact that patents protected the active process of creation (the *art*), presented a number of difficulties. It was 'ambiguous, as it may mean (i) a patent for a product pure and simple, apart from the art by the exercise of which it is produced; (ii) the art by the exercise of which the product is produced': *ibid.*

[21] Nevertheless early patent privileges were concerned with buying and selling products. It was also unclear until *Crane v Price* (1842) 134 ER 239 that a patent could be granted for a process.

[22] F. Bastide, 'The Iconography of Scientific Texts: Principles of Analysis' (tr. G. Myers) in (eds.) M. Lynch and S. Woolgar, *Representations in Scientific Practice* (London: MIT Press, 1990), 206. 'Of course it seems easier to show an "object" (such as skeletons of worms or of sponges) than an action (*un faire*)': *ibid.* See also J. Derrida, 'Psyche: Inventions of the Other' (1989), 27.

[23] The tension was exacerbated by the fact that representations were interpreted visually. As Turner said, it is not the 'muscle that acquires possession' of intangible property 'but the eye': T. Turner, *Remarks on the Amendment of the Law of Patents for Inventions* (London: Elsworth, 1851), 3.

[24] Nevertheless the 1710 Statute of Anne, which spoke of encouragement of learning, and the 1624 Statute of Monopolies, which talked of the *manner* of new manufacture, clearly embody the dynamic nature of the property protected as intellectual property.

static terms, the performative aspect of the intangible took on a somewhat ambivalent status within the law.

Should we treat this, as many have, as evidence of a transformation in the way the intangible was represented in law from action to thing,[25] that is, as commodification of the intangible? There are two reasons why our answer to this is 'no'. The first is this: while when dealing with the intangible pre-modern law found it necessary to represent action in a static rather than a dynamic fashion, nonetheless in other aspects of its dealings with the intangible the primary focus of the law remained on the process of creation. While there may have been moves in other areas in the eighteenth century to treat, for example, the text as a thing rather than as an action, it was not until the latter part of the nineteenth century that similar changes took place in other areas of intellectual property law.[26] Prior to this, in law the intangible was seen as a form of action; albeit one that was frozen in time and identified in the traces that it left behind. Although the law was only able to represent performance in static terms, it is incorrect to assume that as a result it necessarily saw the intangible as a thing. To do so not only misrepresents the position of the intangible in law, it also causes us to overlook the tension and instability generated by the law's attempt to grant property status to intangibles. Moreover, it also leads us to overlook the various techniques that the law has employed over time when negotiating between the dynamic and the static, and the impact that this has had on intangible property.

The second reason why we reject the argument about the commodification of intangible property is that if we resist the temptation to comfort ourselves with the theoretical assurance of a simple opposition between action and thing or between the performative and the constant, we are able to recognise that the juridical categories employed in pre-modern intellectual property law operated in a middle ground that oscillated between action and thing. The result of the development of this intermediate zone was that the law came to deal in elements which were neither actions nor things:[27] a situation which reinforced the ambiguous position occupied by the intangible in pre-modern intellectual property law.[28]

[25] 'In the early modern period, it was ... usual to think of the text as an action, as something done. Now, in the context of the developing marketplace society, the text was being represented as a kind of thing': M. Rose, 'The Author in Court' (1992), 492.

[26] While it is difficult to date the precise time when this way of thinking ended, it is clear that it continued at least up until the end of the nineteenth century when mental and creative labour were all but excluded from the law's immediate concern. See further ch. 9.

[27] See J. Derrida, 'Psyche: Inventions of the Other' (1989), 45.

[28] Pottage captured the awkward nature of the intangible in pre-modern law when he said 'one might say that whereas the "things" of law should be seen as products of subjective

Reproduction and identification

The ambiguous status of the intangible was compounded by the law's willingness to accept that, in order to have any real effect, the subject matter of intellectual property law needed to be susceptible to repetition and reinscription. Indeed, it is almost a truism that in intellectual property law the protected subject matter must be both reproducible and repeatable. In reflection of this it has long been recognised that the property right in the intangible must extend beyond its first embodiment (the manuscript, painting, or prototype) to cover the production of replicas and equivalents. Typically, this has been taken to mean that the intangible needs to be presented in abstract and universal terms. This is necessary so that when comparing physical objects, it is possible to determine whether or not there has been a reproduction of the intangible.

At the same time, one of the primary tasks confronting the law in its dealings with the intangible is the need to be able to identify the property, to trace the protected subject matter as it is translated into new formats. While the task of identifying the intangible can be seen in a number of different ways, it is best understood as an evidential question. As Ginzburg reminds us, evidential matters of this type are 'highly qualitative' processes in 'which the object is the study of individual cases, situations and documents, precisely *because they are individual*'.[29] Temple Franks, Comptroller-General of Patents at the beginning of this century, highlighted the important role played by individuality in identifying intangible property when he said in relation to copyright infringement that 'a thing to have protection must have individuality, otherwise how can it be proved that it has been copied?'[30]

By juxtaposing reproduction and identification in this manner, we are better able to appreciate the conflicting demands that are embodied within the legal notion of the intangible. More specifically we see that the law is faced with the problem that, on the one hand, the intangible must be, at least potentially, reproducible and susceptible to repetition; at the same time, one of the primary tasks facing intellectual property law is the need to identify the scope and nature of the intangible

---

apprehension and appropriation, or as an intermediate stage of a dialectic of subject and object, law hypostatises this middle term, and deals with it as though it were a "material" thing': A. Pottage, 'Autonomy of Property', paper presented to Hart Workshop, London, 1991, 14.

[29] C. Ginzburg, 'Clues: Roots of an Evidential Paradigm' in *Clues, Myths and the Historical Method* (tr. J. and A. Tedeschi) (Baltimore, Md.: John Hopkins University Press, 1989), 106.

[30] L. Temple Franks, 4 March 1910, BT/209/835.

property – a qualitative task which highlights the individual nature of the intangible.[31]

Despite or possibly because of the complexity of these tasks the law responded with a simple and powerful argument. In relation to literary property the law set out to manage these apparently conflicting demands by limiting the scope of the property to that which was captured in the printed word. The focus on print, as Ginzburg says, 'meant that even while dealing with individual cases, one avoided the principal pitfall of the human sciences: quality'.[32] In short, by focusing on the printed word, the task of identification was able to be presented as being quantitative, objective and universal. Moreover, as it enabled the law to determine whether two objects were similar without the need to engage in qualitative judgment, the gap that existed between repetition and identification was, at least temporarily, overcome.

As we have seen, with the realisation that a print-based approach unduly limited the potential of intellectual property, the law shifted its attention away from print towards the expression of the creator. Importantly, expression was thought to carry with it a number of characteristics which provided the means by which the conflicting tasks the law had set for itself were accomplished. On the one hand, expression was abstract and isomorphic enough for it to be reproducible and repeatable. At the same time, the expressive contribution of the author, as well as that of the inventor, engraver and designer, was such that it always enabled the property to be identified.[33] The reason for this was that it was believed that whenever (creative) objects were produced, creators always left an indelible mark on the work which enabled it to be identified. Moreover, it was also assumed that the mark left by the creator was unique and individual. As Hargrave said, 'a literary work *really* original, like the human face, will always have some singularities, some lines, some features, to characterise it, and to fix and establish its identity; and to assert the contrary with respect to either, would be justly deemed equally opposite to reason and universal experience'.[34] The

---

[31] Benjamin captures a similar tension in his comment that 'the uniqueness of a work of art is inseparable from its being imbedded in the fabric of tradition': W. Benjamin, 'The Work of Art in the Age of Mechanical Reproductions' (tr. H. Zohn), in (ed.) H. Arendt, *Illuminations* (New York: Harcourt, Brace and World, 1968), 223.

[32] C. Ginzburg, 'Clues: Roots of an Evidential Paradigm' (1989), 107.

[33] The inventor 'stamps the character of his mind on his invention as well as an author is known to do on his book': W. Spence, *The Public Policy of a Patent Law* (London: Printed for the Author and sold at 8 Quality Court, 1869), 16.

[34] F. Hargrave, *An Argument in Defence of Literary Property* (1774), 6–7. 'No instance can be given, of two men's separately writing books on the same subject, agreeing in words or sentiments from beginning to end. Every man's book (if an original composition), as well as every man's face, must be capable of distinction from another's': D. Rae,

longevity of such a claim is reflected in the fact that, almost a century later, Copinger said, in the first edition of his now famous book on copyright law, that for 'copyright, the claim is not to ideas but to the order of words and this order has a marked identity and a permanent endurance. The order of each man's words is as singular as his countenance'.[35]

Given the belief that creations always exhibited the unique mark or traces of their creators it was always possible, so the argument went, to identify the intangible property, no matter how much it was transformed.[36] The fact that the unique mark of the creator always remained etched in the intangible meant it was always possible to determine, for example, whether an abridgment of a book infringed the literary property in that book.[37] Just as the naturalist could determine the nature of an animal from a single bone, or graphologists were said to be able to recognise traits of the inner person from their writing, it was said that if the 'lost books of Livy were found without a clue to their authorship, there would not be wanting those who would quickly recognise in them the proprietary marks of the great historian'.[38]

Despite the force of these arguments, gradually the idea that expression could be used as a means of identifying intangible property began to unravel. In some circumstances this arose with the realisation that it was simply not possible to identify, for example, either the author of a book or the scope of the literary property by looking at the book in

Information for John Hinton (1773) 18–19. As Blackstone said as counsel in *Tonson v Collins*, 'style and sentiment are the essentials of a literary composition. These *alone* constitute its identity': *Tonson v Collins* (1760) 96 ER 189. See also W. Blackstone, *Commentaries* (1809), vol. II, ch. 26, 405 ff.

[35] W. Copinger, *The Law of Copyright in Works of Literature and Art, including that of Drama, Music, Engraving, Sculpture, Painting, Photography and Ornamental and Useful Design* (London: William Clowes and Sons, 1870), 6. Erle J, *Jefferys v Boosey* (1854) 10 ER 703.

[36] The Scholastic motto 'we cannot speak about what is individual', *individuum est ineffabile*, was effectively transformed in law into 'we do not need to speak because it is individual'.

[37] This meant that the 'literary or artistic compositions of one person are perfectly distinguishable from those of every other ... Hence the copyright privilege is conceded in the absolute certainty that the grantee is their true and only originator or first producer or creator. No second person can come forward, after the copyright privilege is secured to an artist or author, and allege that the poem or picture he composed also. To infringe copyright means to slavishly or meanly copy the work of another': R. Macfie, 'The Patent Question' (1863) *TNAPSS* 821.

[38] 'Is Copyright Perpetual? An Examination of the Origin and Nature of Literary Property' (1875–6) 10 *American Law Review* 22. Speaking of a musical composition, it was said that it 'is a creation without material form in the realm of imagination; but so complete is the form of its being, so marked in its individuality, so distinctly and perceptible to the musical mind that another will produce it by ear, without the aid of written or printed notes': *ibid.*

question. In particular, doubts were raised about the uniqueness of creativity, which was crucial to the argument that expression acted, in effect, as an *identikit* of intangible property.[39] More specifically, doubts were raised about the idea that in creating a new work or invention the creator necessarily left traces of himself in the final product which could later be used to identify the intangible property.[40] Put simply, when confronted, for example, with a work written in English and another in French (which was said to be a translation and abridgment of the English work), expression provided very little, if any, assistance in determining whether the two works were the same.[41] There was no magic formula, no fingerprint or DNA which followed the intangible property as it mutated into new formats that enabled the law to look at two works and proclaim – 'yes, that is a copy of the other'. Paradoxically, because expression served to focus attention on the image of the individual as a unique empirical entity, not only did it fail to answer the twin demands of replication and identification as was supposed, it actually served to heighten the tension that existed between them. These problems were compounded by the fact that the more the scope of the intangible was broadened (to include equivalents, translations and the like), the more abstract and hence illusory the intangible became.

While it gradually became clear that expression was unable to fulfil

[39] According to one eighteenth-century account, '[a]ll men whose sensations are equally well ordered, ought to have the same perceptions. It will be extremely difficult therefore to ascertain whose ideas they originally were, or to say that they are proper to one man more than another'. As a result all that the writer was willing to concede was that 'an ingenious and speculative man improves his intellectual powers more, and makes a better use of them than his neighbours'. Consequently he concluded that 'this cannot come under the denomination of *property*, and more than the circumstance of one man's blood circulating faster than another's, is property, or the circumstance of being more expert in walking, riding, or fencing': *Information for John Robertson* (1771) 9.

[40] This was because while 'some few may be known by their style ... the generality are not known at all': Yates (as counsel for defendant) in *Tonson v Collins* (1760) 96 ER 185. In his typically astute way, Kenrick recognised the limitations of relying on expression as a mode of identification. Instead he argued for the need for legislative intervention to determine 'more precisely ... the limits of appropriation, so that both writers and booksellers may know how far they are authorised to abridge, copy or make quotations from the works of their predecessors ... without which they cannot safely exercise their calling, and all improvement in works of *history, philology,* and *science* must speedily have an end': W. Kenrick, *An Address* (1774), 47. Speaking of the problem of drawing a line in terms of ownership Lord Thring said to the 1898 Select Committee on Copyright, 'it is all very well when you come to great works ... you can register them and distinguish them by known signs; but when you come to the innumerable small works' a different situation prevailed: Lord Thring, *Report from the Select Committee of the House of Lords on the Copyright Bill (HL) and the Copyright Amendment Bill (HL)* (1898) 184.

[41] *Burnett v Chetwood* (1720) 35 ER 1008.

the demands that were made of it, and that it did not solve the problems of identity so much as defer or suppress them, this is not to deny that expression and the model of creation that it embodied played and continue to play an important role in shaping intellectual property law. Nor is it to deny that expression provided a narrative of legitimacy and lent its structure to matters such as the rules of originality and obviousness. While the fate of expression and its continuing impact on intellectual property law remain important and contentious issues, our interest lies less with expression as a means of identifying intangible property – and its ultimate failure – than with what it potentially teaches us about intangible property.

Upon reflection it becomes clear that no matter how much the law longed for the intangible to be presented in abstract, universal terms, because of the individualising perspective which is at the heart of the task of identification, the law has never able to fully satisfy the demands of replication (or abstraction) and identification. We are alerted to the fact that these twin demands, which pull the law in different directions, not only remain unresolved but also continue to play an important role in shaping contemporary intellectual property law. Indeed many current debates (such as those which have arisen in relation to copyright and patent protection of computer programs and computer-related inventions) can be seen as the law attempting to work through these conflicting demands in new environments..

The essence of creation

The ambiguous and somewhat enigmatic nature of intangible property was compounded by the law's willingness to accept that the subject matter of intellectual property law could be infringed beyond the immediate form in which it was expressed. As we saw earlier, with the formation of pre-modern intellectual property law it became clear that for intangible property to have any real value it was not enough for the owner only to be protected against identical copies. Rather, what was needed was that protection also be given over non-identical copies, to copies that were in some sense similar. As soon as it was accepted that it was possible to infringe a patent other than by directly copying an invention (for example by taking the pith and marrow of the invention), that the scope of literary property extended beyond the right to print and re-print to include such things as abridgments, compilations and translations, and that a design could be infringed by fraudulent imitations, the nature of intellectual property law changed fundamentally. This was because by admitting that copying need not imply that the works be identical, the law necessarily moved from the concrete to the abstract,[42] from the relative security of the text or the external appearance of the design and the machine to the shadowy ephemeral world of the *essence* of the creation.[43] Because it was necessary for the intangible to be both identifiable and at the same time malleable enough to move from work to work, it was forced to take on a transcendental quality. With this single gesture, which was perhaps the most important that took place in this area in the eighteenth century, intellectual property law was set on a course from which it has been unable to escape.

The shift from the surface of the text to the essence of the creation had a number of important consequences for intellectual property law. One of the factors that flowed from the decision to admit that the scope of the property extended beyond its immediate form is that the intangible only ever reveals itself in a partial way. Given that when disputes arise over intangible property the law is only ever presented with a partial image of the intangible, what the law deals with is always already secondary; it is a representation or sequel of the physical object that it has before it. As the essence of the intangible always remains hidden from view, this means that, unlike the case with print, which is visible and easily identifiable, one of the primary tasks that confronts intellectual property law is that of recreating or locating the essence of the creation. So, for example, before being able to determine whether the property interest has been appropriated the law first has to locate and identify the essence of the intangible property.

In the account of the legal concept of the intangible outlined above, it was presupposed that the law deals with pre-existing subject matter, that its task is to locate and identify pre-existing intangible property.[44] Added to this was the assumption that creation proceeds in a chronolo-

---

[42] 'Property in the order of words is a mental abstraction, but so were many other kinds of property: for instance, the property in the stream of water, which is not in any of the atoms of the water, but only in the flow of the stream': W. Copinger, *The Law of Copyright* (1870), 6.

[43] 'The incorporeal or immaterial element ... of the manufacture, the book, or the picture, has to be identified under a different form of corporeal or material element in settling the question of difference from two others, that is to say, from something which has preceded, or from something which has succeeded': T. Webster, 'On the Protection of Property in Intellectual Labour as Embodied in Inventions, Books, Designs and Pictures, by the Amendment of the Laws of Patent-right and Copyright' (1859) *TNAPSS* 239.

[44] It is as if the law assumes the existence of a reality independent of the physical object, a realm of what Kant called the things-in-themselves or noumena, of which no complete representation is possible. Perhaps the most famous modern formulation of this is to be found in Judge Learned Hand's comment in *Nichols v Universal Pictures Corporation*: 'Upon any work ... a great number of patterns of increasing generality will fit equally well as more and more of the incident is left out.' At the centre lies the essence (or totality) of the work, further out the title (characters), yet

gical line that flows from author to work, or inventor to invention. It was also assumed that there is some inaugural event or a supposed point of origin which produces the intangible.[45] While there is no denying the power of this way of thinking about intellectual property, to replicate it as a template of the model of creation used in law only serves to distort our understanding of intangible property.

A more helpful way to proceed is to acknowledge the positive role that the law plays in creating its own subject matter. That is, we need to take account of the fact that the legal process is *itself* creative;[46] that the law, in effect, creates or at least plays an important role in shaping the (essence of) intangible property – that, contrary to what so many suggest, there is no naturally existing core or essence of a work or invention that the law simply discovers. It is this creative faculty which enables the law to perceive similarities and invent correspondences between apparently dissimilar objects, to trace the intangible (albeit with difficulty) through different media. In highlighting the creative dimension of intellectual property law, our understanding of intangible property moves from a focus on the model of creation that the law employs, to include the creativity that the law *itself* exercises in completing this model; from poesis (or production) to autopoesis (or self-production). In recognising the creative nature of intellectual property law, we are also better able to appreciate the dynamic nature of intangible property.[47]

---

further still the ideas which fall outside the remit of legal protection: (1930) 45 F. 2d 119, 121.

[45] Invention also presupposes an 'originality, a relation to origins, generations, procreation, genealogy, that is to say a set of values often associated with genus or geniality, thus with naturality. Hence the question of son, of the signature, and of the name': J. Derrida, 'Psyche: Inventions of the Other' (1989), 28.

[46] If we follow the idea that 'mimesis is always concerned with a relational network of more than one person; the mimetic production of a symbolic world refers to other worlds and to their creators and draws other persons into one's own world . . . mimesis implies an acceptance of tradition and the work of predecessors', it is tempting to describe the legal process as mimetic: G. Gebauer and C. Wulf, *Mimesis: Culture, Art, Society* (tr. D. Reneau) (Berkeley, Calif.: University of California Press, 1993), 3.

[47] Derrida's comments about patent law, which apply equally to all forms of intellectual property, succinctly capture the nature of this tension. On the one hand there exists the abstract, universality. 'Universality is also the ideal objectivity, thus unlimited recurrence.' The problem with this however is that this 'recurrence is lodged in the unique occurrence of invention', a process which 'blurs, as it were, the signature of inventors', or what we treat as the individual. The upshot of this is, argues Derrida, that 'the name of an individual or of a unique empirical entity cannot be associated with it except in an inessential, extrinsic, accidental way. We should even say aleatory. This gives rise to the enormous problem of property rights over inventions, a problem that, in its legislative form, dates from a relatively recent moment in the history of the West': J. Derrida, 'Psyche: Inventions of the Other', (1989), 53.

Although we are drawing attention to the positive role that the law plays in creating intangible property, we should not be taken as suggesting that intangible property is purely a figment of the legal imagination. Rather, what we are hoping to highlight is that the law finds itself in a situation where it both uncovers and produces intangible property: the relative weight of each depending on the circumstance and the subject matter in question.[48] While it may be impossible for the law to reduce the subject matter of intellectual property to a material form or to exhaustively define intangible property, it is not as some suggest – or hope – an optional exercise.[49] Rather, in a process as impossible as it is necessary, the law is forced to pursue something that it can never completely imagine, which is always beyond representation.[50]

Moreover, while the creative (or mimetic) faculty employed by the law plays an important role in shaping intangible property this is not to suggest that it somehow resolves the tensions that underlie the juridical category of intangible property. Instead, just as the law continues to find itself grappling with issues of reproduction and identification, questions as to the essence of the intangible property continue to reappear when the law finds itself confronted with new subject matter.

By highlighting the tensions which characterise intangible property we are not suggesting that it inevitably leads to the demise or collapse of intellectual property law. Indeed it could be argued that rather than undermining the law such tensions are the source of potential strength – that, for example, the circularity and ambiguity which lie at the heart of the subject matter of intellectual property law endow it with the flexibility to accommodate unexpected forms of subject matter. In addition, recognising that conflicting demands pull the subject matter of intellectual property law in different directions helps to explain why it is that this area of the law is so often referred to as the 'metaphysics of the

---

[48] See S. Stewart, *Crimes of Writing* (1991), 5 ff.

[49] 'As the content becomes less dependent on the medium in which it is made available to the public, a system of law conceptually linked to the medium, such as copyright, must inevitably undergo some dramatic rethinking': Copyright Convergence Group, *Highways to Change: Copyright in the New Communications Environment* (Canberra: Microdata, 1994), 5–6.

[50] As Peters argues, 'there can be no return to a pre-representational system – no hope for a world of reals as the foundation for language, no hope of fixed commodities as the foundation for trade. Humans were bound to that process of continual motion which could prevent the representational systems from collapsing, bound to the continued translation of representations (money into goods into money, words into things into words)': J. Peters, 'The Bank, the Press and the "Return of Nature": On Currency, Credit, and Literary Property in the 1690s' in (eds.) J. Brewer and S. Staves, *Early Modern Conceptions of Property* (London: Routledge, 1995), 377.

law';[51] 'where the distinctions are ... very subtle and refined ... and sometimes almost evanescent':[52] a claim first made in relation to patents but soon applied to other forms of intellectual property.

While in order to understand intangible property and the role it plays in intellectual property law it is necessary to take account of the tensions that are embodied within the juridical category, we also need to take account of the ways in which the law accommodates and accounts for these tensions.[53] In a sense much of the history of intellectual property law can be seen as one of the law attempting to contain and restrict the intangible – to capture the phantom – only to find that the object of representation reconfigures itself in a new medium: the latest example being in relation to digital works. The particular way in which the law has responded to these demands is one of the focuses of the next part as we move to look at intellectual property law in the early period of the nineteenth century.

[51] M. Renouard, *Traité des brevets d'invention*, quoted in T. Webster, *The Law and Practice for Letters Patent for Inventions* (London: Crofts and Blenkman, 1841).

[52] *Folsom* v *Marsh* (1841) 9 F Cas 342, 344.

[53] While Stewart suggests that tensions of this type were resolved by the cult of authorship, originality and genius, we hope to highlight the role played by more bureaucratic means: S. Stewart, *Crimes of Writing* (1991), 32.

Part 2

The emergence of modern intellectual property law

The early nineteenth century was an important period in the development of the British law which granted property rights in mental labour. As well as witnessing the beginnings of the administrative and legal reform of patent law, a number of unsuccessful attempts to introduce a general Law of Arts and Manufacture, and a resurgence of concern with the duration of literary property, it also saw proposals to extend existing rights to analogous subject matter, the development of bilateral literary property agreements, and the first treatises and digests to focus exclusively on this area of the law. While these changes all played an important role in shaping modern intellectual property law, we will concentrate on the series of reforms which took place from 1839 to 1843 in what we would now call design law.

Given that the design legislation enacted at the time stands at the conjunction of pre-modern and modern intellectual property law, it is unsurprising that it proved to be important not only in the formation of modern design law, but also in that of intellectual property law more generally. We see during this period the development not only of many of the salient features of modern design law but also of modern intellectual property law and, more specifically, the emergence of two important features of modern intellectual property law. First, with the establishment of the Designs Register the first modern system of registration for intellectual property came into being. One of the notable aspects of this new mode of registration was that proof was rendered a matter of public rather than private control. At the same time, we also see the first concerted efforts to regulate intangible property by bureaucratic means.

Secondly, with the reforms that took place in the 1840s the law became increasingly interested in the aesthetics of law; in the shape that the law itself took. In this we see the first moves towards the formation of the modern mode of organisation which, in contrast to the subject-specific and reactive nature of pre-modern law, was abstract and forward looking. The process of abstraction was a crucial stage in the development of a design law and the categorisation of mental labour more generally. This is because the shift from a reactive, specific law to a law which was abstract and forward looking produced a change in the ontological status of the law, 'a move from linguistic patterns mastered at the practical level to a code, a grammar, via the labour of codification, which is a juridical activity'.[1] The abstraction in the legal categories not only shaped the way the categories were organised, it also influenced what were taken as problems to be resolved: of how the new categories were to be organised and the boundaries between the categories policed. Interestingly we also see that the attempts to organise the categories according to what we would now call the principles of law failed. Instead the law resorted to more bureaucratic means: to the newly established registration system as a means of organising and regulating the categories.

---

[1] P. Bourdieu, 'Codification' in his *In Other Words: Essays Towards a Reflexive Sociology* (tr. M. Adamson) (Cambridge: Polity Press, 1990), 80. This is reflected in the 1844 International Copyright Act whereby 'four several Acts' were reduced to the category of 'fine art'.

3   Designing the law

The first statute to deal explicitly with the legal protection of designs was the Calico Printers' Act of 1787.[1] This Statute, which was passed not long after the end of the literary property debate, conferred two months' protection on 'every person who shall invent, design and print ... any new and original pattern ... for printing linens, cottons, calicos or muslins'. The Act, which was championed by William Kilburn on behalf of the London calico printers,[2] was modelled on the existing statutes giving protection to authors and engravers.[3] Although passed as a temporary measure, the Act was renewed in 1789[4] and then again in 1794 when the length of protection was extended to three months and the provisions were given permanent effect.[5]

While this legislation served its ends fairly well, it became apparent early in the nineteenth century that there was an urgent need to improve the state of British design. Britain was able to produce manufactured goods more cheaply and in greater quantity than many of its competitors, but when these goods were compared with those produced by other trading nations, particularly France, it was thought that their sale suffered from their inferior aesthetic quality. In order to improve this

---

[1] An Act for the Encouragement of the Arts of Designing and Printing Linens, Cottons, Calicos and Muslins by vesting the Properties thereof in the Designers, Printers and Proprietors for a Limited Time 27 Geo. III c. 38 (1787) (1787 Calico Printers' Act). For the background see S. Chapman, *The Cotton Industry in the Industrial Revolution* (London: Macmillan, 1972); S. Chapman and S. Chassagne, *European Textile Printers in the Eighteenth Century: a Study of Peel and Oberkamps* (London: Heinemann Educational, 1981).

[2] A. Longfield, 'William Kilburn and the Earliest Copyright Acts for Cotton Printing Designs' (1953) 45 *Burlington Magazine* 230; D. Greysmith, 'Patterns, Piracy and Protection in the Textile Printing Industry, 1787–1850' (1983) 14 *Textile History* 165.

[3] CJ (1787) 546. The London calico printers objected to their patterns being copied by the new cotton factories of the north. The latter group opposed the pleas for protection to such effect that the duration of protection granted by Parliament was confined to two months and also that the Act was only passed as a temporary measure.

[4] An Act for Continuing an Act Made in the Twenty Seventh Year of the Reign of His Present Majesty 29 Geo. III c. 19 (1789).

[5] An Act for Amending and Making Perpetual an Act Made in the Twenty Seventh Year of His Present Majesty 34 Geo. III c. 23 (1794).

situation, a number of changes were proposed.[6] These included the establishment of design schools to improve the skills of British designers and the opening of a museum (later called the Victoria and Albert Museum) where, with a view to improving standards of taste, 'good designs' were to be exhibited to the public.[7] Attention was also given to improving the legal regime which provided property protection for designs. To this end, the 1787 Calico Printers' Act was repealed and replaced by the two new acts.[8]

The first of these, the Copyright of Designs Act, which was passed on 4 June 1839, widened the category of subject matter which was protected under the 1787 Calico Printers' Act from its initial limitation to certain vegetable fabrics (such as cotton, linen, calico and muslin) to include animal fabrics (wool, silk or hair and mixtures thereof).[9] It also extended the jurisdiction of the Act to include Ireland. The protection provided by the 1839 Act, which arose automatically on publication of the design was, like the Calico Printers' Act of 1787, limited to three months.[10] The second Act, which became known as the Designs Registration Act, was passed on 14 June 1839.[11] This Act extended the scope of protection beyond woven fabrics to include all articles of manufacture; and moved protection away from patterns and prints to provide protection for the shape and configuration of any article of manufacture. The Act also conferred longer protection on such designs varying according to the nature of the substance to which the design was to be applied from three years to twelve months and specified that protection was only to be granted if the design was registered. It is important to note that only one of the Acts passed in 1839 – the so-called Designs Registration Act – required registration as a prerequisite for protection. In contrast, the protection offered by the other Act of 1839 arose automatically on publication of the design.

Although these Acts were hailed as improvements upon the previous law, they were soon repealed and replaced by two new statutes: the 1842

[6] See, generally, 1836 *Select Committee on Arts and Manufacture*.
[7] On the design schools see Q. Bell, *The Schools of Designs* (London: Routledge and Kegan Paul, 1963); A. Rifkin, 'Success Disavowed: The Schools of Design in Mid-Nineteenth Century Britain' (1988) 1 *Design History* 89.
[8] For a history of the Designs Acts see E. Potter in 1862 *Report from the Select Committee on Trade Marks Bill, and Merchandise Marks Bill: Together with the Proceedings of the Committee, Minutes of Evidence* 98 (Q. 2181 ff) (hereafter 1862 *Select Committee on Trade Marks*).
[9] An Act for Extending the Copyright of Designs for Calico Printers to Designs 2 Vict. c. 13 (1839) (hereafter 1839 Copyright of Designs Act) .
[10] T. Webster, *The Subject Matter of Letters Patent for Inventions and the Registration of Designs* (3rd edn) (London: Elsworth, 1851), 78.
[11] An Act to Secure to Proprietors of Designs for Articles of Manufacture the Copyright of Such Designs for a Limited Time 2 Vict. c. 17 (1839).

Ornamental Designs Act[12] and the 1843 Utility (or Non-Ornamental) Designs Act.[13] The main change instigated by these Acts was to extend the subject matter protected under the 1839 Designs Registration Act to include calico (which in return received nine rather than the three months' protection it received under the 1839 Copyright of Designs Act).[14] The other change introduced by these Acts, which marked an important shift in approach, was to divide design into two separate categories: into ornamental and utility design.

As with much intellectual property legislation, these statutes can be seen as particular responses to changes in the environment in which the law operated.[15] More specifically, they can be seen as attempts to modernise the law, to bring it into line with the cultural and technological changes which had occurred over the previous fifty years: with changes in technology which enhanced methods both of production and of copying; with developments of new industries and new types of cloth (such as the printing of silks and woollens);[16] and with shifts in consumer demand. The legislation also sought to take account of the fact that by the 1830s certain practices, such as the printing of linens, were virtually obsolete.[17]

In many ways the changes which took place over this period are unremarkable in that they merely built upon legal techniques and concepts already in existence.[18] These included a reliance on the individual as the focal point for the way in which the law was organised[19] and an understanding that the basis of protection lay in the labour and expense of producing the design.[20] Utilising a similar model of creation

[12] An Act to Consolidate and Amend the Laws Relating to the Copyright of Designs for Ornamenting Articles of Manufacture 5 & 6 Vict. c.100 (1842).

[13] An Act to Amend the Laws Relating to the Copyright of Designs 6 & 7 Vict. c. 65 (1843).

[14] Section 3, 1842 Ornamental Designs Act.

[15] See T. Kusamitsu, 'The Industrial Revolution and Design' (PhD Thesis, Sheffield University, 1982).

[16] P. Thomson (21 Feb. 1839) 45 *Hansard* col. 746; *Memorial from Manufacturers of Norwich to Board of Trade* (2 March 1838) BT/1/338 25G.

[17] E. Tennent (5 Feb. 1840) 51 *Hansard* col. 1266.

[18] In calling for reform it was said, 'it was not the aim to introduce any new principle into the law but simply to give effect to a principle which the existing law already recognised and professed to provide for, but which in the lapse of time had become utterly nugatory': *ibid.*

[19] The 1787 Act recognised the individual as the source of the design giving the property 'to every Person who shall invent, design and print or cause to be invented, designed and printed'. See also section 1, 1839 Designs Registration Act, which spoke of authors or commissioners.

[20] C. O'Brien, *The British Manufacturers' Companion and Calico Printers' Assistant; Being a Treatise on Calico Printing, in all its Branches, Theoretical and Practical; with an Essay on Genius, Invention and Designing* (London: Printed for the Author and Sold by Hamilton and Co., 1795) .

to that which was used in connection with literary property and patents, a design was seen as the unique creation of an individual; albeit that its production was influenced by other designs.[21] Moreover, it was suggested that like a person's signature, the artistic style of a designer was so distinct and unique that it was always possible to identify a designer from the work he produced. The design legislation enacted at this time also drew upon the fact that there was general agreement as to the value of the legal protection which had been modelled on literary property. It accepted too that it was possible to grant property rights in mental labour.[22] While one of the central questions in the literary property debate had been whether it was possible to grant property rights in intangibles, by the 1840s this was accepted as a given. Instead, the main focus of debate was as to the duration of protection, to the role that ought to be played by registration and to the ways in which creators were to be distinguished from copiers.[23] It was also argued that the property right was granted not for the idea or style which lay behind the design, but for the particular way in which the style was expressed: adopting, in effect, a version of the idea–expression dichotomy.

While in many ways the statutes enacted in 1839 are unremarkable in that they merely built upon established techniques and concepts, they do provide us with a useful insight into two important changes that took place in intellectual property law at the time. The first noteworthy feature of the reforms made in 1839 was the establishment of a Designs Register and with it the introduction of the first modern registration

---

[21] 'It is impossible ... for two men working independently to think of the same thing ... as for the kaleidoscope to repeat a configuration ... A subject has been given to two men, both professional designers; both requested to convert a simple natural subject into a certain artificial one; and the results have exhibited no sort of similarity in effect; and if 10,000 men had tried it, every one of their productions would have shown the peculiarities of the artist's style, just as the handwriting of a signature identifies the writer': T. Turner, *On Copyright in Design* (1849), 6. In a similar vein, it was recently said that a 'design is a human expression and therefore personal and unique': H. C. Jehoram, 'The EC Green Paper on the Legal Protection of Industrial Design. Halfway down the Right Track – A View from the Benelux' (1992) 3 *EIPR* 76.

[22] In arguing for copyright in patterns for printing, Peel was able to say in 1840, 'I do not feel called upon to discuss here, either the legal right, or the moral justice of our claim. Intellectual property is recognised by the laws of our country': J. Thomson, *A Letter to the Right Honourable Sir Robert Peel, on Copyright in Original Design and Patterns for Printing* (London: Smith, Elder and Co., 1840), 14. 'I cannot enter into delusive, refined, metaphysical arguments about tangibility or materiality, or the corporeal substance of literary property; it is sufficient for me that such a property exists': T. Turner, *On Copyright in Design* (1849), 28.

[23] 'To make the principle of protection which had been recognised for half a century "real and efficient" rather than merely "deceptive and delusive" it was necessary to extend the protection from three to twelve months': E. Tennent (5 Feb. 1840) 51 *Hansard* col. 1265. See also (9 Feb. 1841) 61 *Hansard* col. 483.

system for intellectual property:[24] a change which was to have a profound effect on intellectual property law. The second notable feature of the 1839 legislation was a growing concern with the form of the law. Combined with the introduction of the registration system, this growing concern with the aesthetics of the law played an important role in the making of modern intellectual property law. In order to explore these developments further, it is necessary to look at the reforms which took place between 1839 and 1843 in more detail.

Towards a modern system of registration

As we saw earlier, two distinct Acts were passed in the June of 1839: one offering twelve months' to three years' protection for certain types of designs on the condition that they had been duly registered; the other establishing three months' protection for designs for printing on cotton, calico, linen and other woven fabric which arose automatically on the creation of the design. The existence of two forms of protection, one automatic, the other conditional on registration, is in marked contrast to the way the design regime was first envisaged by its chief architect and then Chairman of the Board of Trade, Poulett Thomson. Indeed in the draft bill circulated by Thomson in the close of 1838, registration was a prerequisite for *all* types of protection.[25] The explanation for the move away from the initial plans for a regime in which registration was required for all types of protection to a mixed system lies in the objections that the calico printers had to the proposed registration system set out in the draft bill.[26] The objections of the calico printers to a system of protection based upon registration were so vehement that they were willing to sacrifice the longer protection provided under the 1839 Designs Registration Act (initially twelve months but later reduced to nine months) for a shorter three-month period. As we shall see, what

[24] The idea of a registration system had been discussed and supported by the 1836 *Select Committee on Arts and Manufactures*. However, it seems the proposal for such a system as regards calicos was made as early as 1820. On this see (1820) 5 CJ 59, 80, 145, 251, 295, 370, 401; and (1820) 53 HLJ 256, 281, 301, 762.

[25] Potter (a calico printer at Manchester) reported that Poulett Thomson 'wished us to come under the registration, and we declined it: we thought it would not work for our trade': 1840 *Report from the Select Committee on Copyright of Designs* 27 (Q. 480). However, H. Labouchere (President of the Board of Trade) later doubted whether – even if the calico printers had accepted registration – the House would have agreed to twelve months' protection: (9 Feb. 1842) 56 *Hansard* col. 497. The calico printers were also excluded from registration in Mackinnon's Bills of 1837–8 and 1839 (see ch. 5, p. 104).

[26] In 1838, the calico printers petitioned Poulett Thomson for an extension of the 1794 Act to six months and to all mixed fabrics: letter from Orvington and Warwick to P. Thomson (23 Feb. 1838) BT/1/338.

the calico printers were objecting to was, in effect, the introduction of the first modern administrative system for the issuance of intellectual property. Consequently their objections alert us to some of the central differences that exist between modern and pre-modern intellectual property law. The objections are also noteworthy because they provide us with an insight into important aspects of the modern registration system which was taking shape at the time.

The objections raised by the calico printers to the registration system were twofold. The first and most important related to the fact that the register was intended to act as evidence of the originality of patterns.[27] It was anticipated that registration would thereby overcome difficulties in determining whether or not a pattern was new and original. The particular problem that the register was to resolve arose from the fact that if two similar patterns appeared on the market in close succession, it was virtually impossible for independent parties to identify which was the original and which was the copy.[28] The way in which this difficulty was to be resolved was through the process of registration. Under the proposed regime if a pattern was registered before another appeared on the market, it could be presumed that the later pattern had been copied from the one which had been registered. In this way the registration system was to act as a 'legal guarantee'[29] which would function to resolve doubts as to the originality of patterns[30] and, in so doing, prevent litigation. In this sense it was to play an important role in determining issues of priority. As it enabled the owner of the design to be identified, it also made it easier to identify the intangible property, thus helping to resolve one of the problems associated with the law granting property status to intangibles discussed earlier.

Although the calico printers accepted that a registration system was required for objects such as patterns for grates and stove,[31] they argued that in their case there was no such need. This was because they were

---

[27] S. Schwabe, 1840 *Select Committee on Designs* 21 (Q. 182).

[28] 'The same idea frequently struck different individuals nearly at the same time, and it was in such cases exceedingly difficult to determine who was entitled to the priority, but with a system of registration this was perfectly easy': E. Tennent (5 Feb. 1840) 51 *Hansard* cols. 1268–9. On this, see J. Kershaw, 1840 *Select Committee on Designs* 208 (Q. 3665). In the 1830 decision of *Sheriff* v *Coates* (1830) (39 ER 61), the Lord Chancellor said, 'I feel myself wholly incompetent to pronounce whether this is or is not an original pattern': 1840 *Select Committee on Designs* 46 (Q. 7809). As patterns were seen to be the unique expression of their creators there was no possibility of independent creation.

[29] J. Koe, 1840 *Select Committee on Designs* 450 (Q. 7862).

[30] The consequence of this uncertainty was that 'the most well-disposed person might very innocently offend against the law, and be involved in difficulties which might be very serious for him, without the least intention of doing so': 1840 *Select Committee on Designs* 288 (Q. 4985). See further, *ibid.*, 266 and 288.

[31] 'It was impossible to place any mark of publication on the articles themselves. In the

already able to fully prove their own copyright and, therefore, the problem of establishing priority of designs did not apply to them.[32] More specifically, because the calico printers regularly printed the number, the name of the manufacturer, and the date of publication at the end of each piece of textile they produced, they were able to argue that they had a pre-existing system of registration which enabled them to determine the originality of their patterns.[33] Given that they already had in place mechanisms which enabled them to identity their patterns, the calico printers argued that there was no reason why they should incur the further expense that would have been an inevitable consequence of a centralised, financially self-supporting registration system.[34]

The second objection that the calico printers had to registration related to the plan that the register was to act as a source of information: both to provide inspiration for other designers and also to enable manufacturers to ensure that the designs they produced did not infringe existing designs.[35] While the calico printers accepted that it was necessary for there to be mechanisms which would enable a court to ascertain what was a new and original design (but argued that their own measures were sufficient to achieve these ends), they rejected out of hand the idea that the register was to act as a source of information. Their main objection to this stemmed from the proposal that if registration was required as a prerequisite for protection copies of their patterns which were deposited at the Designs Office would on payment of a small fee have been open to public inspection. Moreover, the calico printers complained that such inspection would have been highly detrimental both to their own interests and to those of the nation. This was because it would have prematurely revealed patterns which were not yet mar-

bill, therefore ... a register would be afforded': P. Thomson (21 Feb. 1839) 45 *Hansard* col. 748.

[32] 1840 *Select Committee on Designs* 44. In response to the question of whether it was desirable that patterns should be registered, James Thomson said, 'We did conceive at the time [the 1820 Calico Bill] was applied for that a registry would be desirable, in order to facilitate the proof of the publication; but we have found that there is no difficulty, and there have been proceedings within the last two or three years under this Act, with the result we are satisfied, except the three-month period is too limited': J. Thomson, 1831 *Minutes of Evidence Before Select Committee on Manufactures, Commerce and Shipping* (1831) 240 (Q. 3865).

[33] C. Warwick, 1840 *Select Committee on Designs* 128 (Q. 2370). The reason calico was excepted from the need for registration was because 'we have a registry of our own, which other trades have not': *ibid.*, 129 (Q. 2388).

[34] See H. Labouchere (5 Feb. 1840) 51 *Hansard* col. 1268; E. Tennent (16 March 1842) 61 *Hansard* col. 670.

[35] Occasionally these arguments focused on the problems that may have arisen for third parties who unwittingly copied patterns. As one witness complained, 'There being no registration of patterns, nobody can know when they are copying the patterns of others': 1840 *Select Committee on Designs* 53 (Q. 735).

keted and as such would have provided opportunities for copying and piracy, particularly by foreign manufacturers.[36] The nature of these difficulties was summed up by Salis Schwabe, a Manchester calico printer, when he said the main problem with the proposed register was that it would give 'pirates an opportunity, on payment of 5 s, to search for any design he pleases and try how near he could come to my patterns without being called a pirate. This is one great objection to that plan; publicity of that kind I should most decidedly object to'.[37] Poulett Thomson, who was particularly sensitive to the demands of the calico industry,[38] accepted the objections raised by the calico printers and replaced the draft Bill which he initially circulated with two separate Bills. Drawing upon his position as President to the Board of Trade he successfully manoeuvred these Bills through Parliament.[39] These were to become the 1839 Copyright of Designs Act and the 1839 Designs Registration Act.

While the impact the calico printers had on the legislation passed in 1839 is interesting in its own right,[40] for our purposes what is more interesting is that their complaints, which can be read as a struggle between pre-modern and modern intellectual property law, provide us with a useful insight into aspects of the modern registration system. In particular, they provide us with an opportunity to explore three important characteristics of the registration process.

The first feature which the calico printers' complaints alert us to relates to the way in which proof was manufactured and organised. More specifically they remind us that while the practice of registering mental property was well known to the law prior to the 1840s, the registration system that came into existence at this time differed from the pre-existing regimes in two important respects. Under the old schemes, proof was the product of private and self-contained processes,

---

[36] *Memorial from Manufacturers of Norwich to Board of Trade* (2 March 1838) BT/1/338 25G. Similar arguments were raised in the context of patents. See E. Robinson, 'The Early Diffusion of Steam Power' (1972) 34 *Journal of Economic History* 91–2.

[37] 1840 *Select Committee on Designs* 10 (Q. 159).

[38] It was suggested (to Potter) that Poulett Thomson's 'political connection with the town of Manchester, as its representative, might indispose him and make it undesirable for him to mix up himself' with a question which was much disputed amongst his constituents. Potter asserted that those who had agitated the question before declined to do so again precisely because Poulett Thomson was 'fettered': 1840 *Select Committee on Designs* 28 (Q. 490–1).

[39] While there was some discussion as to the nature and scope of these Bills (mainly in relation to calico), the other aspects of the Bills which were to prove crucial in the development of contemporary design law (such as the extension of protection to three-dimensional shapes) were little debated: 1840 *Select Committee on Designs* 96 (Q. 1694).

[40] On the role played by metal workers see E. Potter, *Select Committee on Designs* 29 (Q. 497); 94 CJ 172.

whereas the system of registration introduced in 1839 brought with it a growing expectation that proof and bureaucratic property more generally ought to be a matter for public rather than private control. As a result we see a shift away from private guild-style modes of regulating evidential issues – such as existed at the Stationers' Hall,[41] the Cutlers' Company[42] and the Kafkaesque offices of the patent system – towards institutions which were publicly funded and organised.[43] In a sense the objections brought by the calico printers can be seen as an attempt to retain their private pre-modern system of manufacturing proof against the introduction of a more modern public scheme. The complaints brought by the calico printers, who were based in Lancashire and Lanarkshire, can also be seen as an attempt to resist the process of centralisation which was taking place; the establishment of a registry in London rather than in Glasgow or Manchester.[44]

The second feature of the modern registration system that came into existence in the early part of the nineteenth century which was highlighted by the calico printers' complaints relates to the role registration was to play in regulating information: to the way knowledge was controlled, stored, transmitted and used. Prior to this, the type of knowledge which was to become the domain of intellectual property law had largely been subject to private or semi-private control. Moreover, memory played a pivotal role in the storage and retrieval of such knowledge. One of the notable features of the modern registration system was that it declined to follow either of these methods. In contrast to previous practices where knowledge was largely subject to private control and reduced to memory, the system of registration which began to take shape at the time aimed to ensure that information was both mobile and visible.[45] Like encyclopaedias

[41] Yates (as counsel for the defendant), *Tonson v Collins* (1760) 96 ER 185.
[42] On the history of the Cutlers' marks, see R. Jackson, 1862 *Select Committee on Trade Marks* 1–13 (Q. 1–43).
[43] The 1839 Act established a publicly funded, centralised administration. After defraying expenses, the Design Registry was to transfer any financial profits to the Consolidated Fund: Section 8, 1839 Designs Registration Act.
[44] In contrast with the procedure for obtaining patents where, at least until 1852, applications had to be made in Edinburgh, Dublin and London, the Design Registry was based in London and conferred a single right applicable throughout the United Kingdom.
[45] 'Inscriptions are mobile. They are made flat, which facilitates domination and use. The scale can be modified at will without change in internal proportions; they can be reproduced and spread with little cost. Because they offer such optical consistency, everything, no matter where it comes from, can be converted into diagrams and numbers and combinations and tables': B. Latour, 'Drawing Things Together' in (eds.) M. Lynch and S. Woolgar, *Representation in Scientific Practice* (London: MIT Press, 1990), 45–7. See also J. Law, 'On the Methods of Long-distance Control: Vessels,

and libraries,[46] registration acted as a form of collective or public memory. It did this by specifying that in order for a design to be protected, applicants were required to deposit either three copies or three drawings of their designs at the Registry.[47] While these practices had antecedents in the patent specification,[48] this was the first occasion in which representative registration – the process whereby the creation was represented in pictorial or written terms rather than via a copy or a model – was used with any degree of sophistication or thought in intellectual property law.

The changes which took place with the formation of a modern registration system, which drew upon the standardisation of verbal and visual formulae which was taking place at the time, facilitated a number of other important changes. For example, the increased reliance on paper inscriptions produced a shift of orientation away from memory-based retrieval towards print-based methods. Moreover, by reducing a pattern or a design to paper, to a flattened reality, it was easier for design-related knowledge to be classified, measured and communicated. Because this facilitated better regulation and control, it helped the law to achieve its new goal of ensuring that information, which was increasingly considered as public knowledge, was placed into a more accessible and manageable form.[49]

The third and more general feature highlighted in the discussions about the introduction of the Designs Register was a particular way of thinking about registration. More specifically, it alerts us to the view – now pervasive – of registration as an area of little conceptual interest, involving only the complex but routine bureaucratic game of paper shuffling. As Bruno Latour reminds us, however, paper shuffling is a powerful technology that constantly escapes attention:[50] a theme which we shall return to in more detail later. Another image of the registration

Navigation and the Portuguese Route to India' in (ed.) J. Law, *Power, Action, and Belief* (London: Routledge, 1986).

[46] See R. Yeo, 'Reading Encyclopaedia: Science and the Organisation of Knowledge in British Dictionaries of Arts and Sciences, 1730–1850' (1991) 82 *ISIS* 24; Yeo, 'Ephraim Chambers' *Cyclopaedia* (1728) and the Tradition of Commonplaces' (March 1996) *Journal of the History of Ideas* 157.

[47] Section 6, 1839 Designs Registration Act.

[48] While the requirement that a specification be enrolled was enunciated in *Liardet v Johnson* (1780) 62 ER 1000 it seems that it was not until late in the nineteenth century that the patent specification took on the role of disclosing the invention. In fact the publication function was achieved, if at all, prior to 1851 by the medium of journals – the *Repertory of Inventions*, the *London Journal of Arts and Sciences* and the *Mechanics' Magazine* – in which recent specifications were reproduced.

[49] On this see B. Latour, 'Drawing Things Together' (1990), 19; F. Bastide, 'The Iconography of Scientific Texts' (1990), 211 ff.

[50] B. Latour, 'Drawing Things Together' (1990), 55.

process that was apparent at the time was the widely held belief that the primary task performed by registration was to create a situation whereby a person could readily show that he or she was the originator (or owner) and not the copier of a particular design. Thomas Turner summed up such an approach when he said the service provided by registration consists in 'simply receiving, recording and preserving the claim of the owner'.[51] While these tasks were and remain central to intellectual property law, to suggest that this was the *only* function the registration system performed leads us to ignore the important role played by registration in determining the scope of intangible property. Closely associated with the tendency to ignore the positive role played by the registration process in shaping the property interest is the belief that the introduction of representative registration merely simplified the existing processes of proof and that, as such, it gave rise to few substantial differences from the pre-existing regimes. As we shall see, however, the process of representing the creation, as distinct from merely depositing the object or even a model of that object, led to an new understanding of what was being proved and as such heralded an important change in the logic of intellectual property law.

The aesthetics of law

The second notable feature of the legislation passed in 1839 was that it was prompted not only by a desire to provide better protection for designs, but also by a growing concern with the shape that the law took; a concern, if you like, with the aesthetics of the law. This is in contrast to the situation in the eighteenth and the early part of the nineteenth century where little interest was shown in the form that the law took. Under pre-modern intellectual property law there was minimal legal input, at least in so far as the organisation of the legal framework was concerned. The legislation passed during this time, which was even more facilitative than it is now, consisted primarily of *ad hoc* responses to particular problems which had arisen in certain industries: the petitioners' primary concern being to establish continuity between the various forms of property protection (mainly borrowing from the goodwill that had grown up around literary property and related forms of protection). As such, the form that the law took was, at least up until the early part of the nineteenth century, haphazardly shaped by the subject-based way it developed, each piece of legislation reflecting the interest group that promoted it: whether it be a particular guild (as with the

---

[51] T. Turner, *On Copyright in Design* (1849), 35.

1710 Statute of Anne), a particular branch of trade (as with the 1787 Calico Printers' Act) or an interest based social grouping (such as the Sublime Society of Beef Steaks in the 1735 Engravers' Act).[52] While prior to 1839 there was little concern with the form that the law took, it is clear that by the time the design legislation was enacted the law which granted property rights in mental labour had become increasingly interested in itself and the shape that it took. It had become, in short, self-referential.

This new-found interest in the aesthetics of law manifested itself in two ways. With France acting as a role model,[53] the growing concern with the form of the law revealed itself in the belief that there was a need for the law to be made as simple, uniform and precise as possible. As well as reconciling apparent inconsistencies and arranging 'the whole in a logical manner',[54] there was also a desire to reduce the complexity of the legal system; to rationalise and order the law that dealt with intellectual labour. Based upon the idea that complicated systems were evidence of the unsoundness of the principles on which they were based,[55] the design legislation passed at the time aimed not only to provide more effective protection for designs (by expanding its scope), it also set out to simplify and consolidate the legal arrangements that achieved these ends. The reformers hoped thereby not only to control unwieldy legal materials, but also to replace 'the uncouth, incongruous and mendacious hash forming the common law' and the 'mongrel empiricism' of statute law with a more systematic and ordered legal system.[56]

The second way in which the growing concern with the aesthetics of the law manifested itself was in terms of the way in which the subject matter was defined. While under the 1787 Calico Printers' Act subject matter had been defined in product-specific terms, under the 1839 Designs Registration Act a more abstract and open-ended formulation

---

[52] On which see D. Hunter, 'Copyright Protection for Engravings and Maps in Eighteenth Century England' (1987) 8 *Library* 128.

[53] G. Foggo, 1836 *Select Committee on Arts and Manufactures*, 53.

[54] R. Godson, *A Practical Treatise on the Law of Patents for Inventions and of Copyright with an Introductory Book of Monopolies* (London: Joseph Butterworth, 1823), ix.

[55] One of the problems with the existing law was that 'calico printing had so many different branches, varying in so many different degrees and from each other that it was impossible that one system of copy right for designs could apply to them all. If then uniformity could not be established, it would be far better to let all legislation on the subject alone': E. Potter, *A Letter to Mark Phillips Esq MP in reply to his speech in the House of Commons, Feb. 9th 1841, on the Designs Copyright Bill* (Manchester: T Forrest, 1841), 3.

[56] M. Leverson, *Copyright and Patents; or, Property in Thought, Being an Investigation of the Principles of Legal Science Applicable to Property in Thought* (London: Wildy and Sons, 1854), 54.

was adopted. In particular protection was extended from patterns for printing linens, cottons, calicos or muslins, as in the 1787 Act, to 'designs for the shape and configuration of any article of manufacture'.[57] What we see in the provisions of the 1839 Act is not only an expansion in the scope of subject matter from textiles and fabrics to metals, and from patterns to shape and configuration, but also a move away from detailed subject-specific definitions to a more abstract wording.[58]

In the abstraction and consolidation that took place with the passage of the 1839 legislation, we see the beginnings of an important change in the legal logic; and a shift from pre-modern to modern intellectual property law.[59] In particular we see a gradual move away from the subject-specific legislation which characterised pre-modern intellectual property law – such as the 1787 Calico Printers' Act, and Bills for patterns on ribbons[60] or designs for lacework[61] – towards the idea of design law: a general area of law which was applicable, at least potentially, to *all* forms of design, towards the development, in Weberian terms, of a formal law which only takes into account the general characteristics of the case under consideration.[62] In this we see the shift towards the modern manner of organising the categories of intellectual property law. While in its pre-modern guise the law had been happy to let the shape that it took be a passive response to the subject matter protected, this subject-specific mode of organisation was increasingly

---

[57] Section 1, clause 3, 1839 Designs Registration Act.

[58] The 1839 Act extended protection not only to silk weaving, carpet making and paper hangings, but to all articles 'in which the value of the patterns forms an essential element in computing the value of the whole': E. Tennent (16 March 1842) 61 *Hansard* col. 670. An earlier example of the broad, abstract right can be seen in clauses 16 and 17 of Godson's 1833 Patent Bill which proposed to extend protection to 'the inventor or designer of every new pattern to be applied to any manufactured article, or to be used in manufacturing any article'. This was to be combined with a definition of invention as 'new manufactured article' with no reference to utility. See S. Billing and A. Prince, *The Law and Practice of Patents and Registration of Designs with the Pleadings and all the Necessary Forms* (London: Benning, 1845), 205.

[59] While the adoption of a more abstract definition gave the appearance that trades were treated in a like manner, the needs of particular trades were accommodated via other means, such as the length of protection and the cost and class of registration.

[60] See Joseph Merry's petition for protection of new and original patterns for ribbons: (1829) 84 CJ; J. Merry also wrote two letters to the Board of Trade, praying protection for the invention of machinery for ribbon velvet (filed 16 July 1829): (1829) 35 *Minutes of the Board of Trade*, Letter No. 33, 266; 1829 *Select Committee on Patents* 89–90.

[61] 1831 petition by the lace trade for protection of patterns: J. Millward, 1836 *Select Committee on Arts and Manufactures* 18.

[62] 'The objectification brought about by codification introduces the possibility of a logical coherence, of a *formalisation*. It makes possible the establishment of an explicit normativity, that of grammar or law': P. Bourdieu, 'Codification' (1990), 79.

derided and ridiculed.[63] The disdain which was to develop in modern intellectual property law towards pre-modern modes of organisation was captured in Darras' remark that if 'we make a law on literary property, there is no reason why we should not make a special law for every form of property, so I propose to you a law on each of the following forms: property in hats, property in peaches, property in peaches in brandy, property in green hats belonging to M. Anguis'.[64]

The changes which took place in the form of the law not only brought about the emergence of what is arguably the first modern area of intellectual property law, they also set in play a series of questions and concerns which were to have important, yet unexpected, ramifications for the way the law was to develop. It is to these consequences and the way in which the law responded that we turn in the next chapter.

[63] 'But if new patterns in wool and silk are admitted into the circle of monopoly can we stop there? Clearly not; for there is not an argument which can be urged in favour of the workers in flax, cotton, wool, and silk which may not be urged with equal effect in favour of the workers in gold, silver, iron, brass, wood, ivory, leather, hair, wax, paper, dough, and clay – in short every other workable substance whatever ... The reasoning, then, by analogy leads us to this, that new patterns of every kind and degree should be protected; and this is precisely what the present Bill proposes to accomplish, for it"enacts that the inventor or designer of EVERY NEW PATTERN to be applied to ANY manufactured article, or to be used in the manufacturing of ANY article, shall have the *exclusive* right to use the same pattern" ... for 12 months': 'The Bill for Amending the Patent Laws' (1833) 19 *Mechanics' Magazine* 302.

[64] A. Darras, *Du Droit des auteurs et des artistes*, quoted in W. Briggs, *The Law of International Copyright (with Special Sections on the Colonies and the USA)* (London: Stevens and Haynes, 1906), 25 n. 1.

Although the legislation passed in 1839 significantly extended the scope of the laws protecting designs, they were soon repealed and replaced by two new statutes: the 1842 Ornamental Designs Act[1] and the 1843 Utility Designs Act.[2] The main change instigated by these new Acts was to extend the subject matter protected by registration to patterns for printing on woven fabrics including calico (which in return received nine rather than the three months' protection it had been given under the 1839 Copyright of Designs Act): thus bringing it into line with the protection given to designs woven into rather than merely printed upon woven fabrics. The other change introduced by these Acts, which marked an important shift in approach, was to divide design into two separate categories: into ornamental and non-ornamental design.

When Poulett Thomson first set out to reform design law in 1837 he hoped to unify the law and at the same time also expand the scope of subject matter protected. As we saw earlier Thomson's plans were hindered by the objections of the calico printers. Shortly after the passage of the 1839 legislation, however, the attitude of the calico printers towards registration changed.[3] This change of heart can be attributed to the fact that the spatial and temporal relationships that existed between the calico printers and the imitators of their works had altered. In particular, the three months' protection then available to them had been rendered inoperative by increases in the speed of copying. While this period had been sufficient to protect patterns when engraving had been done by the burin and printing by hand, the case was said to be very different 'when every process had been expedited by machinery, and the application of electro-magnetism had reduced the

---

[1] 5 & 6 Vict. c. 100 (1842).

[2] 6 & 7 Vict. c. 65 (1843).

[3] The calico printers were now 'willing to accept the copyright upon the same conditions, namely, with the amended system of registration for their patterns': (1841) 56 *Hansard* col. 485. For a general discussion of this see 'Report of the Registrar of Designs' on a letter from James Fischer of 12 Jan. 1844 (11 July 1844) *Letters to the Board of Trade* BT/1/421, No. 47.

labour of months to the compass of as many hours'.[4] The calico printers also argued that the period of protection was undermined by other factors such as the application of steam navigation to shipping (which placed foreign markets almost upon a par with the home market as regarded priority in design)[5] and to changes in trade practices.[6] The consequence of these developments was that imitators were able to gain access to patterns much earlier in the fashion season than they had before, thus undermining the lead time calico printers had previously enjoyed.[7]

The change of heart experienced by the calico printers can also be attributed to the fact that the private systems of identification that they used were not as effective as initially claimed.[8] More importantly, many of the objections the calico printers had to the registration system were shown to be unfounded. In particular, the calico printers' fears that the information function of the register would act as an aid to piracy was alleviated by the fact that in 1840 the Register was, at the behest of the Registrar, changed from an open system (in which the public had access to the designs which had been registered) to a closed system.[9] The other objection that the calico printers had to registration, that it would be costly and cumbersome, had been allayed by the promises that the cost of registration would be reduced.[10]

The case for reform of the 1839 legislation, which gradually extended beyond the calico printers to include paper stainers and lace designers, was taken up by the MP for Belfast, Emerson Tennent.[11] After the calico printers' capitulation, and the positive recommendations of the 1840 Select Committee on Designs in favour of extension,[12] Emerson

---

[4] E. Tennent (9 Feb. 1841) 56 *Hansard* cols. 484–5.

[5] On the importance of the West Indies and the United States in this context see E. Tennent (5 Feb. 1840) 51 *Hansard* col. 1262; E. Potter, 1840 *Select Committee on Designs* 38 (Q. 486); S. Schwabe, *ibid.*, 12 (Q. 202).

[6] For example, in order to have materials ready for a new fashion season, it was necessary for designers to deliver their patterns to warehousemen so that their 'riders might exhibit them to [their] customers, and thus enable [them] to compute the extent of [their] orders': E. Tennent (5 Feb. 1840) 51 *Hansard* col. 1263. See also T. Turner, *On Copyright in Design* (1849), 21.

[7] See E. Potter 1840 *Select Committee on Designs* 28 (Q. 482).

[8] 'When any design in metal or pottery is registered, the denoting mark is impressed upon each article and the purchaser is at once made aware that the protection is claimed; but this is evidently impossible in the case of textile goods, each piece having generally to be subdivided into many portions': J. Clay, 'The Copyright of Designs, as Applicable to Articles of Textile Manufacture' (1859) *TNAPSS* 246–7.

[9] F. Long, 1840 *Select Committee on Designs* 454 (Q. 7740).

[10] See T. Turner, *On Copyright in Design* (1849) 23, 34–5.

[11] By this time, Poulett Thomson had been granted the peerage of Baron Sydenham and had become governor of Canada.

[12] On the Select Committee see E. Tennent (1841) 56 *Hansard* cols. 483, 498.

Tennent in 1841 introduced a new Bill into Parliament which offered twelve months' protection to designers of patterns for printing on or working on any woven fabric on the condition that their designs were registered.[13] Despite widespread support for these proposals, Tennent experienced many difficulties in his attempt to complete the process of abstraction and consolidation begun by Poulett Thomson: he failed to gain a consensus amongst calico printers and the Bills were subject to delaying tactics and hostile criticism in Parliament.[14] Tennent's campaign to amend design law ultimately collapsed when he lost his seat with the change of government in 1841.[15] Despite this setback, the task of reforming the law was taken over by William Gladstone, the Vice-President of the Board of Trade, in Sir Robert Peel's new administration.[16] With the support of the new government the programme of reform succeeded. This culminated in the repeal of the 1839 legislation and the enactment of two new statutes: the 1842 Ornamental Designs Act[17] and the 1843 Utility Designs Act.[18]

Given that the reason why two Acts had been passed in 1839 rather than the one as was initially planned – viz. the calico printers' objections to registration – had by the 1840s all but disappeared, it is somewhat surprising that nonetheless *two* Acts, rather than one, were passed in 1842 and 1843. This is all the more puzzling given that the reformers aimed not only to provide longer protection for calico printers, but also to consolidate the five existing Acts in this area into one 'so as to bring the law of the subject within a small compass'.[19] It is also odd that a statute which set out to unite and consolidate the law in this area simultaneously divided it into two separate categories: into ornamental and non-ornamental design.

The simple explanation as to why two statutes were passed can be traced to the change in the form of law, to the newly found concern with legal aesthetics which was reflected in the 1839 legislation. More specifically, the simple explanation for the shape of the 1842 Orna-

---

[13] A Bill for Extending the Term of Copyright in Designs for Printing on Woven Fabrics and Paper Hangings (9 Feb. 1841).

[14] Charges of bribery were later levied against Tennent who had received £2000 in support of his re-election campaign. The Manchester merchants rewarded Tennent for his efforts with 3,000 ounces of plate. See T. Turner, *On Copyright in Design* (1849), 23.

[15] W. Gladstone (2 Aug. 1842) 65 *Hansard* col. 970.

[16] 97 CJ 576; (3 Aug. 1842) 65 *Hansard* col. 978. For the background to the Board of Trade at this time see L. Brown, 'The Board of Trade and the Tariff Problem, 1840–2' (1953) *English Historical Review* 394.

[17] 5 & 6 Vict. c.100 (1842).

[18] 6 & 7 Vict. c. 65 (1843).

[19] R. Sheil (8 March 1841) 57 *Hansard* col. 46 – or 'to comprise all the legislation on this subject into one bill': E. Tennent (8 March 1841) 57 *Hansard* col. 46.

mental Designs Act was that it was designed to correct what were perceived as faults in the pre-existing law. As the Registrar of Designs said at the time, the 1842 Act was a means of rendering the law 'as far as regards ornamental Designs . . . as perfect as possible'.[20] The particular 'imperfection' or 'problem' which the 1842 Act was designed to remedy was that the subject matter of the 1839 Designs Registration Act had become confused in popular opinion with the 'subject matter of letters patent'.[21] The consequence of this was 'the unrestricted registration of almost every description of aticle, under pretence of protecting some shape or configuration, or some kind of impression or ornament, or ornamental casting or modelling'.[22] The nature of these difficulties was summed up in a letter written by the Registrar of Designs to the Board of Trade in 1841:

Among the immediate effects of [the 1839 Designs Registration Act] was one, I apprehend, not originally contemplated. Besides the *ornamental* designs for the usual articles of manufacture such as stoves, Carpets etc., many designs were registered the originality of which did not consist in the ornamental part, but in the invention of a new shape or arrangement of parts, by which utility rather than beauty, was the object sought to be attained; and the Authors considering the principle of the invention likely to be protected by the Copyright afforded to the external shape, registered such shape as coming within the third class of Designs mentioned in the Act. Hence a variety of designs consisting of machines or other contrivances appear in the Register, totally distinct from ornamental

---

[20]   *Report of Registrar of Designs to the Board of Trade Respecting the Origin, Nature and Tendency of the Designs Copyright Act* (3 Nov. 1841), *Letters to the Board of Trade* BT/1/ 379, 21. See, more generally, T. Webster, *On the Subject Matter, Title and Specification of Letters Patent for Inventions and Copyright of Designs for Articles of Manufacture* (London: Elsworth, 1848), 83 ff.

[21]   T. Webster, *The Subject Matter of Letters Patent* (1851), 81; W. Hindmarch, *A Treatise of the Law Relating to Patent Privileges* (London: Stevens, 1846), 25; W. Carpmael, 'Registration of Designs' (1842) 17 *Repertory of Patent Inventions* 39–40.

[22]   T. Webster, *The Subject Matter of Letters Patent* (1851), 81. See also Webster, *On Property in Designs* (1853). The *London Journal of Arts and Sciences*, edited by the patent agent, William Newton, remarked that the Registration Act 'appears to be so little understood, that we feel ourselves imperatively called upon to notice the manner in which its powers are administered, and the absurd way that the public have in many instances misconstrued its intentions and provisions': 'Copyright of Designs' (1840) 16 *The London Journal of Arts and Sciences* 95–6. He continued: 'we are surprised at the numerous applications which are made for the registration of matters in no way contemplated or provided for by the Act for protecting the "Copyright of Designs" and we are still more astonished at finding that those persons who have been interested with the discretionary power of accepting or rejecting the subjects presented for registration, should have occupied the pages of their Record with drawings of steam engines, barrel organs, weighing machines, and a variety of other kinds of mechanical and philosophical apparatus, contrary to any intention or provision of the Act, to the manifest annoyance of tradesmen, misleading of the parties who have been induced to register their inventions, and pay their monies for a presumed monopoly, which they will find to exist only in the moon': *ibid.*, 96–7.

patterns, constituting nearly one third of the whole number, increasing daily in proportion.[23]

In short, the wrong type of subject matter was being registered under the wrong Act.[24]

Although the particular problem which the 1842 Ornamental Designs Act was intended to remedy arose in part as a result of the proliferation in the subject matter which was protected, the primary reason for it can be traced to the change in the form of the law which had taken place in 1839. More specifically, it was the move from the specific to the general, towards protection for the shape or patterning of *all* articles of manufacture, which gave rise to the situation where it was possible for artefacts to be protected under more than one regime. In particular, the abstract way in which the subject matter was defined in the 1839 Designs Registration Act gave rise to the possibility of overlap between ornamental designs and patents. In turn this helped to generate the 'imperfection' which the 1842 Act was designed to remedy.[25] These problems were magnified by the fact that the Registrar had limited powers to refuse applications of what he clearly regarded as inappropriate subject matter.[26]

While the *opportunity* for the 'wrongful' registration of inventions was a product of the abstraction embodied in the 1839 Designs Registration Act, the *desire* lay more with the unsatisfactory state of the patent system. In particular, the frustration and distrust engendered by the uncertain but exacting legal rules and the obscure and expensive procedures by which patents were obtained acted as an impetus for inventors to attempt to gain protection via other means. Given that designs offered a cheap alternative to the expense, uncertainty, and insecurity of patent protection, it is unsurprising that the most obvious

---

[23] *Report of Registrar of Designs* (1841), 10–12.

[24] While in many instances (such as with designs for fabrics or patents for chemical inventions) there was no overlap between patents and designs, the question of overlap arose most acutely in circumstances where both concerned themselves with 'articles of manufacture'. Hindmarch summed up these problems when he said, the 'word invention signifies (in its proper sense) something invented, discovered, or found out, a device or contrivance; and therefore it includes many things, such as designs, patterns, models, drawings etc., which are clearly not inventions within the meaning of the patent law': W. Hindmarch, *A Treatise on the Law Relating to Patent Privileges* (London: Stevens, 1846), 78.

[25] While the abstract definition employed in the 1839 Designs Registration Act gave rise to the potential for overlap between design and sculpture copyright the only matter of practical importance arose from the fact that the broad definition of subject matter used in the 1839 Act provided inventors with an opportunity to register their creations as 'designs'.

[26] There is some suggestion that even in the absence of express powers registrations were refused under the 1839 Designs Registration Act: *Report of Registrar of Designs* (1841), 22–3.

choice was the protection offered by the 1839 Designs Registration Act.[27]

Patents were seen as problematic for a number of reasons. One important cause of dissatisfaction can be traced to the fact that the process of patent administration was convoluted, expensive and uncertain.[28] In addition it was not clear exactly what could be patented.[29] As many patents were deliberately vague and general in their claims[30] it was very difficult to ascertain the nature of pre-existing patents. Because patents were frequently set aside or struck out for trivial errors (such as grammatical mistakes)[31] and patentees were often exposed to 'harassing and dubious litigation',[32] patentees could not be confident that a patent was valid until it had been tested in court (adding even more to the exorbitant costs).[33] The confusion surrounding the patent regime was compounded by the fact that little, if anything, had been done to reduce the widespread uncertainty that

---

[27] 'The registration of the design is obtained by a simple application, which is a great feature in favour of this method . . . whereas a patent is . . . obliged to stand the test of an action at law before its validity is completely established': S. Billing and A. Prince, *The Law and Practice of Patents* (1845), 204–5. 'The expense of procuring patents, and the exceeding difficulty under the rigid construction of law adopted, presented the inventor of many useful improvements in manufacture from exclusively enjoying, for such a period as would recompense him for his trouble, the fruits of his ingenuity; so that it was only in matters of great importance (and of a particular character) that persons could afford to apply for the grant of letters patent': *ibid.*, 191.

[28] For a description of the complicated procedures for patent grant see F. Abbott, 1829 *Select Committee on Patents* 48–9.

[29] '[T]he grand difficulty is the uncertainty of the Opinion of the judges as to what is the subject of a patent, in fact, what is the meaning of the word manufacture . . . they are at sea upon the subject.' B. Rotch, *Select Committee on Patents* 126–7.

[30] The confusion was exacerbated by the practice of patentees of concealing as much of their invention as was possible to lessen the chance of their creations being copied. Given this it was unsurprising to read that it 'is one of the most metaphysical problems that I know, to prepare a title to a patent': J. Farey, 1829 *Select Committee on Patents* 19.

[31] In *R v Metcalf* (1817) 2 *Stark* 149 the patent which had been granted for a 'tapered hair brush' was held invalid because the specification only required that the bristles be of unequal lengths. Lord Ellenborough noted that tapering meant gradually converging to a point and thus that 'the difficulty arising from the grammatical consideration cannot be removed': 1829 *Select Committee on Patents* Appendix B, 203. See also *Bainbridge* v *Wigley* (1810) 171 *ER* 636, where Lord Ellenborough disallowed a patent for a flute with 'new notes', because it only had one note. See further 'Unreasonableness of Judge-made Law' (1835), 447.

[32] See, e.g., Spectator, 'The Unanswered Charges of Piracy Against Mr S. Hutchinson – The State of English Patent Law' (1839–40) 32 *Mechanics' Magazine* 390, 392.

[33] A 'patent right can never be considered as transferable property till its validity has been tried before a court at law, at an expense of one or more thousand pounds': *Review of Charles Babbage, Reflexions on the Decline of Science in England, and on some of its Causes* (1830) 43 *Quarterly Review*, 334. This meant that 'patent property is rendered so uncertain and insecure, that many persons are deterred from obtaining Patents for their inventions': (16 June 1820) CJ 316.

surrounded the nature and scope of patent law identified by the 1829 Select Committee on Patents.[34]

The uncertain nature of patent protection not only led to calls for reform (and later abolition of the patent system), it also generated confusion as to the nature of the relationship between the patent system (if we can really call it this at this time) and the developing designs regime. Most importantly of all, however, the trouble, delay and risks associated with the process of patenting acted as an incentive for creators of functional inventions to register them as designs. That is, it actively encouraged creators 'to get an invention into a class it does not really belong [in], as when a subject for a patent right is registered'.[35]

The attempt to squeeze inventions within the 1839 Designs Registration Act, which was made possible by the broad language it employed and desirable because of the poor state of patent protection, was promoted by the professional ambitions of patent agents. While some patent agents saw the introduction of the Designs Registry, which offered a cheap and relatively straightforward alternative to the costly and protracted drafting involved with patents, as a threat,[36] others saw it as an opportunity to expand their business practices, and acted accordingly.[37]

While the move towards abstraction and consolidation which occurred with the 1839 Designs Registration Act and the problematic nature of the patent system go some way towards explaining why inventions were registered under the design legislation, they do not explain why this should necessarily be seen as 'improper': why it was that many argued that inventions did not 'really belong' within the scope of the Designs Registry. We return to this question in more detail later, but it is worth offering a brief answer here.[38]

---

[34] So scarce, contradictory and unsure were the patent decisions that it was said in 1835 that there was no law of patents: Mr Tooke (13 Aug. 1835) 30 *Hansard* col. 466.

[35] T. Turner, *On Copyright in Design* (1849), 35.

[36] 'Most of the patent agents have taken part against either the whole system, or a large portion of its application': *ibid.*, 24.

[37] Shortly after the passage of the Design Registration Act patent agents began to advertise to the effect that 'they would be happy, for a small fee, to undertake the registration of designs for any of our readers or correspondents': J. Robertson (1839–40) 32 *Mechanics' Magazine* 221. Further indication of Robertson's work in this area is that his firm was involved in one of the first cases under the 1843 Act: Robertson, 'Law Report of Registration' (1845) 5 *Repertory of Patent Inventions* 262–4.

[38] While later commentators treated registrations under the 1839 Designs Registration Act as mistaken and contrary to the intention of the Act, those who introduced the 1839 Act had no obvious intention of confining its subject matter to ornamental designs. In fact, Poulett Thomson argued that the system was meant to give protection to those inventors who only wanted their inventions protected for a very short period of time, and who could not afford the expense of obtaining patents in the ordinary way: (21 Feb. 1839) 45 *Hansard* col. 747.

Implicit within the argument that improper subject-matter was being registered under the 1839 Designs Registration Act was an idea of what *properly* belonged within the scope of design law (and other areas of intellectual property). In particular, ideas about the impropriety of certain registrations were premised on a clear idea of the objects which belonged within the ambit of design law and those which belonged within patent law. More specifically they were based on the idea that design registration should be restricted to shapes and patterns whose purpose was to beautify, with shapes which were constructed to achieve useful ends being the proper subject matter for patents.[39]

Another explanation for the distinction which was drawn between objects of beauty and those of utility can be traced to the way in which the subject matter deposited at the Registry was organised.[40] In turn, the administrative arrangements of the Registry were shaped by the ways in which different forms of subject matter were (necessarily) described. It seems that the Registrar took the view that the ways in which inventions were to be represented and categorised required different techniques of representation.[41]

We also see in the approach adopted to the question of overlap between the emergent categories the use of a set of assumptions which continue to play an important role in shaping present-day intellectual property law. While there were a number of ways in which the question of overlap between the categories could have been approached – exemplified most famously in the different approaches taken to artistic copyright designs overlap in France and in the UK – it was assumed that overlap was a problem to be avoided. Although there is some indication that this may have been because the purity of the Register was perceived as a desirable end in itself,[42] there were a number of adverse consequences which were said to flow from the registration of 'improper' subject matter which made it a problem to be avoided. One of the main problems was that as registration amounted to publication, registration of incorrect subject

---

[39] This was dependent upon the notion of the proper function of the design, not the object to which that design was applied. For example, it was not intended that the decorative shape of a stove be excluded, even though a stove was clearly seen as a useful object.

[40] T. Webster, *The Subject Matter of Letters Patent* (1851), 83.

[41] It was suggested (*Report of Registrar of Designs* (1841), 23) that those modes of technical drawing which were akin to those used in patent specifications were more appropriate where the shape was intended to achieve some function. Moreover, while it was argued that some explanatory text would be required in order to explain the function that configurations were intended to achieve textual explanation of ornamental designs, in contrast, were thought to be superfluous.

[42] This was particularly so with the Registrar of Designs who saw as his role 'to watch and regulate the registration': *Report of Registrar of Designs* (1841), 23–6.

matter under the 1839 Designs Registration Act precluded the possibility of protection by way of letters patent. The result of this was that the cost of registration was wasted and the desired protection was not obtained, thus increasing the likelihood of undesirable and expensive litigation. The most worrying consequence of all, however, was the fear that registration of incorrect subject matter would bring the Designs Office and the registration system more generally into disrepute. As the Registrar of Designs complained, the registration of incorrect subject matter 'must ultimately produce litigation among the inventors of similar improvements which have been successfully registered, and if their futility be exposed in a Court of Law the effect thus produced cannot but tend to bring discredit upon the Office and render the Public suspicious of the genuine Copyrights afforded in the case of Ornamental Designs'.[43]

Policing the boundaries of intellectual property law

In pre-modern intellectual property law, the task of managing the legal categories occurred, in effect, automatically, the industry-specific nature of the legislation setting the necessary limits and boundaries. With the change in the form of the law which occurred in 1839, however, the law was no longer able to rely passively upon areas of trade as a way of differentiating between forms of protection. Instead the law found it necessary to develop techniques which would enable it to organise and manage the subject matter it protected. More specifically, the process of abstraction and consolidation which took place in 1839 meant that the law had to draw lines, to demarcate the limits of the categories, and ensure that certain subject matter was included while other was excluded.[44]

While there were a number of ways in which the task of organising the legal categories could have been achieved (for example by reference to the physical nature of the object or to the commercial value of the intangible), the way in which the law initially chose to organise its subject matter was by defining 'as distinctly as possible, the subjects to be protected'.[45] Drawing upon developments that were taking place in

---

[43] *Ibid.*, 23. In rejecting an application to register a stoneware bottle, the novelty of which consisted of it being stoneware, the Registrar said, 'I think their Lordships will see that if some rule is not laid down against the admission of these designs which are so glaringly without the meaning of the Act much confusion and litigation would arise': letter from the Registrar to the Board of Trade re a complaint by Mr Retties (Jan. 1844) *Letters to the Board of Trade* BT/1/421, T16 No. 1.

[44] 'To codify means to banish the effect of vagueness and indeterminacy, boundaries which are badly drawn and divisions which are only approximate, by producing clear classes and making clear cuts, establishing firm frontiers even if this means eliminating people who are neither fish nor fowl': P. Bourdieu, 'Codification' (1990), 82.

[45] T. Webster, *The Subject Matter of Letters Patent* (1851), 81.

legal practice more generally, the task the law set for itself was to identify what it regarded as the common denominator or the defining characteristics of each of the categories in question.[46] To do this it was necessary to identify in more detail what it was that each of the areas in question protected. Armed with this information, it would then have been possible, so the argument went, to determine whether a particular application was more properly protected as a design or a patent. In the case in hand, this meant that it was necessary to determine the particular nature of the property interest protected by design law, on the one hand, and patent law on the other.

Drawing on a developing jurisprudence which suggested that patents protected such things as the mechanical action, principle, contrivance or application as well as the use, purpose, or result of particular objects, it was agreed that the defining characteristic of patent protection was a concern with the *utility* of inventions.[47] While patent law protected the use made of articles of manufacture, it was argued that design law was primarily concerned with their pattern, shape and configuration.[48] In short, the defining characteristic of patents was a shared concern with utility, whereas the organising principle of property in design was a concern with the *form* that objects took.[49]

---

[46] In a sense it is possible that the change in the form of the law not only created the potential for overlap between designs and patents, but may also have suggested ways in which this problem was to be resolved. This was because in order to move from a subject-specific law to a more abstract and open-ended system it was necessary to identify a common denominator which linked the various elements together. Such generalisation requires some organising feature or principle by which coherence can be given. See A. Simpson, 'The Rise and Fall of the Legal Treatise: Legal Principles and the Forms of Legal Literature' in *Legal Theory and Legal History: Essays on the Common Law* (London: The Hambledon Press, 1987), 307.

[47] Designs Office, Somerset House. Quoted in J. Davies, *A Pamphlet on Patents* (London: Weale, Simpkin and Co., 1850), 15.

[48] The language of the designer, which was the 'subject of the right', lay in the external form, the appearance of the object': T. Turner, *On Copyright in Design* (1849), v. Design protection was confined to the combination of lines producing pattern, shape or configuration, by whatever means such design may be applicable to manufacture: T. Webster, *The Subject Matter of Letters Patent* (1851), vi.

[49] 'In registering any new design for a table-lamp, all which could be secured under such registration would be, some peculiarities of form in the stem or oil-vessel, or in the glass shade: no new mode of supplying oil to the wick, nor any new mode of raising the wick, nor any new apparatus for supplying air to support combustion, could be the subject matter of a registration. A patent, on the contrary, can scarcely ever be said to depend on shape': W. Carpmael, 'Registration of Designs' (1842) 17 *Repertory of Patent Inventions* 40. Another important difference between designs and patents in respect of the way in which their property interest was characterised was that while with patents a distinction was drawn between the physical form in which the intangible was embodied and the intangible itself, with designs the intangible property and its physical appearance were inseparable. To coin a modern parallel, the medium was the message. As one commentator said, design was best characterised as 'property in form, distinct

This logic was adopted in the 1842 Ornamental Designs Act as a way of distinguishing patents from designs. It did this by replacing the broad definition contained in the second and third section of the 1839 Designs Registration Act by a more restrictive provision which stated that a property right was given to designs 'applicable to the ornamenting of any article of manufacture or . . . substance'.[50] It was hoped that this would enable a distinction to be drawn between the subject matter of designs and that of patents:[51] as patents protected the principle or utility of manufactured objects, ornamental form was essentially irrelevant.

The failure of the 1842 Ornamental Designs Act

Although the 1842 Act was crafted to ensure that the Designs Register was limited to ornamental designs, it readily became apparent with the continued registration of utility designs in the months following the introduction of the 1842 Act that it was not up to the task which had been given to it. The particular failing of the 1842 Act was that while it provided a more detailed definition of the subject matter to be protected, nonetheless the language used was still unclear. With hindsight it is easy for us to speak of the 1842 Ornamental Designs Act as an ornamental designs act (as some did at the time), yet it is also equally easy to see how it was construed to include non-ornamental design.[52] Given that in thinking through these issues the law was in the process of formulating what is arguably the first developed category of modern intellectual property law, this confusion is all the more understandable.

While the uncertainty surrounding the language used in the 1842 Act partly explains its failure, equally important was the fact that the Act did little to deter inventors from attempting to register their creations as designs; to alter the 'disposition on the part of Inventors to take advantage of the Act as a means of obtaining a Copyright, by registration, either for new instruments and machines or improvements in old

---

from that of the material substance or article in which it was exhibited': T. Turner, *On Copyright in Design* (1849), v.

[50] On the issue of the intention of the 1842 Act to define subject matter more clearly see T. Webster, *The Subject Matter of Letters Patent* (1851), 80–1.

[51] 'It is important that the manufacturer should well understand, that the protection offered by this Act applies only to shape or configuration of an ornamental character, applied to any article of manufacture, and that the protection offered by this Statute does not in any way relate to mechanical instruments, nor to machines, nor to processes of manufacture': W. Carpmael, *Registration of Designs in order to Secure Copyright* (3rd edn) (London: MacIntosh, 1846), 2.

[52] It is unclear from the language of the Act that it was intended to restrict the registrability of designs. Given this uncertainty it is unsurprising that it was unsuccessful in its aim of cleansing the law.

ones'. In short, the main problem with the 1842 Act was that it failed to dampen 'the incessant attempts on the part of inventors of utilities to squeeze in along with their more fortunate brethren the inventors of ornament. Patents were, from their expense, in a multitude of cases quite out of the question ... The registrar refused to register some designs, and issued warnings to inventors; but the evil continued'.[53] The evils of wrongful registration were compounded by the fact that the 1842 Act failed to provide the Registrar with any express powers to refuse the registration of non-ornamental designs.[54]

With the realisation that the 1842 Act was unable to perform what was asked of it, that the continued registration of machines, contrivances and other articles of utility as ornamental designs needed to be avoided, and that patent reform was not a viable option, calls were made for the further reform of design law. These calls for reform were reinforced by a growing consensus as to which subject matter 'properly' belonged with patent law and, consequently, which did not. Based on the idea that patent law should be reserved for more important inventions,[55] there was a growing belief that so-called trivial inventions – such as the kaleidoscope,[56] 'snuffers, stirrups, lamps, cork-screws, and other articles of domestic use', which were said to 'be of no material value to the public'[57] – were not deserving of patent protection (for which they were then eligible). It was to address these concerns[58] that the 1843 Utility

---

[53] T. Turner, *On Copyright in Design* (1849), 24. 'A registration [of an object of utility under the 1842 Act], though evidently of an unsound title, might give, in the eyes of the public a certain protection and if it failed, there was but three pounds lost': *ibid*. As long as copyright extended to the shape and configuration of articles, 'numbers of new inventions will always be sought to be included in it': *Report of Registrar of Designs* (1841), 26–7.

[54] When the Registrar refused to register a number of articles because they were not 'strictly and sufficiently ornamental', complaints were made to the Board of Trade to the effect that as the 1842 Act did not empower the Registrar to judge as to the fitness of a design received for registration, he was acting without authority. S. Billing and A. Prince, *The Law and Practice of Patents* (1845), 206.

[55] One of the arguments frequently put forward against lowering the cost of the patent process was that it would have meant that worthless, non-deserving patents would be granted.

[56] Sir David Brewster took out a patent for a kaleidoscope in 1817. Apparently the patent failed for lack of novelty, the invention having been exposed before the patent was sealed: J. Robertson, 1836 *Select Committee on Arts and Manufactures* 131.

[57] J. Farey, 1829 *Select Committee on Patents* 141. Farey said that 'many inventions; such as the kaleidoscope, and the hobbyhorse called velocipede' were of no public utility: *ibid.*, 27.

[58] A further concern was that the Registrar hoped to increase the workload and income of the Registry: *Report of Registrar of Designs* (1841), 30. While the Designs Registry was intended to be self-funding, a letter from the Registrar, Long, to the Board of Trade shows 'a deficiency of £68 11. 7 for the first quarter of 1841', which was paid for by the Treasury (which, in turn, led to the Registry being more closely audited and controlled by the Treasury): *Minutes of the Board of Trade* (5 Jan. 1841). Increasing the scope of

Designs Act was passed. This provided protection for 'any new or original Design for any Article of Manufacture having reference to some purpose of Utility, so far as such design shall be for the Shape or Configuration of such Article'. Under the Act, proprietors of designs were given 'the sole Right to apply such Design to any Article, or make or sell any Article according to such Design, for the Term of three years' from registration.

While the 1842 Ornamental Designs Act focused upon the circumstances which gave rise to the *opportunity* for wrongful protection (that is, the broad language used in the second and third heads of the 1839 Designs Registration Act), the 1843 Utility Designs Act attempted to remove any *desire* inventors might have had to gain protection under the Act. This was achieved by providing inventors with an alternative form of protection, a 'substitute' as it was called at the time.[59] The Acts were extended so that they provided protection both 'for the application of a new material or for the combination of parts whether external or internal or for the particular contrivance whereby the utility of any article is increased or a new one produced'.[60] In short, a new form of protection was introduced:[61] what we might now call utility model or petty patent protection.[62] Fearful that the incentives offered by the 1843

the subject matter that was potentially registrable was one way of overcoming this loss. By 1844, the loss had been turned into a profit of £598: *Minutes of the Board of Trade* (1843–4), 2/13.

[59] The 1843 Act was introduced not only to cleanse the Designs Register of unwanted subject matter (and thus to avoid the resulting problems), but also to provide a *new* form of protection. As Turner said, 'the practice was only stopped by providing a substitute. The want of such copyright was obvious, and equally so that a revenue was to be made of it. The new act, 1843, was the first recognition of copyright in useful form': T. Turner, *On Copyright in Design* (1849), 24. Long (the Registrar) claimed that this was the known intention of the legislator. See 'Answer to Memorial of Alexander Prince: 3 July 1843', *Letters to the Board of Trade* BT/413/L16.

[60] *Report of Registrar of Designs* (1841), 27–8.

[61] The 1843 Act aimed 'to give small tradesmen a speedy relief at a small expense, in cases of piracy of some invention he had registered': Mr Clarkson, *Boswell* v *Denton* (1845) 6 *Repertory of Patent Inventions* 265, 266. 'As regards all the minor inventions, and therefore the majority of them, the patent, from its enormous and inflexible cost, afforded no protection at all. It is insisted on that the [1843] act was expressly provided to remedy this, and to such inventions it has been widely applied': T. Turner, *On Copyright in Design* (1849), 45.

[62] For example, the 1843 Act was described as an 'act to make patents cheap' ((2 Sept. 1843) 39 *Mechanics' Magazine* 164) and as 'a miniature patent specification' (T. Turner, *On Copyright in Design* (1849), 63). By introducing a form of petty patent protection the 1843 Utility Designs Act satisfied some of the calls which had frequently been made by creators (and investors) for the introduction of a cheaper, quicker form of protection. As Turner said, there were two arguments for the 1843 Act, the *aequo* and the *bono*. The *bono* was to stop the constant attempts at calling an ingenious design for use an ornament; the *aequo* was the evident want of some cheap and convenient protection, and the propriety of making the registration machinery available for it.

Utility Designs Act might have been inadequate, the Registrar of Designs was also given express powers which enabled him to refuse to register designs which he believed fell within the ambit of the 1842 Ornamental Designs Act.[63]

In combination, the legislation enacted in 1842 and 1843 went some way towards achieving the tasks expected of it in managing the boundaries that existed between the legal categories granting property rights in mental labour. While these statutes provided the means by which ornamental designs and patents were to be distinguished, a further problem remained: the possibility was left open that creations many thought ought to be protected by patent law were in fact registrable as utility designs. While the law was able to distinguish between ornamental design and utility designs,[64] as well as between ornamental design and patents, the question remained as to how it was to distinguish between utility designs and patents.[65] These problems were exacerbated by the continued uncertainty which surrounded the scope and nature of the patent grant.[66] In turn, the problem of managing the relationship between patents and designs, like those experienced with the 1842 Ornamental Designs Act, reflected the continued interest in the aesthetics of the law and, at the same time, the perception that overlap between the categories somehow interfered with or unsettled that aesthetic.

Given the success the law experienced in its efforts to distinguish ornamental designs from non-ornamental designs as well as ornamental designs from patents by focusing on the principles by which each of the categories were (supposedly) organised, it is unsurprising that it would employ similar techniques in its efforts to distinguish patents from non-

---

Utility produced by form is as much a matter of principle as a patent': T. Turner, *ibid.*, 54–5. While the utility model is usually seen as having originated in Germany and as foreign to the UK, Britain adopted a utility model style enactment, long before the German *Gebrauchsmuster* was introduced.

[63] Section 9, 1843 Utility Designs Act.

[64] The subject matter was 'not design *simpliciter*, but rather the application of the design to the particular articles of manufacture for the purpose of ornamenting such articles': T. Webster, *The Subject Matter of Letters Patent* (1851), 82. In contrast, the 1843 Act was for 'a design for any article of manufacture having reference to some purpose of utility': *ibid.*

[65] 'Experience of the working of the Designs Acts shows great confusion as to the subjects of those two Acts, and between the subjects of the Non-Ornamental Designs Act and of Letters for Patents for Inventions ... Many designs have been registered under the wrong Act, and the majority of Designs registered under the Non-Ornamental Designs act are not within the Act, that which it was intended to protect being the subject of Letters Patent and not of registration': *ibid.*

[66] One of the consequences of 'extending the scope of protection beyond identical copies, as justice demanded' to include 'colourable evasions' was that it increased the problem of overlap between the various rights: *Hill* v *Thompson* (1818) 129 ER 427.

ornamental designs. It readily became apparent, however, that the methods used in these other situations were of limited use in distinguishing patents from non-ornamental designs: while ornamental and non-ornamental designs had been distinguished by reference to what were taken as the organising principles of the subject matter protected (viz.: beauty and utility), it was not possible to distinguish patents and non-ornamental designs in this manner.

The particular problem that the law faced was that in some circumstances the nature of the property interest protected as a non-ornamental design and as a patent related to the *same* feature of a particular object; viz. its external form. This presented the law with the problem that while non-ornamental designs were limited to the shape or configuration of articles and patents to the utility of objects, in certain situations the utility of the object also flowed from the particular *form* that the object took. This was especially the case with objects such as paddle wheels, stern-propellers, railway-bars, chairs, sleepers, and wood pavements where the peculiar shape or configuration of the object (which was the domain of design law) was also the source of the object's utility (which was the domain of patent law).[67]

Given that the organising principles were the same for both categories, this meant that a manufacturing object whose novelty lay in its shape or form could be classified *either* as a non-ornamental design or as a patentable invention. As Turner recognised, the decision as to whether such creations were to be protected as a patent or as a non-ornamental design was arbitrary, depending on whether it came 'from patent-men'[68] or from a 'member of the mechanical public'.[69] It was possible, for example, to define the steam engine in such a way that it fell within the scope of both the 1843 Utility Designs Act and patent law: 'Either extreme is theoretically possible: the most complex patent may be called a new form'.[70] Turner captured the nature of the

[67] S. Billing and A. Prince, *The Law and Practice of Patents* (1845), 206. While 'the essence of many inventions consists in the general idea of working out some abstract principle ... or in some mechanical action ... yet there are many cases in which the peculiar shape or configuration is the essence of the invention and can receive full protection under these acts': *ibid.*

[68] These so-called patent-men 'were anxious to narrow the range of "principles of invention", or to extend that of inventions of forms and shapes': T. Turner, *On Copyright in Design* (1849), 49.

[69] *Ibid.*, 50. A number of applications were made for the scope of protection provided by the 1843 Act to be extended primarily because patents were too expensive. See, 'Memorial from Moody of London: Aug. 1845', *Letters to the Board of Trade* BT/1/455, B18 No. 26; letter from J. H. Kelk proposing to extend protection of registration to all inventions (March 1844) *Letters to the Board of Trade* BT/1/424, No. 33.

[70] 'A steam engine is a combination of certain hollow vessels, as cylinders and tubes, and solid parts, rods, cranks, etc., in such a way as to be a purpose of utility, viz., the

relationship between non-ornamental designs and patents when he said: 'You cannot have principle without special form, any more than you can have respiration without lungs'.[71] At 'the other possible extreme, principle is never absent; you might put all useful contrivances to the head of patents'.[72]

While in other situations the law was able to identify what it regarded as the essential traits of the property protected in such a way as to enable it to distinguish between the categories, the particular difficulty that confronted it in these circumstances was that the law was unable to utilise similar rationale to distinguish non-ornamental designs from patents.[73] More specifically, the law was unable to provide a logical or principled basis by which it could differentiate between the manufacture (or invention) which was protected by design law and that which was subject to patent protection.[74]

Although the dispute as to the way manufacturing objects were to be construed may, as Turner suggested, have been played out in terms of a struggle between different occupational groups, it was ultimately defused by more mundane means. In particular, while ornamental designs and patents, and ornamental and non-ornamental designs, were distinguished by recourse to what might now be called the principles of law, non-ornamental designs and patents were distinguished by bureaucratic means. This alerts us to the important role played by the registration system in shaping and reinforcing the legal categories.

A number of different techniques associated with the registration process were adopted to enable the law to manage the boundary between designs and patents. One tactic was to set the registration fees as between patents and utility designs in such a way as to reduce the attractiveness of utility designs to patentees.[75] In turn, the increased

---

sustaining a body of water in one receptacle near ignited substance in another, catching the force of the vapour in a third, and condensing it in a fourth.' In this case, 'the purpose of utility is absolutely dependent on form, shape, and configuration': T. Turner, *On Copyright in Design* (1849), 50.

[71] *Ibid.*

[72] 'To repeat the simile, lungs have no purpose of utility except through the principle and mechanical action': *ibid.*, 51.

[73] Speaking of the confusion that arose as to registration, it was said, 'Registration is frequently confounded with that conferred by letters patent, being in fact regarded as a "cheap patent"': H. Murdoch, *Information respecting British and Foreign Patents* (2nd edn) (London: G. Briggs, 1867), 3.

[74] The problem that confronted the law was that there was 'little of an authoritative nature to guide [it] in deciding what proportion of the registered designs might have been or may be maintained': T. Turner, *On Copyright in Design* (1849), 45.

[75] The fee for designs of utility was set at £10 compared with the fees payable under the Ornamental Designs Act of 1s *for* calico. This was to avoid making patentees overenvious: T. Turner, *On Copyright in Design* (1849), 34–5. Long said of the 1843 Act, 'If confined to three years such a regime would in no way interfere with the law of Patents

control placed upon the application – the way it was drafted and the language used – also played a role in enabling the two categories to be distinguished. For example, because the 1843 Utility Designs Act stated that in order to make designs intelligible, applicants were required to attach to the drawings a written description and to set forth the parts of the design which were new,[76] applicants were forced to think more about the nature of their application. While this would have done little to deter those who wished to 'play the system' from registering their inventions as designs, it would have had more impact on those who would otherwise have mistakenly registered in the wrong category. In addition, because applicants – in order to make designs more intelligible – were required to outline in more detail what they were claiming, the task of the Registrar in policing the categories was made easier.

But perhaps the most important change that occurred in the management of the boundary between non-ornamental designs and patents was one that came about quite suddenly and without explanation: the potential for overlap between different categories was no longer seen as a problem. Whether this is evidence of a new-found maturity in intellectual property law or a pragmatic response to what was clearly a difficult task is uncertain. What is clear, however, is that there was a dramatic turnaround in the way overlap was perceived. Instead of being seen as a problem for the law to resolve, individuals were left to choose which form of protection they wanted. The Registrar made this clear in a notice he issued to the public in 1843:

all designs, the drawing and description of which are properly prepared and made out, will be registered without reference to the nature and extent of the copyright sought to be thereby acquired; which considerations must be left entirely to the judgement and discretion of the proprietor of the design.[77]

Although the law had previously taken it upon itself to determine the category into which a particular application belonged, it suddenly reversed its practices and left it up to applicants to decide by which

---

since, if it were worth while, a protection for fourteen years would always be preferred to one of three'. Further, if the registration fee were set high, for example at £10, this would be 'a safeguard against the Registrar being inundated with merely trifling or insignificant Designs': *Report of Registrar of Designs* (1841), 28–9.

[76] Section 8, 1843 Utility Designs Act .

[77] J. Bowen, 'Notice Issued by the Registrar: Copyright of Designs for Articles of Utility' (1843) 2 *Repertory of Patent Inventions* 251. The Registrar of Designs issued a notice emphasising that, under the 1843 Act, the registration conferred was for the 'protection of shape and configuration': W. Carpmael, 'Copyright of Designs' (1843) 2 *Repertory of Patent Inventions* 251

category they wished their creations to be protected.[78] This ostensibly provided applicants with more choice, but at the same time this was underpinned by a veiled threat which served to restrict the effective choices which were available: applicants needed to take care in deciding under which category they lodged their claims. This was because of the fact that as registration amounted to a publication, and patents and designs both required novelty as a prerequisite of protection, once one avenue was chosen, it excluded the possibility of applicants gaining the other form of protection. Thus, if applicants used the 'wrong' regime not only would they lose that form of protection they would also lose the alternative protection. So if an invention was incorrectly registered as a design and this was later successfully challenged, not only would the invention lose its design protection, it would also be precluded from protection by patent law. While this may have been harsh on applicants, it was said to have been balanced by the fact that registration, even when defective, shifted the burden of proof onto the opposing party. Although the self-regulatory techniques provided by the registration process were not a complete solution to the registration of 'incorrect' subject matter, they were successful enough that the question of how the boundary between design and patents was to be managed was no longer seen as an issue worthy of discussion and consideration. This highlights the important role that was to be played by registration in regulating the legal categories that emerged over the course of the nineteenth century and, at the same time, the limited role played by principles in organising the law.

[78] There were some problems in using registration as basis for differentiation, caused primarily by the lack of harmony between the two forms of registration: while with design, the right commenced on publication, patentees first obtained their patent and then published it six months later. There was little to stop patentees from including new creations within the six-month period and putting them in their specifications – an early example of double-patenting (see *Brett* v *Massi* (1847) 30 *London Journal of Arts and Sciences* 357).

Part 3

Towards an intellectual property law

During the eighteenth and early part of the nineteenth centuries there was widespread agreement that manual labour could and should be separated from mental labour. It would be inaccurate to infer from this, however, that intellectual property law had achieved the status of a separate and distinct category of law: while many familiar themes and concepts were then in use, modern intellectual property law did not emerge as a discrete and widely recognised category of law until midway through the nineteenth century. Although frequent use was made before then of terms such as copy-right, patents, designs and even occasionally intellectual property,[1] it is incorrect to assume that these expressions were used in a consistent, meaningful way or that they referred to distinct areas of law. Similarly, while prior to the 1850s or thereabouts occasional use was made of concepts, modes of organisation and ways of thinking that are recognisably modern in their nature, these were placed alongside and given more or less equal weight to that which now appears to be distinctly alien and pre-modern.

It is often assumed that intellectual property law is a timeless, almost ahistorical, area of law that has always existed, but if we look at the way the law was understood at the time, we see that one of the notable features of the period was that up until the middle part of the nineteenth century there was no Law of Copyright, Patents, Designs or Trade-marks, and certainly no Intellectual Property Law (at least as it is perceived today).[2] The fluid and open nature of the law in this area that prevailed during the eighteenth and nineteenth centuries manifested itself in a number of ways. One way in which the fluidity was exemplified

---

[1] E.g. Appendix 1 of Thomson's *A Letter to the Right Honourable Sir Robert Peel* (1840) was headed: 'Intellectual Property Protected by Law in England'. This included literary property, musical compositions, fine arts and industrial arts. In Thomas Turner's 1849 work, *On Copyright in Design*, there is a table illustrating the 'Comparative duration and expense of intellectual property'.

[2] Even as late as 1869 there was said to be 'very general ignorance of the subject': F. Campin, *Law of Patents for Inventions with Explanatory Notes on the Law as to the Protection of Designs and Trade Marks* (London: Virtue and Co., 1869), 1.

was in the fact that there was a lack of consensus as to how the law in the area should be organised. More specifically, although there was general agreement as to the existence of a general category of law which granted property rights in mental labour and which was united by a shared image of creativity, beyond this no one model or image had yet come to dominate as *the* accurate representation of the law. The openness and fluidity manifested themselves in a range of complex and interconnected ways: from the way the legal and administrative categories, textbooks and libraries were organised, through to the language and concepts that were used, as well as the subject matter that was given legal protection.

The fluid and uncertain nature of the law in this area was captured in Turner's lament in 1849 that the 'subject has till lately only occupied the attention of legislators and jurists at uncertain intervals ... it has been but little studied by the jurist or statistician; and information respecting the subject is widely scattered, and must be sought for under any head rather than its own'.[3] Turner was objecting here not only to the absence of relevant treatises and textbooks, but more specifically to the fact that the law which provided property or property-style rights in mental labour was not organised in a consistent or coherent manner. Indeed there were various competing suggestions proposed at the time as to how this field should be organised, all of which were taken seriously. One proposed mode of organisation, for example, argued for the creation of a category of law which would protect the fine arts as well as 'all forms of industrial art',[4] that is, it adopted a unity of art approach.[5] Thomas Turner's idea of a law of form, which focused on the external appearance and shape of objects (and as such encompassed subject matter now incorporated in patents, design and copyright, but expressly excluded literary property), was an interesting variation on this theme. Another option suggested at the time was to do away with what we

---

[3] T. Turner, *On Copyright in Design* (1849), 12. Godson made similar complaints when he said in 1823 that 'the law of Patents for Inventors has never been fully and scientifically investigated, that it is little known among Artists, that it is supposed that not one half of the Patents which have been obtained could bear the test of legal inquiry, and that cases of Copyright have never before been formed into a distinct and independent Treatise': R. Godson, *A Practical Treatise on the Law of Patents* (1823), viii.

[4] 'Thus, adopting at an early period, a correct principle, the French extended the application of copyright to all production of industrial art, and at this time, France affords, at a small cost, protection of sufficient duration, with effectual and speedy redress for the infringement of copyright. In no other country is there so comprehensive a copyright, and in the markets of every civilised country the elegant productions of France are esteemed in preference to those of all other nations': G. Brace, *Observations on Extension of Protection of Copyright of Design, with a View to the Improvement of British Taste* (London: Smith, Elder and Co., 1842), 10.

[5] That is, it protected all artistic works (including industrial works) irrespective of their application or use.

would now call a copyright–patents–designs-style approach and to divide productions of the mind into 'two great classifications – works (whatever their intention) addressed to the tastes, passions, and existing circumstances of the age, and those adapted to all the fluctuations of society'.[6] Yet another approach distinguished forms of property in thought depending on whether they were expressed by visual or vocal signs.[7] Another option, which was favoured by the 'patent men' who looked on themselves as licensed gamekeepers of the manor of the useful arts and the agents for design registration as so many poachers, was to 'contract the limits of utility in form till nothing visible were left', that is, to replace design protection with patents. In contrast, 'a large part of the mechanical public were quite willing that non-ornamental design should absorb the patent right entirely'.[8]

While modes of organisation were occasionally mooted which are recognisably modern in their approach,[9] these were certainly not given priority over any of the other alternatives. At best all that could be said about the disparate series of statutes and decisions which had developed in piecemeal response to specific problems was that they protected particular forms of creation from copying. The thread which connected them together and the basis by which analogies were formed was that they provided property rights in mental labour. At the same time, it was clear that intellectual property law, and its various sub-categories (of copyright, patents, designs and trademarks) did not yet exist.

The fluid and uncertain nature of the law in this area was also reflected in the fact that commentators, both legal and non-legal, expert and non-expert, frequently spoke of 'copyright in inventions',[10] 'patents for art', literary property as a 'universal patent for authors',[11] 'copyright of trade marks'[12] and occasionally even of 'patents for copyright or

---

[6] 'Law of Literary Property and Patents' (1829) 10 *Westminster Review* 465.

[7] See M. Leverson, *Copyright and Patents: or, Property in Thought* (1854).

[8] T. Turner, *On Copyright in Design* (1849), 49–50.

[9] See, e.g., R. Godson, *A Practical Treatise on the Law of Patents* (1823).

[10] Article IV of A Bill to Extend the Benefit of Registrations to Inventions drafted in 1851 defined copyright as 'the exclusive right to work, make, use, and vend an invention': 1851 *Select Committee of the House of Lords Appointed to Consider the Bills for the Amendment of the Law Touching Letters Patent for Inventions* 410, Appendix E.

[11] Lord Hardwicke, in J. Burrow, *The Question Concerning Literary Property by the Court of Kings Bench on 20th April 1769, in the Case between Andrew Millar and Robert Taylor* (London: W. Strahan and M. Woodfall, 1773), 20. In *Jeffreys v Baldwin* (1753) 27 ER 109 Lord Hardwicke suggested that the Engravers' Act 1735 was 'for the encouragement of genius and art' and likened it to the 'statute of new inventions, from whence it was taken'.

[12] John Jobson Smith, 1862 *Select Committee on Trade Marks* 54 (Q. 1134).

patterns'[13] or referred to patents as 'a kind of copyright for trade'.[14] At best 'copy-right' (which included copy-right in designs) referred to the form or style of right protected and, as such, meant something very different from the way it is used today.[15] Moreover, the term 'copyright' was not limited to works now seen as part of copyright law (such as literary and dramatic works) but occasionally extended to include inventions as well as ornamental and non-ornamental designs.[16] Similar confusion was evident in the language used in the other areas of intellectual property law then in existence.

Despite the fluidity and openness that existed during the eighteenth and early nineteenth centuries, it is clear that by the 1850s not only the holy trinity of patents, copyright and designs were recognised as distinct and separate areas of law, but also that these categories were seen as elements of the more general rubric of intellectual property law. While aspects of this law remained unclear, the process of emergence was uneven, and did not yet include trade marks, in 1853 Webster was able to write without any hesitation or qualification that there are now three 'separate and distinct branches of jurisprudence, which may be treated of as copyright of literature and fine arts, of design in Arts and Manufacture and of letters patent for inventors'.[17] This is not to suggest that prior to this there had not been ideas as to the way the law which dealt with mental labour ought to be organised and that in the 1850s, or thereabouts, one suddenly appeared. Rather, it is to argue that over this

[13] The most striking example of this confusion, at least from a modern perspective, was during the hearings of the Select Committee on Patents where questions were asked about the patent protection for patterns. 'Are patterns ever the subject of patents? No; but it is not well defined, nor is it easy to define, what degree of invention shall or shall not be the subject of patents; it is very desirable that patterns should be protected in some ready way, but not by a patent; it would be too expensive and tedious': J. Farey, 1829 *Select Committee on Patents* 27.

[14] Gibbs CJ, *Wood* v *Zimmer* (1815) 171 ER 162 note.

[15] The decision of *Jefferys* v *Boosey* (1854) 10 ER 681 is interesting in that it reflects the transition from copyright as a right to copy (a copy-right) to Copyright as a distinct area of law. This is most noticeable in the way in which the term 'copyright' was used, often referring to the nature of the right, rather than how it now tends to be used, as a shorthand for a body of law defined (primarily) in terms of its subject matter.

[16] Design legislation well into the twentieth century habitually spoke of copyright in designs.

[17] T. Webster, *On Property in Designs* (1853), 10. In proposing to establish a perfect code of laws of England, Edward Lloyd suggested the collection under 'one head of this whole class of Statutes. The law of patent-right being the first and most important of the group; after that the law of copyright, subdivided into literary copyright and copyright in works of art, pictorial and plastic; this might well be followed by the law of copyright in designs, consolidated into a single statute, and the series would be completed by the law of trade and merchandise marks': E. Lloyd, 'Consolidation of the Law of Copyright' (28 June 1862) 6 *Solicitors' Journal* 626.

period there was a gradual change in the grammar or logic of the law: an important shift in the way the law was represented and imagined.[18]

The emergence of modern intellectual property law and its subsidiary categories of design, patents and copyright as separate and distinct categories of law was exemplified by the changes which took place in the subsequent editions of Richard Godson's *A Practical Treatise on the Law of Patents for Inventions and of Copyright*. While the first edition, which was published in 1823, began with a lengthy section on common law offences in relation to monopolies such as forestalling (or buying up produce on the way to the market in order to maintain prices by holding a monopoly), this was omitted from subsequent editions. Moreover when Godson produced the supplement to his second edition in 1844, he had changed the way he organised his subject matter from a focus on the laws protecting 'that species of property which arises more particularly from the exertions of ingenious and learned Men',[19] to the 'Laws respecting Copyright in Books and musical works and in Designs for Articles of Manufacture'.[20] That is, he had moved away from using mental labour as the basis around which his text was organised, to a more modern mode of organisation. Indeed while the first (pre-modern) edition appears somewhat alien to our eyes, later editions do not differ markedly from modern texts, at least in terms of the way the subject matter was organised and the questions asked.

In the following three chapters we explore how and why it was that within the general category of mental labour patents, copyright and design came to be differentiated from and treated as distinct and separate areas of law.[21] In so doing we consider some of the reasons why the option of these three branches of jurisprudence was taken up by the law and not one of the other options put forward at the time. In short, we are interested in why and how intellectual property law took the form that it did.

To these ends, chapter 5 focuses on some of the factors which prompted the crystallisation of the categories of intellectual property law. As we have already examined the emergence of design law as a distinct area of law we concentrate here on the emergence of patent and copyright law as discrete areas of modern law. We then proceed in

---

[18] In presenting the formation of the categories of modern intellectual property law, we have purposively attempted not to prioritise any one factor. Nor are we suggesting that the categories formed, say, linguistically first and that the institutional formation developed afterwards.

[19] R. Godson, *A Practical Treatise on the Law of Patents* (1823), 1st edition.

[20] R. Godson, *A Practical Treatise on the Law of Patents for Invention and of Copyright: Supplement* (London: Benning and Co., 1844), i.

[21] We consider trade marks in ch. 8.

chapter 6 to explain the way in which the obstacles to completion of the intellectual property law framework were overcome and, in turn, how that framework became entrenched as part of the legal tradition. In chapter 7 we explore some of the reasons why intellectual property law was divided up into its now familiar form. In so doing we focus on those factors which both explained and shaped the legal categories. In setting out to explore the emergence of intellectual property law we have separated those factors which prompted the crystallisation of the categories from those factors which helped give the law its now distinctive shape, but this should not be interpreted as suggesting that these processes operated in autonomous intellectual spheres. While we recognise that the processes of categorisation and legitimation were simultaneous and reinforcing and, as such, that the distinctions drawn are artificial, nonetheless such distinctions need to be drawn if we are to achieve our aim of exploring the peculiar shape of modern intellectual property law.[22]

---

[22] Here we echo Latour's remark that these 'great divides', while useful for teaching, polemics and commencement addresses, 'do not represent natural boundaries and do not provide any explanation, but on the contrary are to be explained': B. Latour, 'Drawing things together' (1990), 19–20.

5   Crystallisation of the categories

The crystallisation of patent law

When the 1829 Select Committee on Patents met to discuss the ways in which law and administration of letters patent for inventions could be improved, it encountered a number of difficulties: a fact reflected in the Select Committee's unusual decision to publish its evidence without making any recommendations.[1] While the Committee was unable to reach any specific conclusions, one point on which it was able to agree was that patent law, if it can be called that at the time, was a mess. Indeed, while patents had been granted by the Crown for over two centuries it was said as late as 1835 that 'there existed at present no Law of Patents'.[2] Given that there was great uncertainty as to what could be patented[3] and as to the purpose and requirements of the patent specification, this way of thinking is hardly surprising.[4] The fact that what we now call patent law was at times subsumed with a Law of Arts and Manufacture, a Law of Form and even treated as a type of copy-right attests to the unsettled nature of the legal categories;

---

[1] The Select Committee chose to publish its evidence without recommendations, saying that they would appear later: they never did.

[2] Mr Tooke, 'Letters Patent' (13 Aug. 1835) 30 *Hansard* col. 466. In *Boulton and Watt* v *Bull* (1795) 126 ER 651, Eyre CJ said, 'Patent rights are no where, that I can find, accurately described in our books.' 'The subject of patents for new inventions has not been treated with due precision, as a branch of law by itself, in any of our law books. It is only indeed within a few years that they have become so important a part of our commercial machinery': Gibbs CJ, *Wood* v *Zimmer* (1815) 171 ER 162 note.

[3] See, e.g., the evidence of B. Rotch, 1829 *Select Committee on Patents* 116.

[4] R. Godson noted that 'the law books had become filled with cases arising from the doubt and obscurity in which the law for the regulation of patents is involved': (19 Feb. 1833) 15 *Hansard* col. 975. It is noteworthy that while the precise nature and content of patent *law* was uncertain, nonetheless the grant of letters patent had a strong and identifiable image. In part, this was because of the longevity of the Crown grant of patents and the administrative regime that had grown up around it. In this sense, the emergence of patent law as a discrete category of law was somewhat different from the crystallisation of copyright and design law.

to the fact that patent law, at least as we understand it today, did not yet exist.[5]

Despite the uncertain and open nature of the law, by the 1850s there was a much clearer idea as to the nature of patent law, what its main elements were, and where its boundaries were to be drawn.[6] While certain aspects of the law were yet to be formulated, the law then in existence bears a very close resemblance to present day patent law.[7]

A number of different explanations can be given for the emergence of modern patent law over this period. In part it can be attributed to the fact that the early part of the nineteenth century was characterised by a growing concern with the state of arts and manufacture in Britain. As a reviewer of Charles Babbage's *Reflexions on the Decline of Science in England, and on Some of its Causes* wrote in 1830, the 'return of the sword to its scabbard' following the end of the Napoleonic wars seems 'to have been the signal for one universal effort to recruit exhausted resources, to revive industry and civilisation, and to direct to their proper objects the genius and talent, which war had either exhausted in its services or repressed in its desolations'.[8] While there existed pride in the state of the nation's skill in the arts of war, it was argued that the arts of peace, which were said to be the basis of manufacturing and commercial wealth, were in need of improvement. This was made all the more urgent by the fact that the sciences and the arts of England, like the economy more generally, were said to be in 'a wretched state of depression'.[9] Given that the procedure for the grant of patents was costly, complex, time consuming and obscure, and that there was widespread confusion as to the scope of patentable subject matter, it is unsurprising that, after a long period where little interest had been shown in exploring the patent system, it was chosen as a target for reform.[10]

---

[5] On the confusion as to the meaning and use of word 'patent' see R. Prosser, 'Use of the Word "Patent"' (1840) 32 *Mechanics' Magazine* 740–1.

[6] Cf. E. Burke Inlow, *The Patent Grant* (1950), 29.

[7] This can be seen in the fact that while the central focus of the 1829 Select Committee was upon the state of patent law, the 1851 Select Committee on Patents felt that whereas patent law was clear enough, reform was needed in relation to its administration. See D. Van Zyl Smit, 'The Social Creation of a Legal Reality: A Study of the Emergence and Acceptance of the British Patent System as a Legal Instrument for the Control of New Technology' (PhD Thesis, University of Edinburgh, 1980), 96–8, 156.

[8] 'Review of Charles Babbage, *Reflexions on the Decline of Science*' (1830).

[9] *Ibid.*, 341. It was also said that rewards should be provided to 'those great benefactors of the human species – those "kings of mind", whose victories are bloodless and immortal': 'Mr Mackinnon's New Patent Law Bill' (1839) 32 *Mechanics' Magazine* 352.

[10] There were a number of scattered and unsuccessful attempts to reform patents prior to this, the most well-known example being that proposed by James Watt in the 1780s. See E. Robinson and A. Musson, *James Watt and the Steam Revolution: A Documentary History* (New York: A. M. Kelley, 1969); D. Van Zyl Smit, 'The Social Creation of a Legal Reality' (1980), 97.

In response to the growing calls for reform,[11] Thomas Lennard called on Parliament in 1829 to establish a Select Committee to inquire into the state of patent law.[12] While the Select Committee proved inconclusive, nonetheless it still played an important role in bringing about the emergence of modern patent law: it both operated to expose the confused and uncertain nature of the law and drew together many of the divergent criticisms that existed at the time. More significantly, the evidence of witnesses as to their understandings of the law provided the materials for the processes of reformulation that were to take place over the next two decades.[13]

The first attempt to rectify the many grievances which the Select Committee had identified occurred when Richard Godson, author of one of the earliest treatises on patent law, introduced a Bill to Parliament in 1831.[14] After this Bill was rejected, Godson introduced further Bills which again met with opposition from many of those who advocated reform.[15] As compensation for proposing the postponement of Godson's Bill, Lord Chancellor Brougham promised to 'devote his attention, as early as possible, to the branch of the law to which it related'.[16] While Godson's Bill had directly confronted many of the problems which were identified in the 1829 Select Committee, Lord Brougham's efforts, which culminated in the passage of the 1835 Act to Amend the Law Touching Letters Patent for Inventions, were much more modest in scope. Notably, while Lord Brougham had promised to consider 'wholesale change', his Act only introduced two significant reforms: to allow

---

[11] During the 1820s a number of petition and bills were drafted to reform various aspects of patent law: all failed.

[12] (9 April 1829) 21 *Hansard* col. 598. See also 84 CJ 214.

[13] The evidence of the witnesses to the Committee revealed that dissatisfaction with the existing system was virtually unanimous. There was widespread criticism of the legal requirements relating to the patent specification, in particular the stringent grounds upon which the patent would be declared invalid, and to the procedures for obtaining patents. Other complaints concerned the duration of patents, the form that the specification should take and whether there should be an examination system and if so the role that scientists should play in that process.

[14] R. Godson (9 July 1831) 29 *Hansard* col. 383; 2 *PP* 177. Godson's Bill failed to make it through the Lords (17 July 1833) 65 HLJ 504. It was later stated that the Bill 'had been thrown out in the House of Lords on the ground of its being better to wait till a more comprehensive measure, which was then promised, could be brought forward': T. Lennard (13 Aug. 1835) 30 *Hansard* col. 468. The *Mechanics' Magazine* congratulated itself, claiming that it alone, amongst the press, opposed the Bill and decisively influenced the Upper House against it: (1833) *Mechanics' Magazine* 352.

[15] On the fate of these Bills see (1833) 19 *Mechanics' Magazine*, 26, 43, 317; (27 Feb. 1833) 3 *PP* 169.

[16] Quoted in M. Coulter, *Property in Ideas: The Patent Question in Mid-Victorian Britain* (Kirksville, Mo.: Thomas Jefferson University Press, 1991), 36.

for amendment of the patent specification and for extensions of the patent term beyond the fourteen years then permitted.[17]

Given that, as the *London Journal of Arts and Sciences* put it, 'excepting numerous technical amendments, Brougham's Bill does not embrace any improvements',[18] it is unsurprising that further efforts were made to reform the law. What is surprising was the way in which the calls for reform of the patent system slowly became subsumed within more radical proposals for the introduction of a general law to promote arts and manufacture in the United Kingdom. These suggestions for a law of arts and manufactures (which is similar, in many respects, to the more modern idea of industrial property law),[19] were perpetuated and accentuated by the 1836 Select Committee on Arts and Manufactures,[20] which was set up to inquire into 'the best means of extending the knowledge of the arts and of the principles of design among the people (especially the manufacturing population) of the country'. The clearest example of a general law of arts and manufactures can be seen in the Bills which William Mackinnon and Edward Baines presented to Parliament in 1837,[21] 1837–8[22] and 1839.[23] These Bills, which built upon and developed the proposals which had been made by Godson and the 1836 Select Committee on Arts and Manufactures, provided that 'any person who invents, designs or contrives or becomes the proprietor of any invention, design or contrivance, which produces some new or beneficial operation or result ... in any art, science, manufacture or calling whatsoever, may and shall hereafter have the sole right and property in every such new invention, design or contrivance for and

---

[17] An Act to Amend the Law Touching Letters Patent for Inventions 5 & 6 Wm. IV c. 83 (1835) (1835 Lord Brougham's Act). See C. Drewry, *The Patent Law Amendment Act* (London: John Richards and Co., 1838).

[18] The editors went on to say that the Act 'left all the principal grievances of which men of inventive talent complain, perfectly unremedied': J. Schroder, 'Observations on Mr Mackinnon's Bill' (1837) 10 *The London Journal of Arts and Sciences*, 109.

[19] Moreover, we see within this general law of arts and manufactures not only an association of patents and designs, but also the first example of petty patent and utility model protection.

[20] 1836 *Select Committee on Arts and Manufactures*. 'Arts' are increasingly used in the sense of fine arts, of drawing, engraving and painting as distinct from art as skill.

[21] (14 Feb. 1837) 36 *Hansard* col. 554; 1837 Bill to Amend the Practice relating to Letters Patent for Inventions, and for the Better Encouragement of the Arts and Manufactures (15 Feb. 1837) 3 *PP* (315).

[22] 1837–8 Bill (No. 71) For the Better Encouragement of the Arts and Manufactures, and Securing to Individuals the Benefit of their Inventions for a Limited Time (1837–8) 1 *PP* 27.

[23] 1839 Bill for the Better Encouragement of Arts and Manufactures, and Securing to Individuals the Benefit of their Inventions for a Limited Time (19 Feb. 1839) 4 *PP* 363. It was the 1839 Bill which was called the 'Patterns and Inventions Bill': (19 Feb. 1839) 94 *CJ* 39.

during the term of Twelve months from the time of registering the same'.[24] Unlike Godson's Bills, which were primarily seen as patent bills which also proposed amendments to the law in relation to patterns, Mackinnon and Baines' Bills were specifically called Bills for the Better Encouragement of the Arts and Manufactures. Moreover, their emphasis was not so much upon patents and designs, as on the promotion of arts and manufacture more generally.[25] As with the various efforts to reform patent law, these failed .[26]

While the various attempts to reform and codify the law which took place in the early part of the nineteenth century,[27] and the Select Committees and commentaries that these prompted, proved unsuccessful,[28] nonetheless they still played an important role in the emergence of patent law. This was because in order to reform the law or to draft legislation it was necessary to think of what patent law might look like, and to ascertain what this abstract category included and excluded. For example, in carving out a separate domain for patent law from the proposed law of arts and manufactures, it was necessary to have some idea of what patent law was, where its boundaries lay and how it differed from other forms of protection. Moreover, the process of drafting patent bills and legislation had the effect of concretising ideas, of forcing commentators to determine in more detail the nature of the law.[29] For example, one of the features of the Bill Godson produced in 1831 was that it set out to clarify the meaning of the word 'manufacture'. When combined with the 1829 Select Committee on Patents, where attempts were made to produce statutory formulations of existing judicial practice and to provide rational definitions of what was a 'patentable inven-

---

[24] Clause 16.

[25] 'In the protection desirable to be extended by an equitable and improved patent law, we include all the useful results of scientific discovery; all the improvements of mechanical invention; all the amelioration produced in our manufactures by the encouragement of the Art of Design; and, finally, the protection of *Pattern Right* in our great calico-printing, cotton, and silk manufactures. It will be evident in the last departments of national industry alone – the protection of the *Pattern Right* – (otherwise the copyright of the new design or pattern, upon which the sale of goods chiefly depends) is a subject of paramount interest to the whole manufacturing class': 'Mr Mackinnon's New Patent Law Bill' (1839), 32 *Mechanics' Magazine*, 351–2.

[26] Mackinnon's Bill of 1838 was 'frustrated ... by the pressure and mismanagement of public business, the balance of parties, and the obstructive proceedings of the Upper House': *ibid.*, 351.

[27] On the question of the codification of patent law see B. Rotch, 1829 *Select Committee on Patents*, 108. On the establishment of 'a code of general right', see [no initial] Symonds, 'Summary of Proceedings of the Trade and International Law Department: Patent Law' (1862) *TNAPSS* 887.

[28] With the exception of the much derided Lord Brougham's Act of 1835.

[29] R. Godson (9 July 1833) 15 *Hansard* col. 976.

tion',[30] these efforts played a crucial role in the crystallisation of patent law as a separate area of law. Although these processes were presented as if they were reducing the pre-existing law to a codified form, given that patent law did not exist in any recognisable form at the time it is more accurate to say that they were creating rather than finding the law.

One of the notable features of these attempts to outline the nature and limits of this nascent patent law was the positive role that was played by foreign patent systems. While present-day commentators often boast about the insularity of patent law in the United Kingdom, it is clear that foreign patent laws played an important role in the crystallisation of British patent law.[31] As John Farey, civil engineer and scientific investigator of the pencil, said when presenting the patent laws of the United States (which somewhat oddly had been re-translated into English from an official French version), France, Belgium, Austria and Spain to the 1829 Select Committee on Patents, these laws 'are very superior to our system, and will be useful to study as models'. These were 'not to be adopted exactly for this country; but a selection of some articles (with such modifications as our different state of commerce and manufacture require) would serve as guides for us'.[32]

The emergence of patent law as a distinct area of law was also prompted by the growth of design law and the registration of inventions as designs after 1839. As we saw earlier, this not only led to the crystallisation of design law but also served to focus attention on the ambit of the subject matter protected by patent law. Moreover, as with the examples offered by foreign patent laws, the security provided by the formation of design law also provided a point of reference with which patent law could be contrasted.[33]

As with other areas of intellectual property law, the appearance of

---

[30] 'I myself wish it to be made the statute law. These heads [which Rotch had set out] ... would embrace all the decisions on what are now held to be the subject of patents': B. Rotch, 1829 *Select Committee on Patents* 110. Rotch said that invention should extend to include (i) vendible articles; (ii) a new process of making either a new or a known manufacture, engine, or article of sale; (iii) a new application of a known manufacture, engine, or article of sale; (iv) an improvement on any known manufacture or article of sale not being patented; (v) inventions imported from abroad not before used in this Kingdom.

[31] For the position re trademarks see R. Jackson, 1862 *Select Committee on Trade Marks* 3–4; A. Ryland, *ibid.*, 13.

[32] J. Farey, 1829 *Select Committee on Patents* 132. Numerous references were made in the Report of the Committee to foreign patent laws, to how they differed from and were better than British law. For example see the evidence of W. Wyatt, 119; Millington (on France), 98–9; J. Hawkins (United States), 125.

[33] The dispute between designs and patents not only helped to set the boundaries of what was to become known as design law, it also played an important role in the crystallisation of patent law.

specialist treatises which set out to explain the law (as distinct from the earlier more polemical tracts and pamphlets) played an important role in shaping patent law.[34] This was because the production of a text required the law to be reduced to writing and in so doing to a particular format. Indeed as Collier said in his *Essay on the Law of Patents* (1803) (which was somewhat immodestly modelled on Locke's *Essay on Human Understanding*), he aimed to arrange the subject of enquiry with accuracy and to detail the leading principles applicable to them in the respective divisions where they were proposed.[35] While the treatises which were produced at the time, which do not differ that much from contemporary textbooks, were presented as if they were finding the law or reducing it to a coherent set of principles, they played a much more creative role than is often recognised.[36]

The growing importance of treatises, the various efforts to reform the law, and the public debates, Select Committees and Reports that these spawned all played their part in the emergence of patent law, but the most important role was played by the judiciary.[37] Prompted by chan-

---

[34] In the *Supplement* to the first edition, Godson complains of the appearance of *A Practical Treatise on the Law of Patents for Inventions* (presumably by E. Holroyd) which failed to acknowledge the work of those (i.e. Godson) who had 'collected all the cases together, having analysed their contents, and having systematically arranged the rules of law extracted from the judgements given in them', have abridged their bodily labour and mental exertions': R. Godson, *A Practical Treatise on the Law of Patents: A Supplement* (London: J. Butterworth, 1823). Both texts were preceded by J. Collier, *An Essay on the Law of Patents* (1803) and W. Hands, *The Law and Practice of Patents for Inventions* (London: W. Clarke, 1808). The first collection of patent cases was J. Davies, *A Collection of the Most Important Cases* (1816). Alongside the texts and collection of cases there emerged a series of specialised journals dealing with patents and related matters. These included the *Repertory of Patent Inventions, Gill's Technological Repository, The London Journal of the Arts and Sciences* and the *Mechanics' Magazine*.

[35] J. Collier, *An Essay on the Law of Patents* (1803), vi–vii. Interestingly he adds that 'the legal erudition of those illustrious contemporaries, Seldon, Coke and Bacon, to the political philosopher and juridical archaeologist, would have afforded abundant amusement, but would have been wholly superfluous to the persons for whom the work is chiefly intended': *ibid.*, xiii.

[36] These texts were written by practitioners and patent agents who were often involved in the drafting of legislation. (One of the most prolific writers and patent barristers, Webster, drafted An Act for Amending the Law for Granting Patents for Inventions 15 & 16 Vict. c. 83 (1852) (1852 Patent Law Amendment Act).) Davies' Digest, which was 'a list of cases from which the subject was to be determined', was written as much as possible 'to avoid using language of our own, but shall chiefly make use of the language of the learned judges, referring to the cases in which they have made the observations stated': J. Davies, *A Collection of the Most Important Cases* (1816), 415.

[37] Carpmael suggested that the 'extensive publication of the modern [patent] decisions in courts of law, have . . . for the most part, removed all doubts as to the patent property being secure': W. Carpmael, 'Introductory Observations of the Law of Patents for Inventions' (1835), 70. See also E. Hulme, 'Privy Council Law and Practice of Letters Patent for Inventions from the Restoration to 1794' (1917) 33 LQR 180. For an overview of the changing nature of precedent during this period see J. Evans, 'Change

ging attitudes towards technology and science which were influenced by the growing professionalisation of the scientific community,[38] the courts helped to clarify the scope and meaning of the subject matter protected.[39] More specifically, building upon earlier decisions such as *Boulton and Watt* v *Bull*,[40] *R* v *Arkwright*[41] and *Hornblower* v *Bull*,[42] the courts clarified the extent to which principles as well as improvements or patents of addition could be patented. Perhaps the most important judicial intervention of the period came with the 1842 decision of *Crane* v *Price* which settled the question as to whether a method or process as distinct from the thing produced could be the valid subject matter of a patent.[43] Hindmarch went so far as to suggest that it was not until *Crane* v *Price* was handed down that patentees could be said to have been fairly sure of what the courts meant by a manner of new manufacture: the definition of the subject matter for which the grant of patents was permitted by the 1624 Statute of Monopolies.[44]

The upshot of these decisions, which were reported and discussed in the growing number of treatises and specialist periodicals on patent law

in the Doctrine of Precedent during the Nineteenth Century' in (ed.) L. Goldstein, *Precedent in Law* (Oxford: Clarendon, 1991), 35.

[38] On which see D. Miller, 'Into the Valley of Darkness: Reflections on the Royal Society in the Eighteenth Century' (1989) 27 *History of Science* 155; C. Macleod, 'The Paradoxes of Patenting: Invention and its Diffusion in 18th- and 19th-Century Britain, France and North America' (1991) *Technology and Culture* 905. 'Repugnance to the adoption of labour-saving machines in general, as detrimental to the interests of industry, was one of the peculiarities of early prejudices, which found its firmest stronghold on the Bench, but which we may hope at the present day is shown to be utterly unfounded': J. Coryton, *A Treatise on the Law of Letters-Patent for the Sole Use of Inventions in the United Kingdom of England and Ireland: To which is Added a Summary of the Patent Laws in Force in the Principal Foreign States* (London: H. Sweet, 1855), 54.

[39] Hardly any patent decisions were reported between 1650 and 1750. Dutton estimated that twenty-one cases took place between 1770 and 1840, with 128 reported cases between 1840 and 1849. Despite problems with such statistics, he concluded that 'they do suggest a turning point in the late 1830s and early 1840s': H. Dutton, *The Patent System and Inventive Activity during the Industrial Revolution 1750 -1852* (Manchester: Manchester University Press, 1984), 71. Holdsworth suggested that the shift in the jurisdiction over the validity of patents from the Privy Council to the common law courts which took place in the middle of the eighteenth century was influential in laying down the foundation of modern patent law. Sir W. Holdsworth, *A History of English Law*, vol. XI (4th edn) (London: Methuen and Co., 1936), 426–30.

[40] (1795) 126 ER 651.

[41] (1785) 1 Web Pat Cas 64; Dav Pat Cas 61; Bull NP 76; 1 Carp Pat Cas 53.

[42] (1799) 101 ER 1285. The reporter in *Wood* v *Zimmer* (1815) 171 ER 162, note, said that 'From these two cases' of *Boulton and Watt* v *Bull* and *Hornblower* 'may be deduced almost all of the learning and law on the subject of patents for new inventions'.

[43] (1842) 134 ER 239. See also *Hill* v *Thompson* (1818)129 ER 427; *Morgan* v *Seaward* (1836) 150 ER 874.

[44] W. Hindmarch, *Law and Practice of Letters Patent for Inventions* (London: Stevens, 1848), 84; An Act Concerning Monopolies and Dispensations with Penal Laws and Forfeitures Thereof 21 Jac. I c. 3 (1624) [1624 Statute of Monopolies].

and reinforced by the rise of specialist patent agents who understood both the requirements of the courts and the subject matter protected,[45] was that the nature of patent law came to be defined more clearly. Webster captured this situation when he said of his first work on patents written in 1839 that 'it was of a smaller size and character than perhaps would have been advisable'. As he said, this was because 'I found the state of the law, on many points, in so much uncertainty that I thought it would not be prudent to do much more than to present the practical forms with notes, and a very general review and outline of principles.' While in his earlier work he found the law uncertain and ambiguous, in 1849 Webster was able to say 'that the law has from the number of fresh cases latterly become a good deal more settled ... I think that the principles of the law are pretty well settled now'[46] – a point which was reiterated by a number of other commentators at the time.

While the close relationship between the patent system and the royal prerogative made reform of patent law a slow and complicated process, nonetheless it was clear by the 1850s that modern patent law began to be perceived and presented as a separate and defined area of law. Importantly, the law which took shape at the time carried with it a number of traits which shaped and continue to shape patent law. Although numerous examples could be given, we wish to focus here on those characteristics which played a role not only in moulding patent law but also in demarcating patent law from the other categories of intellectual property law.

The first characteristic which helped to differentiate patents from the other forms of protection was in terms of the subject matter which patent law protected, or more accurately the image that developed as to what patent law ought to protect. While it was acknowledged that patent law extended to include a range of inventions (from the trivial to the more important) it was asserted that patent protection should be reserved for what were taken to be the more deserving inventions. This

---

[45] On the development of patent agents see H. Dutton, *The Patent System and Inventive Activity* (1984), ch. 5; D. Van Zyl Smit, 'Professional Patent Agents and the Development of the English Patent System' (1985) 13 *International Journal of the Sociology of Law* 79; J. Harrison, 'Some Patent Practitioners Associated with the Society of Arts, c. 1790–1840' (July 1982) *Journal of the Royal Society of Arts* 497. Until the beginning of the nineteenth century 'the obtaining of patents was primarily a part of the business of solicitors and having obtained the patent grants, these solicitors often prepared specifications. With the rise of specialist specification drafters the bulk of the business moved into other hands but, nonetheless, of the "Patent and Designs Registration Agents" listed in the London Post Office Directories of the mid-1860s one in six indicated that they were also solicitors': *ibid.* (pt 3), 670–1.

[46] 1849 *Report of the Committee Appointed by the Lords of the Treasure on the Signet and Privy Seal Office* 34 (Q. 720).

meant that so-called trivial inventions such as weighing machines and kaleidoscopes did not belong in patent law but, as we have seen, deserved their own form of protection: viz., utility model protection.[47]

Hand in hand with the growing perception that patents ought to be reserved for more important inventions was the belief that patents were intended to promote the introduction of new trades and manufactures. For example, speaking of the statutory basis of the patent monopoly it was said that it may be 'fairly inferred that it is not the manufacture, but the manufacturing, which appears to be contemplated. It is the opening of a new channel of industry, the establishment of a new trade, the beneficial employment of capital and labour in a new direction, that is intended to be promoted'.[48] While patents were granted for the creation or production of products *per se*, designs presupposed and required the existence of manufactured products: they were in this sense both derivative and secondary. This not only reinforced the separation of patents from designs, it also led to design law being subjugated to what was taken to be the more important and superior patent law.[49] The prioritisation of patents over design, which matured into the false belief that patent law preceded and shaped design law, was reinforced by an evolutionary view of history, which a number of commentators used in order to explain the law.[50]

---

[47] The belief that patent protection ought to be reserved for more deserving inventions was reinforced by the growing association of patents with science (as distinct from arts and manufactures). In turn this served to reinforce the distinction between patents and designs. The reforms proposed in the 1820 and 1830s were primarily driven by those whose livelihood was directly affected by the existence of patents: inventors, manufacturers, engineers, attorneys and patent agents. In the 1830s and 1840s, however, those interested in reform expanded to include the 'gentlemen of science' (such as Sir Humphrey Davy, Charles Babbage and David Brewster): the men of the upper and middle classes whose common interest lay in the promotion and professionalisation of scientific activity. See M. Coulter, *Property in Ideas* (1991), 37. This situation was reinforced by the fear that the UK was about to lose its position of self-proclaimed 'scientific pre-eminence': J. Morrell and A. Thackray, *Gentlemen of Science: Early Years of the British Association for the Advancement of Science* (Oxford: Clarendon Press, 1981), 3–12. These changes were reflected in the fact that patented inventions were only included within the awards granted by the Royal Society in 1841: J. Harrison, 'Some Patent Practitioners' (1982), 671.

[48] W. Spence, 'Patents as Channels of Industry' (1868) *TNAPSS* 256.

[49] 'The Designs Copyright Acts [of 1842 and 1843] may be said to assume the manufacture to be old, and to rest upon the application of some new or original design to articles of known or existing manufacture': T. Webster, *The Subject Matter of Letters Patent* (1851), 83. A 'design cannot be the subject of a patent privilege, because, although it is new, it is not a new *art*, nor is it an art of working, or making manufactures, or articles of commerce; but on the contrary, it is merely the produce of an art, or produced by the exercise of one of the fine arts, the art of designing, which is an old and well-known art': W. Hindmarch, *Law and Practice of Letters Patent for Inventions* (1848), 101. See also R. Macfie, 'The Law of Patents for Inventions' (1858) *TNAPSS* 147.

[50] 'The history of such protection in this country presents three epochs or stages, so to

The crystallisation of copyright law

In many ways the emergence of copyright law in the middle part of the nineteenth century as a distinct and recognisable category of law was prompted and influenced by similar factors to those acting on design and patents: the development of the legal textbook,[51] attempts at legislative reform[52] and the growing desire for a more rational and organised legal system all playing their part in the transition from copyright as the right to copy applicable to many types of creations, to a 'Law of Copyright' as a distinct and discrete area of law.[53] Despite these similarities one important difference, which we will focus on here, was in terms of the role that the bilateral agreements entered into between Britain and other European countries in the 1840s and 1850s played in this process. While frequently dismissed as mere forerunners of more important multilateral conventions that followed (namely the 1886 Berne International Copyright Convention)[54] it will be argued that the bilateral treaties and the negotiations surrounding them played a significant role in shaping the law of copyright we have inherited.

As with many of the changes that occurred in this area of law in the eighteenth and nineteenth centuries, the idea for international copyright

speak: during the first, the manufactures themselves, and the processes and combinations of matter for the production of the required article, were alone the subject of protection; during the next, or in a more advanced stage, when the necessities and wants of mankind had to a certain extent been satisfied, attention came to be directed to the encouragement of design, whereby the articles so produced might be presented of a form and appearance agreeable to the eye; in a third stage, protection was extended to such shape and configuration as was subservient to utility as distinguished from such shape and configuration as was ornamental; thus the design became, so to speak, superadded to and is not of the essence of the manufacture in which it is applied or embodied': T. Webster, *The Subject Matter of Letters Patent* (1851), iv.

[51] Although legal treatises and textbooks played an important role in shaping copyright law, they seem to have been less important than in other areas of law. Cf. A. Simpson, 'The Rise and Fall of the Legal Treatise' (1987), 273.

[52] 'I propose to render the law of copyright uniform, as to all books and works of art, to secure to the proprietor the same term in each, to give one plan of registration and one mode of transfer': S. Talfourd (18 May 1837) 38 *Hansard* col. 871. See C. Seville, 'Principle or Pragmatism ? The Framing of the 1842 Copyright Act' (PhD Thesis, Cambridge University, 1996).

[53] While prior to this frequent use was made of the term 'copyright' (or 'copy-right'), it is incorrect to assume that the term was used in a consistent, meaningful way or that it referred to a distinct area of law: there was at the time no 'Copyright Law'.

[54] This attitude is summed up in Ladas' comment at the end of his chapter on bipartite conventions, treaties and agreements that the 'net outcome of the bipartite conventions entered into by the various countries before 1883 for the protection of industrial property rights was not important': S. Ladas, *Patents, Trademarks, and Related Rights: National and International Protection*, vol. I (Cambridge, Mass.: Harvard University Press, 1975), 54.

protection was initially suggested by the French.[55] The belief that 'intellectual property should pass frontiers and sheets of water and still be property' was quickly adopted by British writers and publishers.[56] While there was occasional concern about the impact of pirated works upon the quality of literature[57] and widespread acceptance that the free exchange of literary information that the treaties would promote was desirable, the primary motivation behind the calls for international copyright in the United Kingdom was the protection of British interests (which extended not only to the United Kingdom but also to its colonies and dominions).[58] More specifically, the requests for international

[55] In 1832, it was reported to Parliament that there was 'already an interchange of public and parliamentary documents between UK and France': Spring Rice (30 July 1832) 14 *Hansard* col. 897. As the French representative, Count Mole, said, 'some arrangement should be entered into between [the UK] and France calculated to remedy the inconvenience resulting from the reprinting in England of French books and English books in France'. The Foreign Office reported 'that the matter has been referred to the proper department and that the question raises so many important considerations that the government must postpone any express opinion on it. The French ambassador asked for relevant Acts of Parliament': 22 Nov. 1836, FO/27/518 No. 207.

[56] J. Fraser, *Handy-Book of Patent and Copyright Law* (London: Sampson and Co., 1860), 223. 'In 1851 Europe agreed, by International Copyright Treaties, that intellectual property should pass frontiers and sheets of water and still be property.' In April 1837 Le Marchant (of the Board of Trade) reported to Backhouse (of the Foreign Office) that he had received 'strong representations on the part of some of the most Eminent writers of this country and of the principal publishers, that from want of an International law of Copyright the interests of literature are seriously affected'. The Board of Trade had found these representations to be well founded and that this was indeed a 'case which calls for the active interference of government'. The Board of Trade noted that this issue was already under consideration by the governments of France, Prussia and the United States so that there was every possibility that negotiations might be successful. As a result it was suggested that Palmerston might make overtures to interested parties, for 'it would be unbecoming the position of this country, to be slow to further so important an object to the advancement of its moral rank and the deserved claims of our men of letters and men of science who have contributed so largely to exalt the character of the nation'. Furthermore, such action by Palmerston would contribute to the 'extending and cementing the friendship of nations, by subduing the prejudices and widening the sympathies of the most intelligent and influential classes of their respective populations'. The Board of Trade forwarded papers to Lord Palmerston and asked him to 'enter into any general arrangement for effecting the purposes to which this letter refers': 14 April 1837, FO/27/551. For a history of the negotiations see FO/27/860.

[57] Reprints in Brussels were frequently so hasty that 'serious misprints take place and the public is inundated with incorrect editions': 14 April 1837, FO/27/551. Lytton Bulwer sent Poulett Thompson papers on international copyright saying that such a law 'would indeed effect for English literature advantages greater than any government in any age has ever conferred upon authors' *ibid.* On the problem of international piracy (especially in France) see Lytton Bulwer (14 Dec. 1837) 39 *Hansard* col. 1091.

[58] 'The grievances suffered by authors and their publishers from spurious publications printed in other countries, have greatly increased during the late few years, and they have no power at present to protect themselves against the evil and the loss it occasions to them. Every work written by a popular author is almost co-instantaneously reprinted in large numbers both in France, Germany and in America and this is done now with much rapidity, and at little expense, generally less than one eighth of the price at which

protection stemmed from the fact that despite the growing interest in British literature overseas, British works were not protected in foreign jursidictions: in most countries at the time literary property protection only arose for works of nationals published in that country.[59] This meant that while a British author could get copyright protection in the United Kingdom, no equivalent protection existed to prevent piracy of his works in say Prussia or the United States. In short, a growing sense of loss brought about by the fact that British works could be pirated with impunity outside of the United Kingdom precipitated the move towards finding some way of protecting British works in other countries.

The means favoured to achieve this was for Britain to enter into arrangements with other interested countries for the mutual protection of literary property. These treaties were to be 'based on the principle of extending the works of foreign authors the amount of protection afforded in each country respectively to the works of the native Authors'.[60] Initially the mechanism suggested to ensure reciprocity of protection was the establishment of a multilateral treaty.[61] After some interest in this approach, however, it was rejected. As was said at the time, this was because of the belief that it would not be possible 'to pass one general law, based upon the principle of our own law of copyright, because the law of copyright varied so much in different countries'.[62] More specifically, the reason why the option of a multilateral treaty was rejected as the means of establishing international copyright protection can be traced to the belief that just as literature was said to reflect national character, copyright laws reflected the national character of the

the original editions bearing the cost of the copyright can be furnished. All the works of Sir Walter Scott, Lord Byron, Messrs Robert Southey, Thomas More, Thomas Campbell, Rogers, Milman, Hallam, Wordsworth, Bulwers, James, Chamier, Monyatt, The Countess Blessington and indeed most popular authors are so reprinted and resold by Galignani and Bardens [pirate publishers] at Paris': 14 April 1837, FO/27/551.

59 There was some uncertainty in Britain at the time as to the manner and extent of copyright protection given by British Statutes. For example, Talfourd said in 1837, 'if a recent decision on the subject of musical copyright is to be regarded as correct, the principle of international copyright is already acknowledged here': S. Talfourd (18 May 1837) 38 *Hansard* col. 878. For a detailed examination of the question of whether foreigners could get copyright protection in Britain (whether as resident or not) see Lord Brougham, *Jefferys* v *Boosey* (1854) 10 ER 681 (discussing the conflicting decisions of *Tonson* v *Collins* (1760) 96 ER 180; *Bach* v *Longman* (1777) 98 ER 1274; *Chappell* v *Purday* (1845) 153 ER 491; *Delondre* v *Shaw* (1828) 57 ER 777; *Bentley* v *Foster* (1839) 59 ER 641).

60 Earl of Westmorland, 25 Jan. 1843, FO/64/244.

61 Referring to the address made by British authors to the US Congress, it was said that 'the government of Britain should also assist in endeavouring to bring about one great system of international law for the protection, in all European countries, and in America, of Literary Property, convinced that the result will be beneficial to the authors of all countries and the interests of literature in general': FO 27/551.

62 P. Thompson (20 March 1838) 41 *Hansard* col. 1110.

country in which they operated. As such it was considered too difficult to develop a treaty which could singularly transcend and unite all the variation that existed between the proposed member states. As a consequence of these envisaged difficulties, the plans for a multilateral treaty were rejected in favour of more flexible bilateral agreements which the Crown would be able to pass in specific circumstances. To this end, in 1838 the International Copyright Act[63] was passed. This provided Her Majesty with the power to direct that authors of books published in foreign countries have the sole liberty of printing and printing such books within the British dominions. In so doing, it opened the way for the establishment of bilateral copyright agreements.

Without exception, all the negotiations entered into on the basis of the 1838 Act failed.[64] The simple explanation for this was that the protection offered by the 1838 International Copyright Act was much narrower than the equivalent provisions available in the countries with which Britain hoped to develop reciprocal protection. The consequence of this was, as the French said in response to the proposed Anglo-French treaty mooted in the early 1840s, 'that the effect of these articles would be to benefit English interests exclusively'.[65]

By 1843 the arrogance which underlay the early British negotiations was replaced by a renewed desire to protect British interests. This led in 1844 to the passage of the Act to Amend the Law Relating to International Copyright which repealed and replaced the 1838 Act. This new Act empowered Her Majesty, by Order in Council, to give protection to the authors of books and works of art first published in a foreign country. No order was to be made however unless reciprocal protection had been granted by the relevant foreign power. The 1844 International Copyright Act allowed copyright protection to be conferred on the foreign authors of works of literature and art, which comprised the publication of books, dramatic works, musical compositions, drawings, paintings, sculptures, engravings, lithography, and any other works whatsoever of literature and of the fine arts. The 1844 Act differed from the 1838 Act both in terms of the subject matter protected (the earlier Act focused exclusively on literary property) and in terms of the mechanisms available to police and enforce the rights.[66] It also differed from the 1838 Act in that it was successfully used by the British

---

[63] 1838 An Act for Securing to Authors in Certain Cases the Benefit of International Copyright 1 & 2 Vict. c. 59 (1838) (1838 International Copyright Act).

[64] After initial discussions with France, meetings were planned in Berlin, Brussels, Washington and The Hague: 30 Sept. 1837, BT/1/337.

[65] Memorandum by J. Bergue on the history of the Anglo-French negotiations: 19 Dec. 1849, FO/27/860.

[66] Another problem with the 1838 International Copyright Act which the 1844 Act

government to enter into copyright conventions with a number of countries. In particular, the 1844 International Copyright Act acted as the basis for treaties with Prussia (1846 and 1855), Saxony (1846), Brunswick (1847), the Thuringian Union (1847), Hanover (1847), Oldenburg (1847), France (1851), Anhalt-Dessau and Anhalt-Bernbourg (1853), Hamburg (1853 and 1855), Belgium (1854 and 1855), Spain (1857), Sardinia (1860), and Hesse Darmstadt (1861).

Although the International Copyright Acts of 1838 and 1844 played a central role in establishing a regime of international copyright protection and are important in their own right, our interest here lies with the impact these Acts and the negotiations and treaties which surrounded them had upon domestic law in the United Kingdom.[67]

The reshaping of domestic law

The first and most obvious consequence of the so-called laws of international copyright law was that they led to direct changes in domestic law. This was the result of the fact that the negotiations proceeded on the 'assumption that the expediency between two countries depends upon a *precise and minute equality* of advantage to be derived by each contracting party respectively'.[68] This meant that before a treaty could be completed, it was necessary to ensure that the protection available in both countries was virtually identical.[69] It therefore became important not only that British laws bore some formal resemblance to the laws of the countries which the United Kingdom wished to enter into agreements with, but also that the benefits they offered were substantially equivalent.

As the scope and effectiveness of the protection available in Britain tended to be less extensive than that provided in other countries, and a reduction in the level of protection was never considered, changes had to be made to British law in order to bring about an 'approximation of

---

remedied was that it did not enable Her Majesty's Government to extend protection to prints and engravings made overseas.

[67] Another factor which contributed to the development of copyright law was the question of imperial copyright. As was said, 'it is probably not too much to say that, were it not for the difficulty arising from the constitution of the Empire, the Copyright Law [of the UK] would have been remodelled long ago': 'Copyright Law Reform' (1910) 216 *Quarterly Review* 486.

[68] 25 Jan. 1843, FO/64/242; emphasis added.

[69] 'It is desirable that copyright laws, whatever they may be, should be as nearly as possible the same in all English-speaking countries, and should be extended throughout these countries to all authors, without distinction. In this way the author would get the largest possible market': T. Farrer, 'The Principle of Copyright' (1878) 24 *Fortnightly Review* 850.

laws'.[70] We can see the impact that the bilateral agreements had upon domestic law in relation to the 1846 Anglo-Prussian treaty. Initial discussions aimed at establishing a treaty between the United Kingdom and Prussia began in the mid 1830s. In 1840, however, the Prussian government decided to discontinue its negotiations with Britain because it 'considered that the reciprocity which was contemplated by [the 1838 International Copyright Act] to be only an apparent reciprocity',[71] because the protection offered under the 1838 Prussian Law for the Protection of Property in Respect to Works of Science and of Art against Counterfeiting and Imitation[72] was greater than that available in Britain. Prussia's greater protection was due to three factors: it extended 'to a much greater variety of objects than in England ... over a much longer period'; the means of 'redress in cases of infraction of copyright were much more easily attained in the former country than in the latter'; and higher duties were imposed on books imported into Britain than were charged on those imported into Prussia.[73]

In spite of the breadth of these objections, by 1843 British representatives were able to report to the Prussian government that the law in the United Kingdom had 'undergone important changes which will have the effect of materially increasing the protection at present enjoyed in England by literary property'.[74] In particular, the British government was able to say that, as a consequence of the 1842 Copyright Act, it had the satisfaction 'of being able to intimate to the Prussian Government that a change to British law *has* taken place which will have the effect of materially extending the protection at present enjoyed by literary property, as to terms of duration'.[75] The objections raised about copyright infringement and the enforcement of remedies was rectified by changes introduced by the 1844 International Copyright Act and also by changes in Customs House

---

[70] FO/64/242.
[71] 25 Jan. 1843, FO/64/244.
[72] Published at Berlin, 18 Dec. 1837. Translated 15 Jan. 1838, BT/1/337, No. 6169/32a.
[73] Earl of Westmorland, 25 Jan. 1843, FO/64/244. Prussian booksellers who had been consulted on the 'proposed arrangement with the Great Britain government had requested that import duty on books into Great Britain be lowered in the same manner as duty on prints had been, and they attached great importance to this point and it would contribute especially to dispose favourably of feelings of the German people [*sic*] towards the projected Treaty, which was hurtful to some private interests': *ibid.*
[74] FO/64/242. Encloses copies of Acts of last session (5 & 6 Vict. c. 45, 1 July 1842; 5 & 6 Vict. c. 47, 9 July 1842). Lord Westmorland requested attention 'be drawn to sections 23–25 of the late Customs Act concerning pirated editions in this country. He hoped that this will be sufficient to reach an agreement re Literary Property': *ibid.* Since earlier legislation, 'the position of International copyright has materially changed': 15 March 1852, BT/1/491/343/52.
[75] FO/64/241.

regulations.[76] The complaint that the scope of subject matter protected under the 1838 International Copyright Act was too narrow was resolved with the passage of the 1844 International Copyright Act which extended the category of works protected from literature[77] to include the 'fine arts'.[78] This was despite the fact that at the time fine art was not protected under domestic law in Britain.[79] In turn, the requests that the duty imposed on books imported into Britain be lowered were agreed to and corresponding amendments made.

As a result of these changes, the British negotiators were able to say that 'an approximation between the two countries has thus been produced, which Her Majesty's Government trusts will have the effect of rendering the Prussian Government less averse to an arrangement'.[80] Although the Foreign Office constantly intimated that the changes which had taken place in British law had come about in order to appease Prussian objections, it is difficult to determine the extent to which this was actually the case. Certainly, there is little evidence to support this in the domestic proceedings. Nonetheless, it is clear that Prussian objections played a role in alerting the Foreign Office and in turn the Board of Trade and Parliament to deficiencies in domestic law as well as offering alternatives for change. While it is difficult to determine beyond this the precise impact that the Anglo-Prussian agreement had upon municipal law in Britain, a situation where we can more readily identify the ramifications of the bilateral treaties is in association with the 1851 Anglo-French Treaty. In many respects this treaty was similar to the other treaties which the United Kingdom had entered into, but it differed in that it *purported* to provide reciprocal protection for translations of literary works, before such rights existed in domestic law in Britain. Although there was some uncertainty about the changes that

[76] Section 17 of An Act to Amend the Law of Copyright 5 & 6 Vict. c. 45 (1842) (1842 Copyright Act) allowed for the destruction of pirated copies of books when seized on importation. Speaking in 1845 Peel said, 'it was alleged on the part of Prussia that the law of copyright in this country was defective, and ought to be amended. Since that time two Bills had passed Parliament to amend the law of copyright, and diminishing the objections raised by Prussia': R. Peel, 'International Copyright' (1845) 77 *Hansard* col. 1043.

[77] Even with the extension of international copyright to include artistic works in 1844, the primary concern in the UK was with literature.

[78] FO/64/241. Unlike the 1838 International Copyright Act, the 1844 Act took into account the 1833 An Act to Amend the Laws Relating to Dramatic Literary Property 3 & 4 Wm. IV c.15 (1833) (1833 Dramatic Property Act).

[79] The Law Officers of the Crown advised the Board of Trade that, with some exceptions, fine arts were not protected by municipal copyright law: 'so far as I have been able to learn, the law of copyright in pictures is open to doubt. I cannot find any law which prevents my having any man's pictures copied if I gain access to it': 16 April 1847, BT/1/502/402.

[80] FO/64/242.

came about as a result of the Prussian objections, there is no doubt that translation rights were introduced into British law in 1851 so as to bring domestic law into line with the pre-existing Anglo-French copyright treaty.[81]

While it is clear that the bilateral treaties influenced the development of domestic copyright law, this is not to suggest that British law was dictated by the Prussian or French governments;[82] rather, in these situations the UK government was more concerned to protect British interests overseas and therefore in establishing treaties than it was with the fate of domestic law. The degree to which the British government was willing to alter domestic laws differed depending upon the nature of the market in question and the quantity of British works (typically books) that were pirated.[83] For example, in situations where there was little interest in books written in English (as distinct from translated works as was the case in Russia) or in English prints or designs, there was more of a concern to protect British law. In contrast, in circumstances where there was more of a market for pirated books, as in France and Prussia, the fate of domestic law was less of a priority.[84]

---

[81] An Act to Enable Her Majesty to Carry into Effect a Convention with France on the Subject of Copyright, to Extend and Explain the International Copyright Acts, and to Explain the Acts relating to Copyright in Engravings 15 & 16 Vict. c. 12 (1852).

[82] As the French were said to have shaped copyright law in Belgium. On this see P. Geller, 'Legal Transplants in International Copyright: Some Problems of Method' (1994) 13 *University of California at Los Angeles Pacific Basin Law Journal* 200.

[83] For example, in Russia the 'reproduction of English engravings, other works of art or designs for earthenware stuff, papers etc. does not take place to any extent worth mentioning; artists as well as manufacturers chiefly use French models which are preferred by the public'. Letter from Robert J. King (in Moscow) to Napier, 5 Aug. 1861, BT/1/556/1092/61. See also the letter sent to Lord John Russell from Napier (St Petersburg), 14 June 1861, FO/65/576 No. 166 and the 'Report on English Book Trade in St Petersburg', to Napier from Saville Lumley, 12 Aug. 1861, FO/65/578/ 296.

[84] Similar pragmatic motives were also at work amongst French treaty negotiators. 'Their letters have always pressed for the conclusion of the Treaty as gaining an object of importance for this country by putting a stop to the French piratical reprints of English works; and in order to accomplish this, they have always given way on points not essential to or incompatible with their main object': Memorandum by J. Bergue, 19 Dec. 1849, FO/27/860. This willingness to dispense with principle can also be seen in the Prussian treaties. It was reported that 'by its treaty with England, the Cabinet of Berlin evidently recognised the justice of the claims of foreign authorship, [but] it has not yet consented to conclude a similar convention with France, cheap French books (i.e. pirated editions from Brussels and Leipsic) being more necessary to Prussian enjoyment than English works of the same illegitimate origin': 'A Few Words on International Copyright' (1852) 95 *Edinburgh Review* 148.

The self-image of copyright law

Concomitantly with the direct changes in municipal law that came about as a result of these forays into international copyright law was a more important change in the grammar and logic of the law: a shift in the way the law was represented and imagined. Importantly it is this logic, or a version thereof, which operates today. While the law of the eighteenth and early nineteenth centuries was primarily a backward-looking, subject-specific law which tended to respond to specific (sometimes minor) problems, the copyright law which took shape in the 1850s and 1860s was an abstract law which extended 'to *all* works of literature and art in the widest sense'.[85] Moreover, as well as being an abstract law, the copyright law was also a forward-looking law: it was formulated in such a way as to encompass new forms of subject matter, 'those productions in which the laws ... now or may hereafter give their respective subjects privilege of copyright'.[86] What occurred with the shift from a reactive, specific law to a law which was abstract and forward-looking was a change in the ontological status of the law, 'a move from linguistic patterns mastered at the practical level to a code, a grammar, via the labour of codification, which is a juridical activity'.[87] This transformation marked an important stage in the formation of the modern system of copyright law in the United Kingdom. With this change we see not only that copyright law was given a label, but that it also came to take on an identity which was widely accepted both inside and outside of law. This can be seen in the manner in which commentators increasingly began to talk both meaningfully and consistently about 'our' law of copyright as a distinct and separate entity.[88] Related to this

---

[85] BT/1/476/3065. Literature was defined to include dramatic and musical works. In turn, 'copyright of a picture is understood to be the right of allowing it to be engraved or made public. Copyright in a picture, or a right to permit or forbid its being made public by a copy, is a right prior to and distinct from copyright in any particular copy or engraving in it. This is what the expression artists or possessor of the picture ... means': 18 Sept. 1850, FO/27/889 (to BT). In the care taken over the language used in the treaties more generally see Foreign Office to Lord Normanby, 10 Nov. 1851, FO/27/897. By 1855 the protection by British law of 'art' as an abstract category was so well established that the absence of equivalent provisions was seen as a weakness of other treaties. On this see the criticism made of the suggestion that the Holland–France treaty, which was limited to 'œuvres scientifiques et littéraires', be used as a model for an Anglo-Dutch treaty: 'The UK treaty was wider than that between Holland and France': to Lord Tennent from Lord Hobart, 24 Nov. 1858, BT/1/548/1741.

[86] BT/1/476/3065.

[87] See p. 62, n.1.

[88] In response to a letter from Russia asking for similar treaty with the UK as Russia had with France, the Foreign Office said that 'this was at variance with the British law on copyright': Foreign Office to Lord Napier, 24 July 1861, FO/65/572, No. 134.

was the fact that for the first time, at least overtly, the law in this area became self-reflexive: it became concerned with *itself*, with the shape that it took, and the image that it offered to the world.[89]

A number of different factors associated with the bilateral agreements helped to facilitate the crystallisation of copyright law. Perhaps most importantly of all, in responding to the requests which were made for 'an accurate and authentic report of the present state of the law of copyright'[90] it was necessary to think of and conceptualise the law of copyright (as distinct from the specific forms of copy-right protection which had been considered previously), and to ascertain what this abstract category included and excluded. In the same way in which the production of a treatise or a textbook requires the law to be reduced to writing and thereby to a particular format, in order to negotiate the international copyright treaties it was necessary to have a picture of what copyright law was, what its minimum standards were, and what it was that a Prussian or Saxon bookseller could expect in London or Glasgow. In short the international copyright treaties presupposed and required a representation of domestic law. To determine whether the laws of two countries were equivalent to each other it was not only necessary to have a clear idea of what the law was, it was also important that these representations were fixed and secure. As such, although there was a great deal of confusion as to the nature of domestic law, in negotiating the bilateral copyright treaties this uncertainty was ignored or, perhaps more accurately, resolved.[91]

As well as helping to facilitate the crystallisation of the law of copyright, the bilateral treaties also played a role in shaping the particular *form* that the law took. The abstract nature of copyright law arose in part from the need to communicate about the copyright system, from the pressure for a standardised language of communication.[92] This was because in order to determine whether the protection available in two

---

[89] This was reinforced by the consolidation in legal publishing which played a role in establishing the proper shape of the legal text and in turn copyright law.

[90] 13 Jan. 1837, FO/27/538, 'which contained a memorandum on the state of the law of England relative to the protection of literary property'.

[91] In 1837 Earl Granville sent a letter to the Foreign Office which was to be forwarded to the French government in which he said, 'I herewith transmit to Your Excellency a Copy of a note which I have addressed to M. de Bourguenay inclosing copies of 6 acts of Parliament together with a memorandum on the state of the law of England relative to the protection of literary property and I have to instruct Your Excellency to apply to Count Mole for an accurate and authentic report of the present state of the law of copyright in France both as regards natives and foreigners, in return for the information thus furnished to M. de Bourguenay. Her Majesty's Government still reserves for further consideration the proposal for negotiation between the two governments': 13 Jan. 1837, FO/27/538.

[92] See generally Earl of Westmorland, 25 Jan. 1843, FO/64/244.

countries were equivalent to each other, it was necessary to find a common denominator, a basis from which this task of evaluation could be carried out. It was also necessary to find some mechanism which would enable the negotiators to move beyond the traits of national character which were said to bind the copyright laws to the idiosyncratic features of the nations involved. The process of codification and abstraction met these needs by ensuring a basic level of communication and interchangeability. In order to assist in this process there were also demands for the law to be standardised and made uniform. To this end there were frequent calls for simplicity, clarity and precision in the drafting of the treaties.[93] Again, what we see is a concern with the *form* that the law took; the law taking an interest in the *shape* of the law. Hand in hand with this heightened self-reflexivity was an increased desire to rationalise and order the law that dealt with intellectual labour. With France acting yet again as a role model,[94] there was a demand for the law to be made as simple, uniform and precise as possible.[95] Working from the premise that complicated systems were evidence of the unsoundness of the principles on which they were based,[96] there were frequent attempts to consolidate and reduce the complexity of the law – a trend which was reinforced by the more general moves towards legal codification which were taking place in Britain at the time.[97]

Another factor which explains both the abstract and the forward-looking nature of the copyright law that developed at this time, why it was that the treaties were said to extend 'in principle to those productions in which the laws in both countries do now or may hereafter give their respective subjects privilege of copyright',[98] relates to the difficulties experienced in negotiating the treaties, and to the time, cost and delay this involved. An abstract, forward-looking law had the advantage in that it decreased the likelihood of the need to reopen negotiations whenever a new subject matter was given protection in a particular treaty country.

The abstract, forward-looking nature of the copyright model can also be explained by the constitutional framework within which the negotia-

---

[93] Duchy of Brogher to Lord Palmerston, 26 Oct. 1847, BT/1/476/3065.
[94] See ch. 3, n. 53, ch. 5, n. 32.
[95] In a similar vein it was said, 'it is one of the evidences of the unsoundness of the principle upon which patents are based, that a complicated system of jurisprudence and of legislative machinery is specially required to maintain it': W. Hawes, 'On the Economical Effects of the Patent Laws' (1863) *TNAPSS* 831.
[96] *Ibid.*
[97] One of the best examples of this can be seen in Sir James Fitzjames Stephen's attempt to codify copyright law which was appended to the 1878 *Report of the Royal Commissioners on Copyright*.
[98] BT/1/476/3065.

tions proceeded. More specifically, it stemmed from the fact that while the Foreign Office and the Board of Trade were responsible for the international copyright treaties, they did not have the authority to alter pre-existing judicial or legislative arrangements. This led to a dilemma. On the one hand, in order to ensure that the treaties entered into would be able to encompass works that might require protection in the future and therefore to avoid the need to renegotiate those treaties, there was pressure on the Crown for the law to be made future-looking and abstract. At the same time, it was clear that the Foreign Office lacked the authority to extend the scope of protection beyond that already provided for under the pre-existing domestic law. The response of the Crown to this dilemma was not to limit the scope of the Foreign Office's negotiations. Rather, it was to *pretend* that the image of domestic law used in the international agreements was an accurate representation of British law. This was despite explicit recognition that the particular image of copyright law utilised and incorporated in the international treaties differed, sometimes markedly, from British domestic law as it then was: most notably in relation to the protection given to fine art[99] and translations, and in terms of the methods of enforcement.[100] The pretence of neutrality was highlighted in Palmerston's remark in relation to the drafting of copyright treaties that it was important 'to avoid the *appearance* of an assumption by the Crown of power to alter by its own authority arrangements fixed by Parliament or to control proceedings by courts of justice'.[101] The tension created by the desire to change the law, combined with an apparent inability to do so, was also avoided by the fact that the process by which the various statutory and judicial arrangements were combined into the abstract category 'art and literature' was described as one which was merely 'declaratory of the pre-existing law'.[102] All that was being done – so it was said – in the move from subject-specific legislation (which were primarily *post hoc* responses to individual problems) to a forward-looking abstract area of law capable of accommodating new forms of creativity was the process of highlighting what was implicit in the statutes and related judicial decisions: what Parliament and the courts had intended but not articulated. As

---

[99] See above, note 78.

[100] The Law Officers (Dodson, Cockburn and Wood) wrote to Palmerston advising him that the 'Crown does not have power to implement Article 10 on duties', that it 'cannot bind Parliament not to raise rates during the continuance of the treaty, nor that any reduction for another country should apply to France': 13 Dec. 1851, BT/1/484/1342/51.

[101] Lord Palmerston (Foreign Office to Board of Trade), 18 Sept. 1850, FO/27; emphasis added.

[102] *Ibid.*

such, the Crown was able to argue (at least to itself) that since they were not creating law but merely replicating it in a different form the treaties generated no constitutional problems.

While the process of abstraction and categorisation was presented as a neutral event which was merely declaratory of the pre-existing law,[103] it is clear that it was a creative task which involved selection and exclusion.[104] In particular, in deciding that copyright protected not only literary works but also artistic works, the law came to embody a particular way of thinking about creativity.[105] Despite the fact that design protection, like that offered for books, engravings, sculptures, and textiles as well as for inventions and other objects of utility, was a right to prohibit copying (a copy-right), in putting together an accurate picture of the law[106] the subject matter of design, along with the subject matter of works of manufacture and utility, were excluded from the remit of copyright law. Unlike the position in France, and contrary to the views of many commentators, the abstract model of copyright which came into being in the United Kingdom at this time related 'exclusively to literature and the fine arts'. In contrast 'patterns, designs, and manufacturers' marks' were 'reserved to be dealt with by a separate arrangement'.[107] While the law adopted what could be called a unity-of-literature approach (namely, it *prima facie* protected all literary works irrespective of their quality), it felt unable or unwilling to adopt a unity-of-art approach. With this we see, for the first time, the institutionalisation of the idea that copyright law protected art and literature but

---

[103] The idea of neutrality, which was compounded by the aesthetic agnosticism and fear of judgment which developed in the later part of the nineteenth century, remains a central trait of contemporary intellectual property law.

[104] There were occasions when the Board of Trade acknowledged the role it was playing in prioritising a particular view of copyright over others. See reply to letter from M. Girgot, 16 Feb. 1846, BT/1/476/3065.

[105] In turn this reflected legal attitudes towards the value and nature of the works protected by copyright law.

[106] See above, note 90.

[107] See 'A Few Words on International Copyright' (1852), 151. The law's attitude in this respect is clear in the amendments that Lord Palmerston made to a copyright treaty which had been drafted by the Foreign Office. 'The word "composer" has been substituted for the words "inventors and designers" because the latter words seem applicable rather to works of manufacture and utility, which are in this country protected by the Patents Laws and by the Acts for the Registration of Designs, than to works of literature and the fine arts, to which alone, as [article 1 of Treaty] expressly states, the provisions of the convention are intended to apply': 13 Dec. 1851, BT/1/484/1342/51. The Foreign Office amended a draft convention sent to it by the Board of Trade 'by deleting the term "design" and replacing it with "drawing"': 31 Dec. 1849, FO/27/860/1069. See also 29 April 1850, FO/27/887 (from Board of Trade to Addington).

excluded designs: a trait which continues to shape contemporary intellectual property law.

Another important and continuing characteristic of the model of copyright law which developed during the nineteenth century was that it came to embody the belief that copyright was beyond the remit of trade and commerce[108] – a concept which finds resonance in the contemporary idea that books are not articles of manufacture. The non-commercial image of copyright prevailed despite the clear connection which existed between literary property and the import duties imposed on paper, and between copyright and the publishing industry more generally. The attitude adopted towards literary and artistic property is in marked contrast to the approach taken towards patents and designs which were seen to have clear connections with commerce and trade.[109] The contrast between the non-commercial image of copyright and the commercial nature of patents, designs and trade marks was reflected in the fact that patents and designs were placed within the Treaties of Freedom, Commerce and Navigation whereas copyright remained in separate treaties. It was further reinforced by the bifurcation in international intellectual property law that took place with the passage of the Paris and Berne conventions later in the century. The institutional manifestation of the romantic idea that copyright works should be considered in a non-commercial light can be seen in the exchange that took place in the 1840s in relation to the proposed Anglo-Prussian Copyright Treaty. In reply to the Prussian argument that there should be 'precise and minute equality in the relief of *merchantable benefits* to be afforded to each side respectively' (that is, that the cost of books should be equivalent), MacGregor argued that it was incorrect to equate what was primarily a moral issue with matters of trade. In an attempt to take copyright outside the scope of trade and commerce and place it in a moral framework he said:

---

[108] The patents system 'concerns trade much more so than does copyright which, however, occupies a higher position, wherein adoption of a false principle affects pursuits loftier than those of commerce': R. Macfie in (ed.) Macfie, *Copyright and Patents for Inventions: Pleas and Plans*, vol. I (Edinburgh: T. and T. Clarke, 1879), vi. A 'machine is in itself, as soon as it is completed, an object of trade, and consequently, the property . . . ought to be limited. On the contrary, a literary copy is only an object of trade *quatenus* its mechanical composition': *A Vindication* (1762), 11–12.

[109] The nature of the difference between copyright and design is clear in the way they were treated under the Standing Order of 9 Nov. 1703 (14 CJ 211), introduced in substitution for the Grand Committee on Trade and renewed on 9 April 1772 (33 HCJ 678), which stated that any bill which affected trade or commerce had to be laid before a committee of the whole house. While design bills, which affected trade, were required to be put before the whole house, this rule did not apply to 'copyright' bills which at best only impacted on trade 'indirectly': (19 Feb. 1840) 52 *Hansard* col. 402.

Although anticipating direct benefit to both parties as an arrangement for the protection of literary property, [the Prussians] do not conceive that an inducement of this description is the only one that ought to operate upon their minds. Copy-right is in [the eyes if the Prussians] a species of property and one not less entitled to the full enjoyment of legal protection within the limits defined to it than are other descriptions; and although it may, in certain respects, be more open to invasion, the moral formation of the right to which it gives determinate force, is not, as it appears to them, in any degree impaired thereby ... Conversely, then, piracy is a species of robbery and as such my Lords anticipate that they will find on the part of civilised states a disposition to discountenance and relinquish it without minute calculations on the part of any of them as to the degree of pecuniary profit which in one quarter or another may be derived from the allotment and distribution of the spoil.[110]

MacGregor's comments are useful in that they capture the non-commercial and romantic perspective from which copyright is often viewed and the tension that exists as a consequence of holding such a view, given the obvious connections that the subject had and continues to have with commerce and trade.

Hand in hand with the non-commercial image of copyright law was the idea that the works protected by copyright law were cultural, unique and local. Again, this was in contrast to the subject matter of patent (and less so design) law which was technical, neutral and universal. More specifically there was a belief that the subject matter that fell within the international copyright treaties (namely works of literature, drama and the fine arts) was closely connected to the national culture in which it was created. Following from this, and by equating the subject matter of international copyright with copyright more generally, it was said that the copyright laws of individual member states were, like the works they protected, inextricably linked to the culture of the particular country in question. In a period when translation rights were virtually non-existent, the localised image of copyright was reinforced by the fact that the vernacular languages acted as a barrier to the movement of literary works and as such to the perceived mobility of copyright law.[111]

[110] To Lord Canning from MacGregor, 14 Oct. 1842, FO/64/241. MacGregor reversed the caricatures of Prussia and the United Kingdom. The Lords were 'most anxious to keep the question of International Copyright entirely apart from other less satisfactory matters and to show the anxiety of the two governments, even while they appear unfortunately to differ in their commercial views, to unite in rendering an important service to the cause of literature': 30 Oct. 1844, MacGregor to Canning.

[111] That is, the market appeal of the book was limited, at least in so far as it was protected as literary property, by the popularity of the national language. In this sense, commentators spoke of the problems British texts had in Russia because the English language was still only a 'foreign guest', whereas French had been 'naturalised': Robert J. King, 5 Aug. 1861 (from Moscow to Lord Napier), BT/1/556/1092/61. In a similar way, Anderson discusses the limited market appeal of the Czech book (which can only be read by readers of the appropriate language) and the Czech car, which can

Representing copyright law

It is clear that the bilateral copyright agreements entered into in the middle of the nineteenth century presupposed an image of domestic law. It is also clear that the image of domestic law presented in the international negotiations was *not* an accurate representation of the law at that time. Beyond the direct changes that these treaties produced, however, the impact that the bilateral copyright treaties had upon domestic law is less clear. This can be explained in part by the fact that the bilateral treaties were negotiated by the Foreign Office and not by the usual legal sources, namely, Parliament or the courts.[112] More importantly, the primary reason why the impact of the copyright treaties upon domestic law may not be readily apparent relates to the epistemological assumptions commonly employed in law. (Similar claims could also be made in relation to the 'false' image of the subject matter protected by patent law.) In particular, it can be traced to the fact that in law it is common to say that a model or image represents something which objectively exists out there. As such, we would expect that the image of copyright used in the international treaties either represented the state of domestic law or, if not, that it was inaccurate and therefore irrelevant. If we reject the realist assumptions which force us to concentrate on what copyright law actually protects (and also ignore the related attempts to cleanse the law of legal fictions),[113] we see that the image of copyright used in the bilateral agreements played an important role in the development of the domestic law. In particular, if we suspend our realist assumptions we see that the model anticipated, possibly created, the legal reality. That is, the image of copyright law was a model *for* rather than a model *of* what it purported to represent. In effect, the laws presented during the bilateral agreements as accurate descriptions of domestic law (which they were clearly *not*) became real laws, real fictions. The image presented and used in the bilateral conventions as

be used by all: B. Anderson, *Imagined Communities: Reflections of the Origin and Spread of Nationalism* (London: Verso, 1983), 34. In highlighting the artistic rather than the commercial nature of designs (and in so doing the ambivalent status of design law more generally), the Registrar of Design said in 1862 that the design system in each country in Europe 'depends on the national feelings and the modes of thought peculiar to each and that unless a total change were made in the system peculiar to one country and adopted *in toto* by the other little satisfaction could be expected from any partial change': 31 Dec. 1861, BT/1/557/212/62.

[112] This is reflected in Lord St Leonard's remark that 'nothing could be more improper than to consider the state of international law in deciding a question upon our own municipal law': *Jefferys* v *Boosey* (1854) 10 ER 681.

[113] See, e.g., L. Patterson and S. Lindberg, *The Nature of Copyright: A Law of Users' Rights* (Athens, Ga.: University of Georgia Press, 1991), esp. 134–43.

being representative of copyright law in the United Kingdom came to be accepted as an accurate, or at least partially accurate, picture of that law. In this sense that 'false' picture became the law, or at least a powerful and influential representation of it.

The reorganisation in the logic and grammar of the law facilitated by the bilateral agreements entered into in the nineteenth century brought with it a number of other changes. At a general level, the image and the empirical reality which this was said to represent had an important impact upon what was expected of copyright law, where its boundaries were drawn and consequently what was included and excluded within its remit. More specifically, once imagined, the model of copyright became an instrument for reform. In particular, the fact that domestic law failed to match up to Britain's international obligations was used as a basis to argue for reform of the law (a ploy used over the last two decades or so in arguing for the introduction of moral rights in the UK and Australia). The gap which existed between domestic and international law, which meant that British laws 'were unjust in their operation upon the Subjects of those foreign States who have entered into International Copyright Conventions with Her Majesty, inasmuch as such treaties are based upon the principle of reciprocity',[114] played an important role, for example, in ensuring the enactment of the 1862 Fine Art Copyright Act.[115]

The image of copyright also became the ideal or standard against which reform was measured.[116] For example, the 1862 Fine Art Copyright Act, which offered protection to painters, draftsmen and photographers, was described as 'another and most important step towards the completion and perfection of the series of parliamentary enactments of Artistic Copyright'.[117] The state of perfection spoken of was the domestic embodiment of the model of copyright which was institutionalised in the international copyright agreements. Many of the reforms instigated during the remainder of the nineteenth century, in particular the numerous attempts to consolidate the various copy-right statutes,

---

[114] (26 March 1858) 6 *Journal of the Society of Arts* 294.

[115] An Act for Amending the Law relating to Copyright in Works of the Fine Arts, and For Repressing the Commission of Fraud in Production and Sale of such Works 25 & 26 Vict. c. 68 (1862) (1862 Fine Art Copyright Act).

[116] Scrutton's text on copyright law sets out to deal with the 'leading ideas upon which an Ideal Copyright should be based' – a copyright which closely follows the model adopted in the bilateral treaties: T. Scrutton, *The Laws of Copyright: An Examination of the Principles which regulate Literary and Artistic Property in England and Other Countries* (London: John Murray, 1883), 2.

[117] E. Underdown, *The Law of Artistic Copyright: The Engraving, Sculpture and Designs Acts, the International Copyright Act and the Artistic Copyright Act 1862* (London: John Crockford, 1863), 5.

can be seen as attempts to codify this model.[118] This process of perfection was formally completed at a statutory level with the passage of the 1911 Copyright Act.[119] With one or two exceptions, much of the history of copyright law since that time has largely been a process of refinement and further entrenchment of this model, which is applied with increasing sophistication and detail.

[118] See, for example, 'Lord John Manners's Copyright Bill for Consolidating and Amending the Law relating to Copyright 1879' (22 Aug. 1879) 27 *Journal of the Society of Arts* 879–80.

[119] 1911 Copyright Act 1 & 2 Geo. V c. 46 (1911). The law at the time, which was 'incomplete and often obscure', was 'governed by no fewer than twenty-two Acts of Parliament, passed at different times between 1735 and 1906; and to those should be added a mass of Colonial legislation, frequently following blindly the worst precedents of English law ... The new Copyright Bill [which became the 1911 Copyright Act] makes a clean sweep of all these enactments and proposes to set up in their place a homogenous code of Copyright Law, drafted on the whole on sound and generous lines': 'Copyright Law Reform' (1910), 489.

6   Completing the framework

The first half of the nineteenth century was, as we have seen, a particularly important period in the development of modern intellectual property law. It was a formative era which saw the crystallisation of the legal categories and of many of the attributes commonly associated with this area of law. Although by the 1850s intellectual property law had taken on a form recognisable to modern eyes, it still had a fragile and precarious existence: however important the developments which had taken place by this time may have been, they were only an initial step towards the formation of modern intellectual property law – the beginning of a process which was not completed until early this century. Indeed, it was not until the passage of the 1911 Copyright Act, which codified and rationalised the pre-existing law, that it can safely be said that the emergent field was transformed into an established area of law, that intellectual property law had become an entrenched part of the legal tradition. It is our aim in this chapter to focus on this period of consolidation and entrenchment (1860–1911): a time in which gradually, haphazardly and following no particular logic, the categories of modern intellectual property came to take on an institutional reality. More specifically we focus on the fact that, in order for the legal rubrics to acquire their contemporary status as natural categories which reflected some higher philosophical order, it was necessary for a number of obstacles to be overcome.[1] This was particularly the case with patents and copyright.

Trusting patents

While by the middle of the nineteenth century copyright and design law were widely regarded as positive mechanisms which protected valuable and deserving subject matter, the patent system was held in a different

[1] The process was neither uniform nor consistent between the different categories with designs, for example, taking shape long before the other areas of intellectual property law.

light.[2] After a brief period in which patents found favour,[3] widespread doubts developed about the worth of a patent system at all. In the 1860s, when hostility towards patents was at its peak, this manifested itself in calls for the abolition of the patent system. There were many reasons for doubting the legitimacy and usefulness of the patent system at the time. On one level the anti-patent arguments were fuelled by a growing support for *laissez-faire* ideas and the reforms taking place in other countries.[4] Another factor which helped to generate doubts about the soundness of the patent system was the state of the registration process. Despite the sweeping changes introduced by the 1852 Patent Law Amendment Act,[5] there were numerous problems with registration: problems which were exacerbated by the ineffective examination system, the uncertain nature of the patent specification,[6] the disputes which took place between patent agents and lawyers as to who should be permitted to act as agents on behalf of inventors for the purposes of obtaining patents,[7] and the widespread ignorance about the state of the law.[8] The consequence of this was that patents granted by the Patent

---

[2] Macfie discussed the question of the abolition of patents at length in Parliament: R. Macfie, 'Patents for Inventions' (28 May 1869) 196 *Hansard* cols. 888 ff.

[3] 'The early prejudice against labour-saving machinery, which according to one writer "found its firmest stronghold on the Bench", had by the 1830s almost disappeared: patents were useful, important and necessary for the growth of industry': J. Coryton, *A Treatise on the Law of Letters-Patent* (1855), 54.

[4] Reform of German patent law was cited in the debate about the abolition of the patent system in the UK. See, e.g., 'The Benefit of a Patent-Law' (13 July 1877) 25 *Journal of the Society of Arts* 818.

[5] Although patent law was much improved as a result of the 1852 Patent Law Amendment Act, it remained an issue of public scrutiny. While some of the criticism was attributable to the rapid growth in patenting, public attention was drawn to the system by the 'Edmunds affair', in which Leonard Edmunds, Clerk of the Patents since 1830, was found guilty of dishonestly handling patent fees, a matter which prompted the resignation of Lord Chancellor Westbury.

[6] Specifications of inventions were frequently prepared in such a manner as to occasion great difficulty in construing them and in ascertaining the nature and extent of the claims of the invention they were intended to make: 1864 *Report of the Commissioners Appointed to Inquire into the Working of the Law Relating to Letters Patent for Inventions* x. See also 'Patents' (Jan. 1859) 105 *Quarterly Review* 140–1.

[7] 'The attention of the Council has also been directed to the encroachment on the professional men by persons engaged in soliciting *patents*, and the subject is under the view to the application of a proper remedy for the evil': (30 May 1848) *Minute Book of the Law Society* 333. 'The Council has also to observe on the existence of a large class of persons who without any legal education or regular qualifications practise as agents in Parliamentary business and solicit Letters Patent for Inventions. The Council thinks that these important branches of business should be confined to Attorneys and Solicitors and they have under their consideration the means by which this object may be obtained': 'Encroachment on the Profession' (19 June 1851) *Minute Book of the Law Society.*

[8] F. Campin, *Law of Patents for Inventions* (1869), 1.

Office were thought to be practically valueless.[9] More importantly, it helped to create a situation whereby the system could not be trusted.

The lack of trust in the patent system was exacerbated by the fact that patents were perceived, pejoratively, as if they were still a part of the *ancien régime* in which the Crown granted individuals exclusive monopolies over particular trades.[10] As well as casting patents as monopolies and thus as contrary to the public good, the tendency to see patents as a product of Crown grant created a stumbling block to reform.[11] Indeed one reason why successive governments felt unwilling to introduce a system of examination for patents, a process which would have increased and ultimately did increase the trust placed in the patent system, was that it 'would have exploded the ancient theory that a patent is special direct grant from the Crown of certain valuable privileges, and that it is only by Her Majesty's gracious favour that these privileges are granted at all'.[12] More specifically, the fact that that there was no obligation upon the Crown to grant patents, but that it did so only as a favour to patentees, meant that there were few expectations on behalf of the users of the system for it to be improved: they were supposed to feel lucky (privileged) that the Crown had lowered itself to grant the rights in the first place.

Despite the hostility which existed towards the patent system, by the 1870s attitudes towards patenting had begun to change. As a commentator argued in 1877, while 'a few years ago the current of public opinion was decidedly running against the law of patents ... there is now a general *consensus* of public opinion that it would be dangerous to

---

[9] A position which in many ways continued until examination was introduced in 1905. See Lord Wolverton (17 Nov. 1902) 114 *Hansard* cols. 1099 ff.

[10] As one commentator said, 'prejudices still exist against patents, as if they were a remnant of the old abuse of monopolies by which an individual obtained from the crown the right to the exclusive exercise of some particular trade': 'Art. V; Publications of the Honourable Commissioners of Patents' (Jan. 1859) 105 *Quarterly Review* 137. See also C. MacLeod, 'The Paradoxes of Patenting' (1991), 885.

[11] The idea that the body granting the patent had no responsibility towards patentees, which was based on the ideas that favours brought with them no duties, was reflected in the belief that patents were granted at the applicant's own risk. 'He takes the risk as to novelty, he takes the risk as to utility, and as to everything else necessary to make a good patent': John Imray (past President of Institute of Patent Agents), 1888 *Report of the Committee Appointed by the Board of Trade to Inquire into the Duties, Organisation and Arrangements of the Patent Office under the Patents, Designs, and Trade Marks Act 1883, so far as Relates to Trade Marks and Designs* 110 (Q. 1910).

[12] H. Trueman Wood, 'The Patents for Inventions Bill, 1877' (9 March 1877) 25 *Journal of the Society of Arts* 342. Trueman Wood continued: 'The theory is that a grant of Letters Patent under the Great Seal of England is a peculiar act of royal bounty. In practice, it can be obtained by the first crotchet-monger who thinks he has discovered the perpetual motion, and is willing to spend £25 for the privilege of saying so. There is plenty of room for reform at the Patent Office; but the reform is administrative, not legislative.'

national interests to abolish patents for inventions, although we ought to reform the laws relating to them'.[13] That is, it was widely accepted that the patent system was worthy of support, albeit in need of reform. A number of factors contributed to the change of attitude which led to the normative closure of patent law. For the most part, the development of trust in patents and its institutions was a gradual process which came with time, with the force of repetition and the familiarity that this generates. More specifically, in the same way in which the literary property debate helped to secure (and close) the normative status of copyright law, the debates as to the validity of patents helped to engender public faith in the *idea* of a patent system.[14]

Although the debates about the need for a patent system played an important role in changing the way the patent system was perceived, the change in attitude depended as much on the integrity and predictability of the routine hidden operations of the Patent Registry as it did on these intellectual debates. While the investment of faith in the registration process which developed slowly over the course of the second half of the nineteenth century can be seen as part of a broader trend in law, it also came about as a result of the fact that the bureaucratic processes used by the Patent Office were refined and improved. This included the introduction of indexes, arranged both chronologically and alphabetically,[15] of the patents which had been granted. Other changes which reinforced the move towards a more rational registration system included the collection of the various Patent Offices in one building, the introduction of job specifications for members of the Patent Office, the clarification

[13] L. Playfair, 'On Patents and the New Patent Bill' (1877) 1 *The Nineteenth Century* 315. The 1871–2 Select Committee on Letters Patent concluded that the patent system was defective but valuable overall, and proposed reforms including the introduction of examination and specially advised tribunals: 1872 *Report from the Select Committee on Letters Patent*. It was argued that the 1871 and 1872 Select Committees 'had put an end to the idea which had previously prevailed in favour of the total abolition of protection for invention. There was a general feeling ... throughout the country, exemplified by the evidence given before the Committee, that it was desirable that there should be protection of inventions': J Hinde Palmer QC (11 Dec. 1874) 23 *Journal of the Society of Arts* 76.

[14] While there were many points of disagreement between the parties, they met on common ground, and shared a faith in progress as well as the language and logic of utilitarianism. See M. Coulter, *Property in Ideas* (1991), 84.

[15] Woodcroft, Professor of Machinery at University College and later Comptroller, drew up an index of patents which he later sold to the Patents Office as the basis for their index. See 1851 *Select Committee of the House of Lords Appointed to Consider the Bills for the Amendment of the Law Touching Letters Patent for Inventions* 486. On Woodcroft see J. Hewish, *The Indefatigable Mr Woodcroft: The Legacy of invention* (London: British Library, 1983), 27. It was said that 'an analytical and elemental system of registration' would be 'as perfect as possible': [no initial] Symonds, 'Summary of Proceedings' (1862), 887.

of their pensions arrangements, and the introduction of new accounting procedures.

The rationalisation of the Patent Office and its activities was enhanced by the fact that patent agents came to be recognised as a distinct and separate professional body,[16] which was incorporated in 1882[17] and granted a Royal Charter in 1894.[18] In turn these changes saw increased attention being given to the way patent agents were regulated: to the qualifications required for entry into the profession,[19] to what it was that patent agents were supposed to do, and the manner in which they were to be disciplined.[20] The increased regulation of patent agents not only led to more defined patterns of work practices but also helped to standardise those practices. In combination, these changes ensured that the documents that the patents agents routinely dealt with could be trusted and relied upon.

When combined with the administrative reforms which took place at the time, these changes meant that trust grew not only in the registration process and in the people who administered that system, but also in the outcomes of that process: in the patent itself. One of the most important consequences of this new-found trust in the patent was that people no longer felt the need to question, at least in the manner they had done previously, the patents which had been granted by the Patent Office. The fact that people were able to rely upon the paper inscription of the invention played an important role in changing the way the patent system was perceived and valued.

While the increased faith in patent administration played a key role in

---

[16] See J. Harrison, 'Some Patent Practitioners' (1982), 494–8; 589–93; 670–4. Campin said in 1848 that there were only about ten patent agents working in London: 1849 *Report of the Committee Appointed by the Lords of the Treasury on the Signet and Privy Seal Office* 15 (Q. 368).

[17] On the incorporation of the Institute of Patent Agents in 1882 see (22 Sept. 1882) 30 *Journal of the Society of Arts* 1014.

[18] The Royal Charter for the Institute of Patent Agents (1891); 1894 *Special Report from the Select Committee on the Patent Agents' Bill*.

[19] Given that the system was one of registration not examination, trust in the value of patent agents was greatly dependent on the standardisation of professional practices. See 'General Notes: Patent Office' (27 May 1887) 35 *Journal of the Society of Arts* 435.

[20] While the number of patent agents and their importance in matters relating to intellectual property expanded greatly in the second half of the nineteenth century, it was said that they were under little discipline or control as to either conduct or capacity: L. Edmunds, in 1864 *Report on Letters Patent for Inventions* (1864) 33 (Q. 576). The 1887 *Report of the Committee Appointed by the Board of Trade to Inquire into the Duties, Organisation and Arrangements of the Patent Office under the Patents, Designs and Trade Marks Act 1883 Having Special Regard to the System of Examination of the Specifications which Accompany Applications for Patents now in Force under the Act* recommended mechanisms to ensure that patent agents were duly qualified before being able to designate themselves as such. See further J. Imray, evidence in 1894 *Special Report from the Select Committee on the Patent Agents' Bill* 62 (Q. 968).

changing the normative status of patent law, the *possibility* for reform came as patents changed from being seen predominantly as a creature of Royal grant or Crown prerogative (which hindered patent reform), to a specifically legal (and administrative) instrument. This process was initially facilitated by the 1851 Protections of Inventions Act[21] which introduced, as a temporary measure, provisional registration for inventions. Similar attempts at registration had previously been rejected because they would have usurped the role of the Crown; but in this case, as it was to be only a temporary measure and in connection with an important public event supported by the monarchy, registration was not considered to be threatening and so it could be tried out. Although intended as a temporary measure, the success of the registration process opened the door for more sweeping legislative reforms.[22] These opportunities were exploited in the 1852 Patent Law Amendment Act which changed the way patent property was perceived from a product of the prerogative of the Crown to a creature of administration.[23] The reason for this was that, as Thomas Webster said, while previously the property in patents had arisen on the grant of the patent by the Crown, with the introduction of a (more) effective system of registration by the 1852 Act the property in the invention arose from the date of *application* rather than *grant* by the Crown (that is, it created bureaucratic property in inventions).[24]

The codification of copyright

Although by the 1850s there was a widespread consensus both as to the form that copyright law should take and agreement that the grant of property rights in things such as artistic and literary works was a worthwhile and valuable exercise, it was not until early in the twentieth century that the model of copyright which had taken shape in the bilateral treaties (and beyond) was adopted at a statutory level. More

---

[21] *An Act to Extend the Provisions of the Designs Act, 1850, and to give Protection from Piracy to Persons Exhibiting New Inventions in the Exhibition of the Works of Industry of all Nations in 1851* 14 & 15 Vict. c . 8 (1851).

[22] See T. Webster, 1851 *Select Committee on Patents* 25 (Q. 104).

[23] W. Carpmael highlighted the change when he told the Select Committee that the 1851 Patents Bill which gave the Commissioners of Patents the power 'for determining what conditions such letters patent shall be granted subject to' took 'away a portion of the prerogative of the Crown' leaving it with the task of merely signing documents over which it had no control: *ibid.*, 311. This was despite the fact that section 16 of the 1852 Patent Law Amendment Act said that 'nothing herein contained shall extend to, abridge or affect the prerogative of the Crown in relation to the granting, or withholding the grant of any letters patent'.

[24] T. Webster, 1871 *Report from the Select Committee on Letters Patent* 44 (Q. 544).

specifically it was not until the passage of the 1911 Copyright Act that the process set in play in the early part of the nineteenth century was completed. Prior to the passage of this Act copyright law, as Lord Monkswell said in 1891, had been in 'glorious muddle'.[25] Moreover, he added, 'since the first Statute on the subject of copyright was passed in the time of Queen Anne, the Law of Copyright seems to have been the sport of some malignant demon as it were, and we find that at present the Law of Copyright is contained in eighteen Acts of Parliament, and in some ill-defined common law principles'.[26] The Royal Commissioners on Copyright, in their *Report* of 1878, spoke for countless reformers when they said, 'the first observation which a study of the existing law suggests is that its form, as distinguished from its substance, seems to us bad. The law is wholly destitute of any sort of arrangement, incomplete, often obscure, and even when it is intelligible upon long study it is in so many parts ill-expressed that no one who does not give the study to it can expect to understand it.'[27] Recognising that the form that copyright law then took belonged to a different (pre-modern) era, the Commissioners called for the shape of the law to be changed. The law 'on this subject should be reduced to an intelligible and systematic form. This may be effected by codifying the law, either in the shape in which it appears in Sir James Stephen's Digest or in any other way which may be preferred.'[28] The Copyright Act of 1911, which sought to bring order out of chaos,[29] set out to respond to calls of this type.[30] It did so by replacing the previous enactments with 'a homogenous code of Copy-

---

[25] Lord Monkswell (11 May 1891) 353 *Hansard* col. 438.

[26] *Ibid.*

[27] 1878 *Report of the Royal Commissioners on Copyright* para. 7, p. vii. The Royal Commission added that 'the common law principles which lie at the root of the law have never been settled. The Fourteen Acts of Parliament which deal with the subject were passed at different times between 1735 and 1875. They are drawn in different styles, and some are drawn so as to be hardly intelligible. Obscurity of style, however, is only one of the defects of these Acts. Their arrangement is often worse than their style ... The law on this subject should be reduced to an intelligible and systematic form. This may be effected by codifying the law': *ibid.*, paras. 5–13.

[28] *Ibid.*, para. 13, p. viii. See also T. Scrutton, *The Laws of Copyright* (1883), vi. This criticism was repeated in 1910 *Report of the Committee on the Law of Copyright* (the *Gorrell Report 1910*) which suggested that the reason for inconsistency especially in relation to the treatment of different works was 'because the subject has never been treated as a whole': Mr Buxton (President of the Board of Trade) (7 April 1911) 29 *Hansard* col. 2589.

[29] 1878 *Report of the Royal Commissioners on Copyright*, para. 13, p. viii.

[30] One such call for the law to be made more intelligible and systematic came from customs officers, who suffered the inconvenience of operating under various enactments, 'some of them conflicting and contradictory': F. Hamel, 1864 *Report from the Select Committee on the Copyright (No. 2) Bill* 7 (Q. 3).

right Law, drafted on the whole on sound and generous lines,'[31] thereby putting in place the model of copyright developed in the early part of the nineteenth century.

What was it that delayed the institutional adoption of copyright law for over fifty years? Certainly, strenuous efforts were made towards that end. Indeed, one of the notable features of the period leading up to the passage of the 1911 Act was the number of attempts that were made to amend, consolidate and simplify copyright law.[32] The main reason for the delay in reform can be traced to the impact that imperial copyright and the colonies more generally had upon domestic copyright law:[33] factors which played an important role in shaping domestic law in Britain.[34] Growing hostility from the colonies and the development of localised feral laws made it increasingly difficult for the British government to achieve its goal of maintaining uniformity of copyright legislation throughout the British Empire.[35] Rather than face the wrath of an Imperial Copyright Conference,[36] or create inconsistency throughout the Empire, the response by Britain was inactivity.[37] Indeed, as a

---

[31] 'Copyright Law Reform' (1910), 489. On the codificatory nature of the 1911 Copyright Act see G. Robertson, *The Law of Copyright* (Oxford: Clarendon, 1912), vi.

[32] As well as eight attempts to codify copyright law (in 1864, 1878, 1879, 1881, 1890, 1898, 1910, and 1911) and the appointment of a number of select committees, attention was also given to specific areas. In the case of artistic copyright, for example, the second half of the nineteenth century saw the introduction of nine Artistic Copyright Bills (1868, 1869, 1882, 1883, 1884, 1885, 1886, 1899, 1900), the appointment of five legislative committees, as well as numerous articles in legal journals, the eclectic Victorian journals and daily newspapers. See generally A. Moffatt, 'What is an Author?' (1900) 12 *Juridical Review* 217.

[33] 'The Copyright question has before now raised very delicate Constitutional questions between ourselves and the Self-Governing Dominions [notably Canada], and a sort of forced uniformity in regard to this matter has led to considerable difficulties between the Mother Country and some of the Dominions, and to interminable, and in some cases, I am sorry to say, to acrimonious correspondence': Mr Buxton (President of the Board of Trade) (7 April 1911) 23 *Hansard* col. 2589. More telling is Buxton's admission of a 'loss of control' over the colonies. While Britain wanted 'uniformity throughout the whole Empire [as to copyright] ... Even if we desired to do so, it is quite clear that, whatever may have been the case in the 'forties, under present conditions, we have no means of exercising such coercion as that': *ibid.*

[34] For example, clause 23 of the 1910 Copyright Bill was taken from Australian law. See 12 Dec. 1910, BT/209/477.

[35] 'It is of the highest importance to maintain uniformity of legislation as regards copyright throughout the British Empire. It is also highly desirable to attain a great degree of uniformity as is reasonably practicable among the principal nations with regard to International Copyright': Board of Trade to Colonial Office, April 1910, BT/209/696.

[36] It was said of the Bill for the 1911 Copyright Act that it had been approved 'by the Imperial Copyright Conference and could not be altered without weakening the Bill': 12 Dec. 1910, BT/209/477.

[37] The colonies' hostility also made it difficult for the UK to implement the Berne Convention. 'Canada is not satisfied with her position in connection with the provisions

commentator on the 1911 Copyright Act said, 'it is probably not too much to say that, were it not for the difficulty arising from the constitution of the Empire, the Copyright Law would have been remodelled long ago'.[38] It was not until early in the twentieth century, when British control of its empire had begun to wane, and the colonial networks had become less important, that the British government felt that it had the freedom it needed to reform domestic copyright law.

Consolidation and entrenchment

At the same time as the obstacles to the completion of intellectual property law were being overcome, the legal categories were being consolidated and fossilised. In part this can be attributed to the fact that the model of intellectual property law that emerged in the middle part of the nineteenth century gradually became more and more inflexible. As the legal categories made their way into and dominated domestic legal culture, as they became entrenched in the legal treaties and commentaries, in the administrative arrangements at the Board of Trade and the Foreign Office,[39] the libraries and bibliographies as well as in the language and statutory frameworks of the law, there was less room for manoeuvre and change. Many factors reinforced the fossilisation of the categories of intellectual property law. In the case of copyright, for example, an image of copyright law utilised in the international agreements was reinforced by the fact that the image of British copyright law was projected to the world. When that world returned to talk to Britain, it did so expecting a particular response. This helped to create a cycle of expectation and dependency in terms of the image that was portrayed of copyright law. In addition, once a particular treaty had successfully been used as the template for agreements with a number of different countries (in the UK's case it was the Anglo-Sardinian model), the Foreign Office

of the Berne Convention, and ... requests have been made for an alteration on that point. If we begin amending or consolidating the law at the present time when subjects of that kind are under discussion with our colonies, we shall add greatly to the friction existing and to the difficulty of passing such a bill at the present time': Lord Balfour of Burleigh (11 May 1891) 353 *Hansard* col. 452. The Berne Convention only began to impact upon UK law as colonial law became less important. One of the reasons why imperial copyright was much more important than that established under the Berne Convention was that the British Commonwealth was the primary market for British publications. For an overview of these issues see S. Nowell-Smith, *International Copyright Law and the Publisher in the Reign of Queen Victoria* (Oxford: Clarendon Press, 1968).

[38] 'Copyright Law Reform' (1910), 486.

[39] On the Board of Trade see E. Cohen, *The Growth of the British Civil Service 1780–1939* (London: Allen and Unwin, 1941); P. Hennessy, *Whitehall* (London: Secker and Warburg, 1989).

was reluctant to negotiate on any other basis than this standard-form treaty for fear that it would lead to pressure to reopen pre-existing treaties. As the model spread to British dominions and colonies, it proved more and more difficult to change. The rigidity of the copyright model and the model of intellectual property more generally was enhanced by the fact that as the number of treaties negotiated increased, the United Kingdom effectively became entrenched in a web of bilateral agreements.[40]

The images of intellectual property law that took shape in the nineteenth century were reinforced by the passage of the Berne and Paris Conventions which marked the culmination of the logic worked out earlier in the century. Another factor which played and continues to play an important role in cementing the legal categories was that by the 1880s or thereabouts the textbooks of intellectual property law had adopted their current form. This was reinforced by the fact that while relatively few textbooks or treatises were published in the first half of the nineteenth century, by 1900 there were some 813 works (114 serials, 699 textbooks), representing some 1,940 volumes published under the classification of industrial property and copyright,[41] most of which were organised along virtually identical lines. As Simpson reminds us, once a field of law has been systematised, organised and written about in this way much of the intellectual excitement associated with it disappears and one of the consequences is, as many present-day writers on intellectual property will attest, that later 'treatise writers are relegated to the laborious task of reworking the same materials or refining matters of detail, and this is particularly true when the branch of law is relatively static'.[42]

The closure of the legal categories which took place over the course of

---

[40] This was also the case with other treaty countries. For example in discussions about a proposed Anglo-Russian treaty, Napier reported that he said to Prince Gottschalk, who was negotiating on behalf of Russia, that 'foreign authors would be admitted to all the rights enjoyed by a native in each country and also possess for a moderate period an interest in the translation of his work'. Napier said that Prince Gottschalk 'stopped me here and said that he regretted he could not hold out the least hope on the subject of translations. The right of authors in translations of [their] work was a principle to which he had given much thought and he had declined to adopt it in the convention with France.' The treaty with France was the basis of his 'model for other countries, and once it had been established "with much difficulty" he could not overturn it. He could not begin again': to Lord Russell from Napier, 26 Aug. 1861, FO/65/578/274. See also Lord Napier to Lord Russell (commenting on letter from Mr Tolstoy), BT/1/556/1092/61. It was also said that it was 'inadvisable to change clauses that have already been agreed with Prussia and Hanover': 18 Sept. 1850, FO/27/889.

[41] HMSO, *Subject List of Works on the Laws of Industrial Property (Patents, Design and Trademarks) and Copyright* (London: Darling and Son, 1900), 5.

[42] A. Simpson, 'The Rise and Fall of the Legal Treatise' (1987), 315.

the second half of the nineteenth century brought with it regularity in approach, a normalisation or standardisation in terms of method and subject of inquiry. This meant that although disputes about intellectual property continued, increasingly they were conducted against the background of a wide number of shared principles and ideas. Moreover, as the shape of intellectual property law came to be settled and the questions which had preoccupied the law for so long came to be answered (or ignored), the focus of attention moved to concentrate upon matters of detail.[43] As trust in the categories of intellectual property grew and constraints upon reform were lifted, more and more energy was given to the equally important but far less glamorous question of the minutiae of intellectual property law. While commentators in the eighteenth and first half of the nineteenth centuries had debated about the nature of intangible property and whether and how boundaries were to be drawn around this property, such questions were succeeded by discussions about the size of the paper and the colour of the ink to be used when drafting patent specifications, the number of people using the Patent Office library, and the gender balance of patentees.[44]

As well as further entrenching the legal categories, the growing attention to detail also promoted the image of intellectual property law as a technical subject whose practitioners would therefore need specialist knowledge.[45] With many issues concerning the shape of the law resolved (or presumed so) it was also easier for the law to expand to accommodate new subject matter. While new forms of subject matter invariably brought with them new problems, during the second half of the nineteenth century the law began to fall into the now familiar pattern in

[43] As Mr Chamberlain said, reform tended to be in terms of 'detail and did not raise any questions of principle': (16 April 1883), 278 *Hansard* col. 349.

[44] We read that in '1898 women inventors contributed 702, or nearly 2.3%, of the total number of applications, about 148 being for inventions connected with articles of dress, and 106 for inventions relating to cycling': 'Patents, Designs and Trade Marks' (June 1898), *The Chamber of Commerce Journal* 125 (which was based upon the fifteenth Report of the Comptroller of Patents, Designs, and Trade Marks). Details were also given of the number of readers at the Patent Office Library.

[45] This was particularly the case with patents and trade marks which required knowledge of science and commerce. The growing specialisation manifested itself in a number of ways. Doubts about the ability of juries to comprehend scientific facts used in patent cases led to calls for abolition of trial by jury. Similarly as the competence of judges was also called into question, an increasing number of calls were made for the introduction of a specialist court, akin to the Admiralty Division (with scientific or commercial knowledge). See, e.g., Society for Promoting Amendment of the Law, *Annual Report 1860–1* (London: McCorquodale and Co., 1861), 9. The drafting of patent claims was another area that increasingly required legal expertise. Godson recognised this in 1833 when he said 'that it was almost impossible for a scientific man to draw a proper specification without the assistance of a lawyer': R. Godson, 'Law of Patents' (19 Feb. 1833) 15 *Hansard* cols. 974–8.

terms of the questions asked and the approach adopted in response to such questions. Whether it was fine art, photography, films or sound recordings, there was an expectation that the law could and should protect new forms of technical and cultural creation; the only real question was how this was to be achieved and what features of the pre-existing structures needed to be changed to achieve this protection. Based on the assumption that the framework was complete and in place, although occasionally in need of adjustment, the primary task for the law came to be to provide the means of notation or inscription necessary to make the object knowable and protectable. The closure of the legal categories also had an impact on the approach taken when thinking about intellectual property law. In particular, instead of being concerned with the shape of intellectual property law and how the categories related to each other, commentators gradually became concerned with ensuring that the categories were not transgressed; they took on the role of policing the boundaries. Moreover as the legal categories were increasingly accepted as givens, there was little effort expended on the part of commentators towards exploring or understanding the nature of the categories.

7 Explanations for the shape of intellectual property law

Valuing intangible property

In previous chapters we argued that mental or creative labour, the sweat of the brain rather than of the body, acted as a common denominator which united those areas of the law which we habitually regard as making up intellectual property law. In this chapter, our aim is to explain how and why it was that, within the more general category, patents, designs, copyright and (eventually) trademarks were carved out as separate and discrete areas of law. Although we recognise the important role played by the environment in which the law operates in shaping intellectual property law, our primary focus here – in line with our primary concern in exploring legal doctrine – is on those factors within the law that helped to shape the particular form that intellectual property law ultimately took. We will show that in spite of what many present-day commentators would have us believe, the emergence of modern intellectual property law was neither natural nor inevitable, nor was it an example of the law coming to occupy its proper philosophical position.[1] Rather, the separation of intellectual property law into its now familiar categories was the product of a complex and changing set of circumstances.[2]

[1] For an example of this see G. Dworkin, 'Why are Registered Designs so Unpopular?' (Feb. 1993) *Intellectual Property Newsletter: Special Report No. 8* 1–2; J. Reichman, 'Legal Hybrids between the Patent and Copyright Paradigms' in (eds.) W. Korthals *et al.*, *Information law Towards the 21st Century* (Deventer and Boston: Kluwer, 1992), 357. In contrast, we agree more with the sentiment that 'the entire field of law is, in fact, continuous, and boundaries which are traced must therefore be to some extent arbitrary': H. Ludlow and H. Jenkins, *A Treatise on the Law of Trade-Marks and Trade-Names* (London: William Maxwell and Son, 1877), 1.

[2] For example, patents and copyright were sometimes distinguished in terms of the speed with which their respective contributions came to be appreciated: Lord Lyttelton (26 May 1842) 63 *Hansard* cols. 803–6. Similar rationales were also employed to justify the different periods of duration given to patents and copyright. This arose from the fact, as the Bishop of London said, that as patents related to 'the ordinary use of human life', they were sure to find success in fourteen years. With regard to the productions of the intellectual world, however, the human mind was slow to comprehend: *ibid.*, col. 808.

In explaining the factors that helped to determine the shape of intellectual property law we wish to highlight two further points. First, we argue that the shape intellectual property law took, as well as the way this mode of organisation was explained, were strongly influenced by the particular type of subject matter that was protected and the way in which that subject matter was interpreted. Whilst we recognise that a range of factors helped to determine the shape of intellectual property law, it is not too far from the truth to say that the way in which the subject matter of intangible property was perceived is the key organising factor used to explain the shape that the categories took. At the same time we wish to show that the organisational role played by the subject matter of intellectual property law itself was to change over time. We hope not only to show the historically contingent nature of the legal categories and the way in which they were explained, but to highlight more clearly the non-natural and non-philosophical nature of intellectual property law.

The quantity of mental labour

There have been a number of attempts in the history of intellectual property law to distinguish between the various forms of intellectual property on the basis of the subject matter protected; one of the earliest and most interesting examples arose in the course of the literary property debate. Before looking at these examples two points need to be borne in mind. First, given that the literary property debate took place prior to the emergence of modern intellectual property law, we need to be careful when drawing conclusions about the impact such arguments had upon the shape that modern intellectual property law ultimately took. Secondly, it was (and remains) common practice to distinguish between the categories of intellectual property law by drawing upon what may be called the ideal typical or representative objects of the categories in question. That is, rather than talking about all the objects that were protected under a particular category (which is clearly impossible), commentators took what were widely accepted as archetypical examples of the form of intangible property under consideration. For example in the literary property debate the book was considered as being representative of literary property, with clocks and machines performing similar roles for patents.

As we saw earlier, the literary property debate turned on the question of the status of perpetual common law literary property.[3] One of the

---

[3] See ch. 1.

most powerful arguments raised against perpetual common law literary property took as its starting point the fact that patents and literary property were both forms of incorporeal property and as such should be treated equally. More specifically, it was argued that since patents were only granted for a limited period of time (seven or fourteen years), there was no reason why literary property should be treated any differently from patents. One commentator on the literary property debate said, 'the right of the Artificer being universally held untenable at common law, if [the proponents of literary property] admitted the Author to stand in the same predicament, they could not support his claim to a perpetuity in his copy-right'.[4]

The proponents of literary property thus found themselves in a position whereby if they were to make out a plausible case for perpetual common law literary property they needed to be able to explain how literary property differed from patents and, in so doing, why it should be treated differently. The writer of *A Vindication* summed up this argument when he said, 'if we can establish a real difference between [patents and literary copyright] we shall demolish the strongest hold, wherein the opponents of literary property have entrenched themselves'.[5]

While today this question would most probably be answered by focusing on whether the property arose automatically on creation or via registration, or in terms of the nature of the monopoly granted, the proponents of literary property took a different approach. Instead they argued that while similar in many ways, notably in their incorporeal status, the 'true and peculiar Property' that was protected by literary property and by patents were so different in their nature that they deserved to be treated differently.[6] Moreover, they argued that because literary property 'totally differs from every other incorporeal Right which the law acknowledges',[7] it was possible to justify the different forms of protection given to literary property and patents.

In order to highlight the difference between property in machines (patents) and that in books (literary property), the proponents of literary property relied upon the dominant conception of composition or creation which existed at the time. This was one in which the mind was seen as a kind of mechanism which produced chains of associated images and

---

[4] W. Kenrick, *An Address* (1774), 6.

[5] *A Vindication* (1762), 8–9.

[6] W. Warburton, *A Letter from an Author* (1747), 8. The difference between the two 'sorts of property' was said to arise from an 'equal difference in the *Things*: As will appear by considering the different nature of the Works; and the different Views of the Operators': *ibid.*, 8.

[7] *An Enquiry* (1762), 2–3.

ideas. Such ideas were the materials from which writers, artisans and architects assembled their composition according to a plan.[8] More importantly, under this schema objects were also viewed mechanistically: they could be broken down into elemental parts, into the amount of mental and manual labour that they contained. Drawing upon this model of creation the proponents of literary property were in a position whereby they were able to characterise and, in turn, to distinguish the various forms of intangible property recognised by the law.

By echoing Joshua Reynolds' dictate that 'the value and rank of every Art is in proportion to the mental labour employed in it',[9] the proponents of literary property argued that different objects (and thus the form of intangible property they represented) could be distinguished according to the *amount* of mental labour they embodied. More specifically, armed with the idea that the various forms of intellectual property could be distinguished by the amount of mental labour embodied in them – which traces in reverse Locke's idea that property originates when an individual's person is impressed upon the world through labour – the proponents of perpetual common law literary property were able to arrange the various types of intellectual property into a continuum, depending on the amount of mental labour (or its relative importance) which was embodied within the archetypical object.[10]

At one extreme of the continuum lay those objects, such as utensils, which were primarily seen as products of the hand and as such contained very little if any mental labour.[11] At the other extreme of the spectrum the proponents of literary property placed objects such as the book. While the proponents recognised that, as with all objects, the book necessarily contained a degree of manual labour, they argued that the intrinsic quality of literary property, which was considered the 'genuine offspring of the mind',[12] lay in its mental elements.[13] In between these two extremes the proponents placed property which arose with the creation of machines. While utensils were seen as being

---

[8] M. Rose, 'The Author as Proprietor' (1994), 34. See also M. Abrams, *The Mirror and the Lamp* (1953), 159–67.

[9] 'As this principle is observed or neglected, our profession becomes either a liberal art or a mechanical trade. In the hands of one man it makes the highest pretensions, as it is reduced to a mere matter of ornament, and the painter has the humble province of furnishing our apartments with elegance': J. Reynolds, *Discourses on Art* (1771) (1959), Discourse IV, 57.

[10] Perhaps the clearest example of this was W. Warburton, *A Letter from an Author* (1747). See the critical remarks on this in *An Enquiry* (1762), 22 ff.

[11] It was argued that the principal expense of objects such as utensils was the materials employed: W. Warburton, *A Letter from an Author* (1747), 9.

[12] *An Enquiry* (1762), 1.

[13] W. Warburton, *A Letter from an Author* (1747), 8. With a '*Book* the principal Expense is in the *form* given: which the original Maker only can supply': *ibid.*, 9.

made up predominantly of manual labour and books primarily of mental labour, because the machine (and hence patents) was made up of a mixture of mental and manual labour, it was said to share things in common with both the utensil and the book.[14]

Although the characterisation of creations in terms of the amount of mental labour they embodied enabled a distinction to be drawn between literary property and patents, this was only the first part of the proponents' argument. Drawing on the model of creativity we outlined earlier,[15] the proponents argued that the more of the creator which was contained in the final product, the more the product was individualised – i.e. the purer the object and thus the property – the less the property could be diluted (or overridden) by other concerns.[16] In the case of utensils, which were seen as being all but devoid of mental labour, it was argued that the property ought to be 'confined to the individual Thing made, which if the Proprietor thinks not fit to hide, others may make the like in imitation of it; and thereby acquire the same Property in their *manual Work*, which he hath done'.[17] That is, while the proponents accepted that property rights could exist in the utensil as a tangible object, they argued that no intangible rights ought to be recognised in the creation of those objects, given that utensils were seen as being all but devoid of mental labour.[18] While the impure nature of the utensil meant that its production did not give rise to any intangible property rights, the proponents argued, in relation to literary property, that it was as close to perfect an intangible property as was possible and, as such, ought not to be impinged by external concerns. In short, it ought to be perpetual.

The image of the pure nature of the property in the literary work is in marked contrast to the way property in the creation of machines was perceived. While it was accepted that machines were made up of a mixture of mental and manual labour, as property in 'mechanical engines' was said to partake 'so essentially of the Nature of manual Works' it was suggested that a strong case could be made for treating machines (and thus patents) in a similar way to utensils.[19] That is, it was suggested that while a case could be made for property rights in the

---

[14] As Warburton said, 'In our Division of artificial moveables, into the two sorts, of mental and manual, we have purposely omitted a Third, of a complicated Nature, which holds of both the other in common': this was the subject matter of patents: *A Letter from an Author* (1747), 13.

[15] Ch. 2.

[16] Cf. W. Kenrick, *An Address* (1774), 6.

[17] W. Warburton, *A Letter from an Author* (1747), 7–8.

[18] These arguments took place before the law had recognised any value in design.

[19] W. Warburton, *A Letter from an Author* (1747), 13.

physical object, no such case could be made for the creation of objects such as machines or clocks. The reason for this was that 'like a common utensil' a machine 'must be finished before it can be of use ... its materials are its principal expense; and ... a successful imitator must work with the ideas of the first inventor; which are all reasons why the property should terminate in the individual machine'.[20] While it may have been tempting to treat the property in machines in a similar way to utensils, the proponents of literary property acknowledged that a case could be made for partial recognition of intangible property in machines. This was 'because the operation of the mind' was said to be 'so intimately concerned in the construction of these works'[21] that the mental element could not be denied. As such, while the machine was made up primarily of manual labour, it also contained a degree of mental labour which warranted protection. Given the impure nature of the property in machines, which meant that they contained at best only a small amount of mental labour, it was said that the only way of dealing with such an 'imperfect right' was by way of a temporary grant.[22]

The proponents of perpetual common law literary property were thus able not only to distinguish between forms of legal protection in terms of the amount of mental labour particular representative objects contained, they were able also to rank the forms of property in terms of their relative level of perfection or imperfection: from the most perfect (literary property) to the partially impure (patents) to the impure (utensils). Given the belief that the duration of a property right should be in proportion to its purity, the proponents of literary property were thus in a position whereby they could explain why patents and literary property were both forms of incorporeal property, but that patents were only granted for seven (or fourteen) years, whereas copyright was to be perpetual. More specifically, they were able to argue that while patents and literary copyright were both forms of incorporeal property, they were so different in their 'natures' that they ought to be given different protection.

A variation on this argument focused less on the nature of the property protected than on what it took to imitate or copy the intangible. In particular it was argued that while the reprinting of a book could be compared to the imitating or copying of an engine, they were very different. The reason for this was that the 'printing of a book is a

---

[20] *Ibid.*   [21] *Ibid.*

[22] The reason for this was that 'because the operation of the mind is so intimately concerned in the construction of these works, their powers being effected and regulated by the right application of geometric science, all states have concurred in giving the Inventors of them a Licence of Monopoly, for a Term of Years, a Claim of Right': W. Warburton, *A Letter from an Author* (1747), 13.

mere mechanical operation, which a man can perform without understanding one word of it. Whereas, no man can copy an engine, unless he
have in his mind the idea of that engine, and know the purpose for
which it is intended, and the mechanical powers by which it operates'.[23]
While a book could be copied with little thought on the part of the
imitator, a clock had to be taken to pieces, its mechanism examined, and
its mode of operation understood. The fact that in order to imitate a
clock it was necessary to reverse engineer it, whereas a book could be
reproduced with relative ease, had several consequences. Practically, the
need to reverse engineer inventions provided them with a natural lead
time that books did not have, thus making the legal protection of
machines less significant than was the case with books. Further, since
the primary component of an invention was perceived to be its material
components, such as the metal cogs or the face of the clock, the copying
of an invention was economically less advantageous to a pirate than the
copying of a book. These practical and economic differences meant that
there was a need for longer protection to be given to books than was the
case with machines. This was reinforced by the fact that as the copying
of a literary work was a mechanical process which did not require the
copyist to understand the work, it was said to be intellectually and
morally a much more offensive type of piracy than that involved in the
copying of an invention, which at least required the copyist to understand the invention and to re-experience the creative processes which
the inventor had experienced.[24]

It is clear that during the literary property debate the *quantity* of
mental labour which was embodied in representative objects played an
important role in distinguishing between the different forms of protection then available. While this mode of reasoning may seem alien today,

---

[23] Lord Monboddo, *Hinton v Donaldson* (1773) *Decisions of the Court of Session* (1774), 12.
The consequence of this was that as the mechanic had utilised his own skill and genius
in copying the work, unlike the mere copier of a book, the use of the work should not
be restricted. See also W. Warburton, *A Letter from an Author* (1747), 10–12.

[24] It was also said that an imitator of a machine only produced 'a resemblance' whereas a
copier of a book produced something identical. As Blackstone said, 'style and sentiment
are the essentials of a literary composition. These alone constitute its identity. The
paper and print are merely accidents, which serve as vehicles to convey that style and
sentiment to a distance. Every duplicate therefore of a work, whether ten or ten
thousand, if it conveys the same style and sentiment, is the same identical work, which
is produced by the author's invention and labour. But a duplicate of a mechanical
engine is, at best, but a resemblance of the other, and a resemblance can never be the
same identical thing. It must be composed of different materials, and will be more or
less perfect in the workmanship ... There is a distinction, then, in the nature of things
compared together; and there is also a distinction arising from public convenience.
Mechanical inventions tend to the improvement of arts and manufactures, which
employ the bulk of people; therefore they ought to be cheap and numerous':
W. Blackstone (as counsel), *Tonson v Collins* (1760) 96 ER 189.

the use of mental labour as a method of organisation was not limited to this period for it continued to be used as a means of distinguishing the various forms of protection throughout the remainder of the eighteenth and well into the nineteenth century. For example the fact that the amount of mental labour embodied in a pattern was said to be less than that contained in a book or a clock was used in the 1840s to separate design law from patents and copyright. In particular, it was argued that designs, which were constrained by the function the object was to perform and the market for which it was designed,[25] should be treated as an imperfect form of property. As Louis Lucas said in evidence before the 1840 Select Committee on Designs, 'I cannot ... consider the designing for prints to be analogous to the case of the author of a book, or any scientific work, or work of art, it is so trifling in nature. The merit is not in the printer; the merit lies in the thousands of men who gain their daily bread by making these designs'.[26] Another more numerically minded witness put the designer's contribution at 1/352 of a manufactured article:[27] thus situating design even further down the scale than invention.[28] This helped not only to distinguish design law from patents

[25] All works were to some extent constrained by external factors: the degree to which creativity was constrained differed depending on the type of work in question. It was generally agreed that fewer constraints operated on artists and authors. In contrast designers and inventors were constrained by functional requirements, by the demands of the market and by laws of nature. In designing a decanter, for example, it was argued that 'the centre of gravity must be kept low and the base wide, to give stability; a certain height, however, is indispensable to its appearance. The grasp of the hand, and the facility of pouring out and filling, cleaning and stopping, regulate the neck; and the design, besides fulfilling these conditions, must be practicable in a material which receives its first shape by blowing into a mould, and its surface from a grinder': T. Turner, *Remarks on the Amendment of the Law of Patents* (1851), 2–3. See also C. O'Brien, *The British Manufacturers' Companion* (1795). While the argument that artists and authors operated under fewer constraints than designers and inventors does not stand up to scrutiny, it is clear such assertions do not withstand any sort of reflection, it is clear from texts at the time that these ideas underpinned the distinctions drawn between copyright, designs and patents.

[26] L. Lucas, 1840 *Select Committee on Designs* 351 (Q. 6018).

[27] As quoted in T. Turner, *Remarks on the Amendment of the Law of Patents* (1851), 10. Speaking of the role of design in relation to articles of dress, Tennent said that the 'material is infinitely more costly and durable, and the uses which they are applied, more permanent and unchanging': E. Tennent (1841) 61 *Hansard* col. 672.

[28] The process of distinguishing patents, copyright and designs according to mental labour that was embodied in ideal typical examples of each category drew on an image of how books, patterns and machines were produced. Particularly important in this context was the complexity of the process of production and the relative input of the 'creator' as compared to mere 'producers' in this process. For example, one reason why designed textiles were seen to embody a small proportion of mental labour was because designing was treated as one element in a complex factory production process. In contrast, books were seen as primarily composed of mental labour because the typical representation of authorship was one of solitary effort. As Turner said, while in 'the higher arts (such as painting and sculpture) ... each individual works by himself', with

and copyright, it also established the basis for the step-child status of design which we frequently read about today.[29]

The quality of mental labour

While the method of organising the categories of intellectual property according to the quantity of mental labour embodied within archetypical objects was used almost exclusively as the way of explaining the shape of the law for nearly a century, changes took place over the second half of the nineteenth century which rendered these modes of organisation increasingly significant. More specifically it became clear during the course of the controversy in the 1860s as to whether the patent system ought to be abolished that changes had taken place in the perception of patents which affected the way the categories of intellectual property law were distinguished.

The patent controversy of the 1860s, which was promoted by the growing influence of political economists[30] and was led by Robert Macfie (MP for Leith and sugar refiner in Liverpool and Scotland), focused on the question of whether or not the patent system ought to be abolished.[31] In response to calls for the abolition of the patent system, those in favour of patents replied, 'if we are to abolish the patent regime there is no reason why copyright law should not also be abolished' (knowing that this was not considered a viable option).[32] The task of those arguing for the abolition of patents thus became one of estab-

---

designs for fabrics 'in a single factory, the bleacher and the printer, dyer and graver, designer and colour-maker, to number sometimes of 1,000 individuals, pursue their calling under the same roof': T. Turner, *Remarks on the Amendment of the Law of Patents* (1851), 7.

[29] The perception of the nature of the subject matter protected also helped to separate designs from patents and copyright. The increasingly subservient image of design law is reflected in the suggestion that designs 'occupy a borderland'. This was because they 'belong to the province of copyright, but traverse the province of patent right, directly interfering, like it, with certain manufactures': R. Macfie, 'The Patent Question' (1863), 821–2.

[30] While figures such as Adam Smith, David Ricardo, Jeremy Bentham and John Stuart Mill had supported patents, in mid-century political economists such as Oxford Professor J. Rogers began to oppose the system. M. Coulter, *Property in Ideas* (1991), 73.

[31] On the 'patent controversy' which began in the late 1850s and continued through to the 1860s and 1870s see *ibid.*; F. Machlup and E. Penrose, 'The Patent Controversy in the Nineteenth Century' (1950) 10 *Journal of Economic History* 1; V. Batzel, 'Legal Monopoly in Liberal England: The Patent Controversy in the Mid-Nineteenth Century' (1980) 22 *Business History* 189; D. Van Zyl Smit, 'The Social Creation of a Legal Reality' (1980), ch. 6.

[32] See J. Rogers, 'On the Rationale and Working of the Patent Laws' (1863) 26 (2) *Journal of the Statistics Society* 135–8.

lishing a real difference between patents and copyright: a repeat of the task that arose in the literary property debate.[33]

While the arguments covered an array of topics, most turned on the question of how the invention ought to be characterised. On the one hand, those who supported patents understood the art of inventing, as with other forms of intellectual property, to be a creative process. Continuing to support the image of the invention which had taken shape during the eighteenth century, the pro-patentees argued that inventing was as *creative* an activity as authoring or designing, that 'Watt may be said to have created his particular steam-engine in the same sense that Milton may be said to have created "Paradise Lost".'[34] The *uniqueness* of the invention was ensured by the fact that although the inventor drew on existing ideas, in reducing these abstract principles to a workable form he gave those ideas a unique expression that no other inventor, even one seeking to apply the same ideas, could duplicate. The pro-patent lobby was thus able to argue that as patents were only granted for (new) creations, for things which did not previously exist,[35] they were not tainted by the monopoly label because nothing was being taken from the public. As such, they deserved continued legal and political support.

In contrast, those who favoured the abolition of the patent system argued that the invention was better understood as a *discovery* rather than as a creation. While the anti-patent lobby believed that the producers of literary and artistic property (and to a lesser extent of ornamental and non-ornamental designs) were properly designated as creators, the same could not be said of inventors. Using a style of language which is closer to that which is used today, it was argued that

a creation of art or literature, a literary or artistic invention, is the man – it is the individual himself; it is the soul, the spirit, the personality of the man who invents it ... Whereas in the case of what is called an invention, in industrial matters, the product, when it is completed, does not represent the inventor, it is rather a material revelation of a thing which is only a solution of a problem which has presented itself to every one.[36]

Hindmarch summed up these arguments when he said, 'an inventor in fact does not create but only invents or finds out something which had a prior existence, although unknown to the world in precisely the same

---

[33] See W. Spence, *The Public Policy of a Patent Law* (1869).

[34] T. Webster, *On Property in Designs* (1853), 32, note f; T. Turner, *Remarks on the Amendment of the Law of Patents* (1851) and *Counsel to Inventors of Improvements in the Useful Arts* (London: Elsworth, 1850).

[35] A requirement now ensured by the fact that patents are only granted for novel inventions.

[36] 'Letters Patent' (27 Oct. 1871) 19 *Journal of the Society of Arts* 847.

way as persons make discoveries in geography and astronomy':[37] that an inventor 'no more creates that art than Sir Isaac Newton did the law of gravitation which he discovered'.[38] By suggesting that inventions were discovered rather than created the abolitionists were able to argue against patents on the basis that because they provided nothing new, they were best seen as unjustifiable monopolies which served to constrain the public. At the same time, however, they could support copyright which, because it was only ever granted for unique and new creations, took nothing from the public.[39]

In opposition to the idea which had been championed by the pro-patent lobby that inventions were the unique expression of their creators, practical experience – it was argued – showed that while literary and artistic works were always the unique expression of their creators, the same invention was often independently made by different people.[40] As Macfie argued, 'there has always been a neck-and-neck chase between men of science and discoveries in arts and physics; and no wonder, for all such discoveries hang one upon another, as natural steps in the progress of a power which can be traced, and every new department of which we can appropriate and apply as soon as it is made cognizable to our senses: whereas the influence of the mind in the other case is purely upon the mind, and no man can trace its working'.[41] As literary and artistic works were seen as the unique expression of their creators, this meant that if Shakespeare had not written *King Lear* or Richardson *Clarissa* these works would never have seen the light of day.[42] However, given that

---

[37] W. Hindmarch, *A Treatise on the Law Relating to Patent Privileges* (1846), 228.

[38] W. Hindmarch, *Observations on the Defects of the Patents Laws of this Country: With Suggestions for the Reform of them* (London: W. Benning and Co., 1851), 23. 'A work of the imagination, whether in literature or the fine arts, such as a poem, a piece of music, a painting, or a piece of sculpture, is actually created by its author, and he gives to the world that which in all probability never would be produced by any other mind. But he who invents a new practical manufacturing art, although the art may be of greater utility than any product of the imagination, does but find out that which had previous existence, in the same way as travellers discover new countries or places': *ibid.* See also J. Rogers, 'On the Rationale and Working of the Patent Laws' (1863), 125.

[39] 'Literary and artistic copyright has for its province visible, tangible works, intended only for the eye, or the ear or inner man through the eye – objects to be looked upon, listened to, thought of; not things to be worked with or employed, nor things consumable, nor new modes of doing a thing, like the subject of a patent right. It has no regard to processes, operations, implements. Therefore, unlike patent right, it interferes not with manufactures, artisans, miners, farmers, shipping. Its sphere is in finished productions, works of art in their completed state – objects that are permanent and unmistakable': R. Macfie, 'The Patent Question' (1863), 821–2.

[40] The possibility of concurrent invention was recognised in the case law earlier in the century. For example see *Ex parte Dyer* (1812) 1 HPC 555; *Forsyth v Riviere* (1819) 1 HPC 785.

[41] 'The Copyright Question' (1841–2), 49 *Quarterly Review* 206–7.

[42] W. Hindmarch, *Observations on the Defects of the Patents Laws* (1851), 23.

scientific discoveries were pre-existing and waiting to be revealed, if Watt had not invented his famous Steam Engine, someone else would eventually have done so.[43]

While the attempts to abolish the patent system were ultimately unsuccessful, they helped to transform the legal image of the invention. In particular over the middle period of the nineteenth century the invention changed from being seen as the unique creation of an individual to a discovery which could be unearthed by any number of inventors.[44] The fact that the juridical view of the invention was recast as a form of discovery, rather than as a unique creation of an individual, had a number of important consequences for intellectual property law. Of particular importance, it was no longer possible to use the amount of mental labour embodied in objects as a basis by which to distinguish the different forms of intellectual property law. Importantly, these changes not only rendered redundant the quantity of mental labour embodied within objects as a way of organising the categories, they also provided the basis for its replacement. More specifically the contrast between the non-creative image of the invention which took hold in law in the second half of the nineteenth century and the belief in more creative endeavours of copyright and design served as a new basis from which the categories of intellectual property law were distinguished. As we will see, while property was still used as the basis to explain the shape that the legal categories took, somewhat paradoxically there was a shift away from *quantitative* examinations of the intangible property towards more *qualitative* examinations. Moreover, while previously the explanatory narratives had tended to operate at a very general level, focusing as they did on the nature of the property protected, the new modes of organisation revealed themselves in more specific situations. These were the manner in which the intangible property was identified, the nature of infringement and the scope of the property protected.

---

[43] Sergeant Talfourd (25 April 1838) 42 *Hansard* col. 565. Carpmael argued that a clear distinction existed 'between the discovery of one of nature's laws, and its application to some new and useful purpose'. In so doing he evoked the style of argument popularised by Locke that 'every man is proprietor of the fruits of his labour; and that to whatever extent he may have impressed additional values on any given thing by the work of his own hands to that extent, at least, he should be held owner of it': W. Carpmael, 'The Law of Patents for Inventions: Part III' (1835) 3 *Repertory of Patent Inventions*, 243.

[44] It is interesting to note in this context Kohler's comment that 'men of science do not create; they simply *reveal* the facts of nature. The scientist may lead us to a *terra incognita*; in so doing he does not become an "author"': J. Kohler, *Autorrecht, eine zivilistische Abhandlung* (1880). Quoted in P. Bernt Hugenholtz, 'Protection of Compilations of Facts in Germany and the Netherlands' in (eds.) E. Dommering and P. Hugenholtz, *Protecting Works of Fact: Copyright, Freedom of Expression and Information Law* (Deventer: Kluwer, 1991), 59.

As we saw earlier, in pre-modern intellectual property law it was presumed that as the law only protected creative (mental) labour, the protected subject matter was presumed to be always unique (and thus identifiable). With the invention coming to be seen as a non-creative discovery the argument that it was possible to identify the scope of the intangible property from the invention itself was undermined: as discoveries merely involved the unearthing of pre-existing ideas, they were said to involve no creative effort or contribution on behalf of the inventor. Given that inventors made no contribution to the final shape the invention took, it could no longer be argued that inventors left their mark or trace on their inventions in the way authors left their marks on their books. More specifically, the fact that inventors failed to stamp their style or expression on the invention or contribute any mental labour to it meant that it was not possible to identify either the inventor (via his mark) or the scope of the invention (similarly by the unique mark that always remained with the intangible) from the object in which the intangible was embodied. These problems were reinforced by the fact that while the unique and individual nature of literary and artistic works meant that they could be readily identified and distinguished, the same was not the case with the patented invention.[45] Given that those things which belonged to the province of patent right were said to be 'in their nature capable of being independently discovered or originated, in the same identical form, by a plurality of persons',[46] it was often not only very difficult to distinguish between different inventions, but it was also often virtually impossible to identify the nature of intangible property.[47]

In response to the growing belief that it was not possible to identify the intangible property from the invention itself, patent law came to rely on other methods of identification: notably upon the process of registration. As Hindmarch said, if inventions were to be identified, 'they must be defined by written specification'.[48] While the language used to describe the patent specification – which was seen as condensing the

---

[45] W. Hindmarch, *Observations on the Defects of the Patents Laws* (1851), 26. 'A painter needs no registration, his work is inimitable': T. Turner, *Remarks on the Amendment of the Law of Patents* (1851), 60.

[46] 'Such, indeed, are as a rule, actually discovered or invented by several persons, and this very often almost simultaneously. It is otherwise with things that belong to the province of copyright – literary and artistic combinations, books, pictures, musical compositions, involving any degree of elaboration. Such, at no interval of time, has ever been produced by even one other person except by a copyist': R. Macfie, 'The Patent Question' (1863), 821. See also Sir W. Armstrong, 1864 *Report on Letters Patent for Inventions* 69.

[47] W. Hindmarch, *Observations on the Defects of the Patents Laws* (1851), 26.

[48] *Ibid.*

'spirit of man' and thus making it transferable[49] – was similar to that used in relation to copyright, the fact that different modes of identification were employed provided an important point of contrast between the two categories of law.

The difference between patents and copyright created by the different modes of identification was further enhanced by the fact that even if the law had chosen to use registration as a means of identifying the copyright work, this was said to have been excluded by the nature of the work protected. While it was possible to reduce the intangible property embodied in a machine to paper, it was said to have been impossible to capture the essence of literary and artistic works: 'who can give a *specification* for the making of an "Inferno"? If any one undertakes to do so, it will not be a Dante, but a Dennis.'[50]

The fact that the inventions were discovered whereas the subject matter of copyright (and designs) were created also had an impact on the way infringement was determined. As Palmer said to the 1871 Select Committee on Letters Patent, 'the doctrine of infringement ... is limited according to the nature of the work'.[51] What Palmer was alluding to here was that the unique nature of literary and artistic works: if two works were the same, they must have been copied from each other. While 'two or more writers may contemporaneously chance upon similar ideas and equivalent expressions; they may even develop the same fundamental conception, but they cannot without copying one from the other, produce books that are the same'.[52] Perhaps most

---

[49] In the specification of the mechanical invention, 'the spirit of the man [is] condensed and made transferable, so that whoever comprehends the specification stands henceforth to the invention, as a thing of practical use, in precisely the same relation as to the inventor': 'The Copyright Question' (1841–2), 206–7.

[50] *Ibid.* Presumably this is John Dennis (1657–1734), poet and critic, perhaps most famous for having been indicated by Swift, Theobald and Pope, and described as a 'horrible poet'.

[51] R. Palmer, 1871 *Report from the Select Committee on Letters Patent* 1871, 690.

[52] 'The Law of Patents' (April 1865) *Edinburgh Review* 588. '[A] book is the simple creation of a man; it is a thing essentially unique which by no possibility any two minds can arrive at in exactly the same way, and, therefore, it is essentially a creation; and not only does it differ in its nature in that respect, but it differs in the result. You have never any difficulty whatever in identifying the thing; and you do not, by protecting any man's book, place fetters upon or limits upon the practical use of knowledge whatever, which other men previously possessed, or stop or impede their progress from one step in knowledge to another ... it being certain that no two minds in the world could have produced the same book'. As a result, 'the doctrine of infringement in these cases is limited according to the nature of the work. Unless it were plain that a man had used the scissors on my dictionary, or whatever it was, and have copied from it wholesale, he is not an infringer ... But inventions are discoveries of something which is not the creation of the discoverer's mind; they are the result of the pursuit of common knowledge, for an end to which the laws of nature are simultaneously directing a number of minds, the whole result depending, not on the actual combinations, and permutations of an individual man's ideas, but on that which is the common intellectual

interestingly of all, it was suggested that, as literary and artistic works always emanated from particular individuals and, as such, there was no chance that two people could independently create the same product, if two works were the same one person must have 'slavishly or meanly' copied the work of another.[53]

The manner in which copyright was infringed is in marked contrast to the way infringement was perceived in relation to patents. This difference can be attributed to the fact that the nature of the subject matter which was protected by patents, which was thought to be different from that protected by copyright, dictated the scope of the property interest (and the way in which patents could be infringed). Unlike the situation with copyright, where if two works were the same the law could be certain that one had been copied, the non-unique nature of the patented invention meant that it was difficult to determine whether an invention had been copied. It also meant that in contrast to the copying of a work protected by copyright, a patent could be infringed unconsciously and unwittingly.[54] The upshot of this was that if a property right was granted in machines, the nature of the invention meant that this would necessarily be an absolute right. As with copyright infringement, where the nature of the subject matter meant that if two works were the same there must have been copying, similarly with patents: the nature of the invention meant that if property rights were granted, they would necessarily have been 'monopolistic'. As such, copyright and patents were distinguished by the way infringement was able to occur, with copyright being limited to copying whereas patents extended to include independent creations.[55]

property of the whole world': R. Palmer, 1871 *Report from the Select Committee on Letters Patent* 690.

[53] R. Macfie, 'The Patent Question' (1863), 821.

[54] 'This ground for differential treatment is connected with others. In particular, the literary or artistic compositions of one person are perfectly distinguishable from those of every other. Hence the copyright privilege is conceded in the absolute certainty that the grantee is their true and only originator or first producer or creator. No second person can come forward, after the copyright privilege has been secured to an author or artist, and allege that the poem or picture he composed also ... Patent right, on the contrary, may be infringed when there is no such exactness, and no copying whatever, but complete originality. Disregarding form, it forbids the embodiment and use of ideas, even of ideas entirely one's own ... Infringements, therefore are necessarily both manifest and of set purposes, whereas infringements of patent right are often doubtful, even when the subjects or results can be exhibited, and when the facts of the case are assented to by all parties; and if it is a question of processes, its infringements are often undetectable after the fleeting moment during which they are alleged to have taken place. Further, as before said, contraventions of patent right may be, and not infrequently are, done unconsciously and unwittingly': R. Macfie, 'The Patent Question' (1863), 821–2.

[55] 'The author in short monopolises nothing but what was made his own by the form he has given to it, which no other mind would have produced with precise similarity. The patentee on the contrary, acquires a monopoly of a thing which it is in the highest

Another important difference between patents and copyright which arose from the fact that patents came to be seen as discoveries rather than creations related to the way in which the scope of the property was perceived. As we saw earlier, the fact that property in mental labour, which included literary property and patents, was only granted for the way in which creators expressed themselves served to restrict the scope of the property. This was because by limiting the property right to the unique expression of its creator, the law did not place fetters upon or limit the practical use of common knowledge; all that it restricted, so the argument went, was the unauthorised use of the creator's unique labour. With the invention being reconfigured as a discovery rather than as a creation, as it had been earlier, the situation was to change. As inventions were now seen as the discovery of pre-existing common ideas, any property rights which were granted would necessarily exclude others from use of the public domain. The upshot of this was, as Macfie said, that there was an 'obvious and broad distinction between copyright and patent right, that to grant exclusive privileges to an author interfered with the compositions of no one else, whereas the granting of them to an inventor continually conflicted with what others had done and were doing'.[56] To use the language now employed in intellectual property law, while copyright was granted for expression and not ideas, patents restricted the use which could be made of ideas (there being no longer any possibility of a scientific expression). In turn, these changes impacted on the way patents were justified. In place of the arguments which relied on the creation or production of labour as the basis for justifying the grant of patent monopoly, increased reliance was placed on the idea of the patent as a contract between inventor and the state. More specifically it was said that the consideration provided by inventors, which warranted the grant of such restrictive rights, stemmed from the fact that they were the first to *communicate* to the public the knowledge of the art which they discovered.[57]

degree probable that others have produced before him, or about the same time. Having the same laws of nature to deal with, the same information from books and scientific discoveries, handling the same materials and the same tools, surrounded by the same facts and analogies, and supplying the same demand, it cannot be otherwise than that many persons should make the same inventions and improvements': 'The Law of Patents' (1865), 588.

[56] R. Macfie, quoted in 'Miscellaneous' (1865) *TNAPSS* 261.

[57] '[O]nly imaginative artists were true creators; the patentee was rewarded for communicating knowledge of the art which he has discovered to the public': W. Hindmarch, *Observations on the Defects of the Patents Laws* (1851), 23. As a result of these changes patents were (again) seen as a form of state regulation. For example, as Macfie said, a material thing 'is visible, tangible, localised, definite, individual, unique. He sees it, can watch it, can defend it. It is entirely under his control. It cannot be mistaken by anybody else as his own.' Importantly this meant that 'independently of law and police,

Given the formative nature of intellectual property law in the middle period of the nineteenth century, the difference between the creative subject matter protected by copyright (and designs) and the non-creative image of the patented invention played an important role in reinforcing and, in so doing, constituting the categories of intellectual property law. Despite this their impact was short-lived. This was because, as we will see, over the second half of the nineteenth century creativity and mental labour were virtually to disappear from intellectual property law. Having said this, two points from this somewhat transient period are clear. First, it highlights the continued role played by intangible property in shaping intellectual property law: albeit that property was now evaluated according to qualitative rather than quantitative criteria. Secondly, while present-day textbooks usually present the presence or absence of registration and the duration or the form of protection (notably whether the property takes the form of a monopoly or a more limited right to copy) as the basis from which the different areas of intellectual property are distinguished, it is noteworthy that in the nineteenth century they played no role whatsoever. At best these factors were, like the categories themselves, dependent on the image of the property protected.

the owner of a farm can, by fencing, keep out intruders – of a house or goods, by bolts and locks, frustrate burglars – of a purse, by weapons, the highwayman; and he does so righteously, and without question or challenge'. In contrast an invention, which is an immaterial form of property, 'is not visible, defined, individual. It is not localised or confined to particular places. It cannot be hedged about, or put under the charge of watchmen ... And [the owner of the invention] cannot ... by his own act secure his property. He must invoke external, State aid': R. Macfie, *The Patent Question under Free Trade: A Solution of Difficulties by Abolishing or Shortening the Invention Monopoly and Instituting National Recompense* (2nd edn) (London: W. J. Johnson, 1863), 12.

Part 4

Transformations in intellectual property law

While the second half of the nineteenth century was primarily a period of consolidation and entrenchment of the intellectual property law which had taken shape by the 1850s, it was also a period of transformation. Some of the changes which took place over this period were the inevitable consequence of the translation of aspiration into practice, while others came about as a result of the spread of ideas and techniques, such as the system of registration developed in the context of designs, to other areas of intellectual property law. Beyond the transformations which were produced by the processes of refinement and completion, a number of other important changes took place.

One set of changes, which we explore in chapter 8, relate to the nature of the relationship between the categories, that is to the way the categories were organised. Another important change was in terms of the way intangible property was perceived. In particular, while creativity and mental labour had long played a central role in various aspects of intellectual property law, over the second half of the nineteenth century the law shifted its attention away from these concepts to concentrate more on the object of protection itself. After charting the shift from 'creation' to 'object' in chapter 9, in chapter 10 we focus on the way intangible property was managed. In so doing we highlight not only the important role played by the registration system in the closure of intangible property, but also the positive role which registration played in managing intangible property. Towards the end of chapter 10 we look at some of the consequences that flowed from the closure of the subject matter, notably in terms of the way intellectual property law was explained and justified, as well as the role closure played in facilitating the gradual inclusion of trade marks into the rubric of intellectual property law. We thereby further draw attention to the interconnectedness of intangible property and the categories of intellectual property law. Although the nineteenth century saw the displacement of creativity and mental labour from the prominent position they had occupied in pre-modern intellectual property law, we end chapter 10 by arguing that although displaced, that creativity continues to play an important, albeit changed, role in modern intellectual property law.

In the final chapter we focus on the fact that at the same time as intellectual property law emerged as a separate and distinct area of law it also developed a series of stories by which the law was explained and justified. These narratives also played an important role in constituting and reinforcing the law. While a number of different narratives took shape alongside the emergence of modern intellectual property law, we focus firstly upon the narratives which explained the origins of intellectual property law; secondly upon those stories which spoke about the purity and insularity of British law; and, finally on the organisational narratives which prioritised theory and principle in explaining intellectual property law. While these narratives dealt primarily with the history of intellectual property law, they also played an important role in shaping its future.

8   Changes in the framework

Industrial property law

As modern intellectual property law emerged in the 1850s, patents, designs and copyright law were given more or less equal weighting. By the 1880s, however, there was an important change in the way the categories were organised. In particular, there was a growing tendency to divide intellectual property law into two classes: into copyright, on the one hand, and industrial property (designs, patents and increasingly trade marks) on the other.[1] While it was sometimes asserted that industrial property was an alien (typically French) concept,[2] it had important precedents in British law. In particular, it could be seen as continuing the short-lived trend towards a Law of Arts and Manufacture which took place in the 1830s. The separation of copyright from the other categories of intellectual property also reflected the idea that copyright was for art and not trade.

Although the idea of industrial property had antecedents in the early history of the subject, it took on a more prominent and influential role in the later half of the nineteenth century. As well as quickly becoming an accepted part of the legal language[3] and shaping the way bibliographies

---

[1] One interesting exception to this was the calls in the 1870s for a Mental Property Act. See W. Bridge Adams, 'Patent Laws' (21 Jan. 1871) 19 *Journal of the Society of Arts* 187 and 'Proposed Bill for the Protection of Mental Property' (21 Oct. 1870) 18 *Journal of the Society of Arts* 186.

[2] In France, the term 'intellectual property ... is divided into literary and artistic property on the one hand, and industrial property on the other. The first of these corresponds almost exactly with what is called in England copyright, except that copyright in designs intended for manufacturing and industrial purposes would come under the head of industrial property. The French classification has made its way over the continent of Europe and is not without influence in this country also because it is observed in the international treaties upon the subject': J. Iselin, 'The Protection of Industrial Property' (18 Feb. 1898) 46 *Journal of the Society of Arts* 293.

[3] See, e.g., 'Title to Sue for the Protection of Industrial Property' (1892) 36 *Solicitors' Journal* 213.

were organised,[4] the industrial property–copyright bifurcation also played an important role in the realignment of the administrative infrastructure of intellectual property law. In particular, it was an important factor in the consolidation of designs, trade marks and patents under the authority of the Comptroller of Patents: a process which began in 1875[5] and was completed with the passage of the 1883 Patents Designs and Trade Marks Act.[6] The division of intellectual property into two domains was reinforced by international developments: notably the passage in the 1880s of the (1883) Paris Convention – industrial property – and the (1886) Berne Convention – literary and artistic works.

Even as these changes were occurring, moves were taking place which prompted and ultimately undermined the industrial property logic. After a brief period in which industrial property acted as a key organising concept, the early part of the twentieth century saw a return to the relative autonomy that had prevailed between the categories in the middle part of the century.[7] The shift away from what was increasingly seen as the 'purely artificial'[8] idea of industrial property was typified by the 1899 Trade Marks Bill which set out to dissociate trade marks from patents and designs.[9]

---

[4] For example, intellectual property books were classified in terms of industrial property (patents, designs and trade marks) and literary, artistic and industrial copyright: HMSO, *Subject List of Works* (1900), 5.

[5] The shift of the Designs Office to the Patent Office and the transfer of the registration of designs from the Board of Trade to the Commissioners of Patents in 1875 led to the closer association of designs with trade marks and patents. On this see L. Edmunds, *The Law of Copyright in Designs* (London: Sweet and Maxwell, 1895), 10–11.

[6] 46 & 47 Vict. c. 57 (1883). See 'The Proposed Legislation as to Designs and Trade Marks: Part III' (12 May 1883) 27 *Solicitors' Journal* 465.

[7] 'One of the most important resolutions passed' at the 1878 Industrial Property Congress 'was to the effect that the rights acquired by patents or the registration of designs and trade marks in different countries, should be independent of each other, and in no respect interdependent, as is now the case in many countries': W. Lloyd Wise, 'Patent Law' (19 Nov. 1880) 29 *Journal of the Society of Arts* 18. See also E. Jackson, 'The Law of Trade Marks' (19 May 1899) 47 *Journal of the Society of Arts* 566; 1888 *Report of the Committee Appointed by the Board of Trade to Inquire into the Duties, Organisation and Arrangements of the Patent Office so far as Relates to Trade Marks and Designs* 37 (chaired by Lord Hershell).

[8] L. Edmunds and H. Bentwich, *The Law of Copyright in Designs* (London: Sweet and Maxwell, 1908), 12.

[9] This ultimately resulted in their separation in the 1905 Trade Marks Act (5 Edw. VII c. 15 (1905)) and 1907 Patents and Designs Act (7 Edw. VII c. 29 (1907)). The preamble to the 1905 Trade Marks Act said that one of its objects was to dissociate the law relating to trade marks from the Acts relating to designs and patents. The 1903 Trade Marks Bill also begins: 'Whereas it is desirable to amend and consolidate the law relating to trade marks, and to disassociate the law relating thereto from the Acts relating to patents and designs now in force . . .'

The denigration of design

Although at a formal level the industrial property–copyright distinction was relatively short-lived, it continued to play an important role in shaping aspects of intellectual property law. The distinction between industrial property and copyright helped to perpetuate the idea that copyright was for art while the other more technical and commercial areas of intellectual property were reserved for those of a more pedantic and technical frame of mind. It also had a lasting impact on the way in which the categories were organised; particularly on the relationship between design law and other categories of intellectual property law.[10]

Whereas design law had earlier acted as a role model in the formation of the other areas of intellectual property law, by the 1870s the relationship had been reversed. While design law was the first area of intellectual property law to mature into its modern form, by the 1870s it had come to take on its now familiar second-class status: an idea which took shape in the historically inaccurate claim that design was the 'stepchild' of patent and copyright law.[11] The denigration of the legal status of design was reinforced by the movement of designs to the Patent Office and the growing belief that design was less important than technology, fine art or literature, an idea which grew throughout the nineteenth century.

Hand in hand with the changing status of design law was the increased attention given to the relationship between designs and copyright. The potential for overlap between the two categories existed for many years. For example, the possibility for overlap between engravings and designs arose as early as 1787, between sculpture and designs from 1839,[12] and between drawings and designs from 1862.[13] Despite this, the question of overlap between designs and copyright was rarely discussed. The first edition of Lewis Edmunds' influential work on design law published in 1895, for example, makes no mention of any overlap between copyright and designs. By the time of the second edition of Edmunds' work in

---

[10] As the editor of the 5th edition of Copinger said, the 'previous editions of this work included the law as to copyright in designs. The law as to designs has, for many years, parted company with the law as to copyright in literary and artistic works, and ... the editor decided to omit the portion of the work relating to copyright in designs from the present edition': *Copinger on Copyright* (5th edn) (ed. J. Easton) (London: Stevens, 1915).

[11] Ladas described industrial designs as 'poor relations in the family group of industrial property': S. Ladas, *Patents, Trademarks and Related Rights*, vol. II (Cambridge, Mass.: Harvard University Press, 1975), 828. Design protection has also been described as a 'neglected child – a younger and less considered brother of those better known individuals, patents and copyright': W. Wallace, 'Protection for Designs in the United Kingdom' (1975) 22 *Bulletin of the Copyright Society of the USA* 437.

[12] The 1842 Ornamental Designs Act *excluded* sculpture from its remit.

[13] 1862 Fine Art Copyright Act.

1908, however, the issue of the overlap between design protection and that offered by artistic copyright, and how this was to be managed, had become a key question for consideration. In part this was a result of the gradual move which occurred in copyright law away from subject-specific definitions of subject matter towards more abstract formulae.[14] Perhaps the most important explanation for the growing concern with the overlap between the two categories, which had not arisen before, can be traced to the proposal, ultimately effected in 1911, that copyright protection, which had long been conditional on registration,[15] was made automatic. The reason for this was that the introduction of automatic copyright protection radically altered the stakes between design and copyright protection: one involving cost and delay, the other offering automatic, free protection. Given this, it is easy to see why the overlap between the two categories suddenly became an issue for the law.[16]

While in answering this problem some consideration was given to following the lead offered by France, Germany, and several British Colonies (New South Wales, South Australia, Victoria, New Zealand and India)[17] whereby designs were treated as works of fine art, ultimately a division was drawn between the two categories of designs and copyright. This was premised on the idea that a distinction could and should be drawn between the two classes of works.[18] On the one hand there were those articles which were said to be 'unique specimens [which] only differ from other works of fine art in having an obvious practical use; a typical example would be a Benvenuto Cellini cup'. On the other hand, there

---

[14] One possible explanation for this was that the relative advantages of copyright protection over that offered by design was not that great. For example, in order to gain copyright protection in drawings, it was necessary to register them at Stationers' Hall. Even when this was done, a work was only protected against the multiplication of copies of the work. Given that it was not clear whether copying on a manufactured artefact would be covered, there seemed little reason to incur the expense of registering twice.

[15] A notable exception being sculpture copyright.

[16] The Textile Designs Committee reported of the probability of 'an attempt being made to treat designs for industrial purposes on the same lines as purely artistic and literary productions': 'New Textiles Designs Committee' (1910) 21 (19) *The Manchester Chamber of Commerce Monthly Record* 265.

[17] Board of Trade Notes on Memorandum of Artistic Copyright Society, 28 Nov. 1910, BT/209/477. For example, under the New Zealand 1877 Works of Art Act works of art included 'useful or ornamental designs' alongside painting, drawing, sculpture etc. See *Correspondence Respecting the International Copyright Conferences at Berne*, vol. II, no. 60 (1887) FO/544/1.

[18] While it was clear that artistic works included works of fine art, there was uncertainty as to whether it included items such as Wedgwood teacups. See, e.g., E. Cutler, 1899 *Report from the Select Committee of the House of Lords on the Copyright Bill (HL) and the Copyright (Artistic) Bill (HL)* 150. Cutler said that he was unable to suggest any definition which could fix and adjust cases on the border line (185). This situation was exacerbated by the fusion of ornamental and non-ornamental design in 1883.

were those more functional articles which were 'intended for indefinite multiplication, such as those which now come under the Designs Act'.[19] While there were many who believed there to be a fundamental difference between pure and applied art,[20] those who worked at the Registry, who would have had to implement this schema, were well aware of the problems that drawing such a 'theoretical distinction' would have generated.[21] Despite the problematic and controversial nature of the fine art–designs dichotomy, ultimately these problems were overridden by commercial considerations.[22] More specifically, the decision to treat designs and artistic works as separate regimes was based on the fear that copyright protection for works of applied art would at best seriously affect and at worst render largely inoperative the registration of designs.[23] These concerns were taken up in the 1911 Copyright Act which distinguished between those designs which were intended 'to be unique' and 'not to be multiplied', which were to be given full copyright

[19] BT/209/835. 'The fundamental distinction between a "design" and a simple "artistic work" lies, it is thought, in the applicability of the former to another article; that is to say, an artistic work is bought purely and simply for its artistic properties: an article to which a design has been applied is bought not simply because of the artistic qualities of the design, but because of the utility of the article apart from the design': *Copinger on Copyright* (1915), 97.

[20] For example, see 'The Law of Copyright and Designs' (31 Jan. 1911) 22 (1) *The Manchester Chamber of Commerce Monthly Record* 4.

[21] Temple Franks (Comptroller-General of Patents) openly acknowledged that 'while it would be controversial to draw a distinction between works of pure art and designs, ... ultimately these problems were outweighed by "commercial" considerations': L. Temple Franks, 4 March 1910, BT/209/835.

[22] 'The Protection Afforded to Artistic Designs' (30 June 1910) *The Manchester Chamber of Commerce Monthly Record* 165 (letter sent to Temple Franks). It was also said that giving designs copyright protection would have been 'disastrous to manufacturing industries, and extremely disadvantageous to designers': 'New Textiles Designs Committee' (1910), 265. In relation to the 1912 *Designs Rules* (*Thirtieth Report of the Comptroller General of Patents, Designs and Trade Marks for the year 1912* at 17 of the Report) which ensured that designs were not to be included within the 1911 Copyright Act, the Secretary of the Manchester Chamber of Commerce, W. Speakman, said in an open letter to the Board of Trade that the rules 'appear to carry out fully what it is desired by this Chamber, viz., that designs for textiles should not come within the purview of or be controlled by the Copyright Act 1911': W. Speakman, 'Copyright Act: Designs' (31 May 1912) 23 (5) *Manchester Chamber of Commerce Monthly Record* 142.

[23] 'It was considered that the grant of full copyright to designs intended to be multiplied by an industrial process would destroy the efficacy of the Patents and Designs Acts, which are regarded as valuable by the manufacturers which use designs (e.g. calico printers). It was therefore decided to exclude such design if registrable under the Patents and Designs Acts from the Bill': Board of Trade Notes on Memorandum of Artistic Copyright Society, 28 Nov. 1910, BT/209/477. The Textile Designs Committee reported that 'as a result of the Chamber's representations, a clause has been inserted in the [1911 Copyright] Bill as follows: "That this Act shall not apply to designs capable of registration under the Patents and Designs Act, 1907"': 'The Copyright Bill' (30 Sept. 1911) 22 (9) *The Manchester Chamber of Commerce Monthly Record* 259.

protection, and manufactured items such as mass-produced door furniture, bell pushes and grates which were to be protected by design law.[24]

In many ways the overlap between designs and copyright was similar to that which existed between designs and patents, but there was one important difference: while the potential for overlap between designs and patents was managed bureaucratically, given the decision that copyright protection should be available automatically and without formality from creation of the work, this option was not available as a way of policing the boundaries between copyright and designs. Faced with this difficulty, in order to draw a workable boundary between the two categories the law opted for a mixture of administrative and legal rules. The subsequent history of this area, where the preoccupation of many commentators has been with the overlap between (artistic) copyright and industrial design protection, attests not only to the relative failure of these techniques but also to the accuracy of the warning by Comptroller-General of Patents Temple Franks about the difficulties that the introduction of such a distinction would create.

Trade marks as a form of intellectual property

When modern intellectual property law first took shape in the 1850s, or thereabouts, trade mark law was not recognised or indeed even considered as a possible candidate for inclusion. This is unsurprising given that modern trade mark law, as we understand it today, did not really exist at the time.[25] Rather the law – which consisted of statutes such as the 1863 Exhibitions Medals Act[26] and offered protection for things such as needle labels and marks for use on cutlery[27] – remained subject specific and reactionary; in short, pre-modern. Moreover, the nature of the law in the middle part of the century was dilatory and chaotic. Indeed as Joseph Travers Smith, a leading trade marks solicitor of the time, said, 'trade marks are not recognised as having any legal validity or

---

[24] Board of Trade Notes on Memorandum of Artistic Copyright Society, 28 Nov. 1910, BT/209/477.

[25] Although the courts did provide protection for 'common law marks'.

[26] In the discussion following a paper by W. Wybrow Robertson this was described 'to a certain extent as a trade marks bill': 'On Trade Marks' (23 April 1869) 17 *Journal of the Society of Arts* 418.

[27] Other examples of the pre-modern nature of the law include A Bill to Amend the Law Relating to the Counterfeiting or Fraudulent Use or Appropriation of Trade Marks, and to Secure to Proprietors of Trade Marks in Certain Cases the Benefit of International Protection (1862) 5 *PP* (Bill no. 17); A Bill to Oblige Printers of Linen to Mark their Names on Linens Printed by them (24 March 1831) 2 *PP*. On 'police marks' or 'liability marks' see F. Schechter, *The Historical Foundations of the Law Relating to Trade Marks* (New York: Columbia University Press, 1925), 38–77.

effect ... there is no written law on the subject of trade marks, and we have consequently no definition by which we can try what a trade mark is, nor consequently what particular symbol amounts to a trade mark, and ... the existing law gives no remedy against an actual pirate, but only against the person who fraudulently uses a trade mark'.[28]

Despite the uncertain and (at least to our modern eyes) somewhat alien nature of the law in this area, over the second half of the nineteenth century trade mark law came to take shape as a discrete and recognised area of law. A number of factors provided the impetus for the crystallisation of modern trade mark law. In part, growing recognition and use of marks in commercial practice led to increased specialisation in this field. In turn this heightened the calls for recognition of trade marks as a separate area of law[29] and for the introduction of a registration system for marks.[30] These changes were reinforced by the fact that a distinct domain for trade marks was slowly carved out at common law.[31]

The move to establish bilateral treaties with European countries, which was prompted by the growing importance of foreign markets to certain sectors of British industry,[32] also played an important role in the move from subject-specific, localised laws to an abstract, forward-looking law. While the bilateral treaties were said to be declaratory of the common law,[33] typically these treaties led to changes in the existing law. This is because although the existing law was chaotic and unwieldy, the mere act of preparing for and entering into negotiations required that the law be set out in more detail.[34] As Ryland said, 'it may be thought

---

[28] Joseph Travers Smith, 1862 *Select Committee on Trade Marks* 119 (Q. 2619).

[29] 'The cases which have been decided upon the law of trade-marks ... are so numerous and additions growing so rapidly that the branch of the law is fast becoming one of large proportions': 'The Law of Trade Marks' (18 Jan. 1879) 2 *The Legal News* 25.

[30] While trade mark registration was not introduced until 1875, moves towards such a system had been made in the preceding decades.

[31] E.g., *Batt and Co.* v *Dunnett* (1899) 16 RPC 413, where Lord Halsbury said, the 'Law of Trade-Marks are [*sic*] not for copyright in marks; they are to protect trade-marks'. It was also said that 'the law has gradually developed by a course of judicial decisions giving authoritative sanction to practices current in the mercantile world': H. Ludlow and H. Jenkins, *A Treatise on the Law of Trade-Marks and Trade Names* (London: William Maxwell and Son, 1877), 1.

[32] 'Unless we have some arrangements with Prussia we can have no protection in that country. We want the freest and fullest freedom of trade': John Jobson Smith, 1862 *Select Committee on Trade Marks* 55 (Q. 1138).

[33] *Ibid.*, 54 (Q. 1132).

[34] As a result of question from Switzerland as to the nature of the law in the UK, the Board of Trade was forced to outline 'everything relating to the property in manufacturing or trade marks, individual design or patterns, or manufacturing of any kind': May 1877, BT/22/18/9. It was said that one of the problems in implementing trade mark agreements arose from fact that there was no common definition of what a trade mark was in the United Kingdom: 1888 *Patent Office Inquiry* para. 40, xiv.

more satisfactory, both to the British minister who has to negotiate a convention with a foreign state, and also to a minister of that state, to be able to refer to a simple, explicit, and complete statement of our laws, as contained in an Act of Parliament, rather than to a library of law reports'.[35] Given that the bilateral treaties were based on the principle of reciprocity, before they could be completed it was necessary to ensure that there was some degree of equivalence between the legal regimes of the parties to the agreement.[36] These treaties placed pressure on Britain to clarify the nature and limits of the law[37] and also to make specific changes: perhaps most importantly the introduction of a trade marks register. As the influential Sheffield Chamber of Commerce said, 'it is important to the interests of merchants and manufacturers that measures should be taken to remove the obstacles now existing in British subjects obtaining redress in the continental courts for the piracy of manufacturers' names and marks'.[38] The need to demarcate the law in a more precise fashion than had hitherto been the case was picked up on in the 1862 Merchandise Marks Act[39] which provided a detailed definition of a mark. While this definition proved problematic (and was not followed in later legislation), the mere act of setting out to define what a mark was played an important role in constituting the limits of modern trade marks law.[40]

At the same time as trade mark law was taking on its now familiar shape there was growing pressure for it to be included within the framework of intellectual property law.[41] The pressure for inclusion came from a number of different sources. For many, factors such as

---

[35] A. Ryland, 'The Fraudulent Imitation of Trade Marks' (1859) *TNAPSS* 230.

[36] In many cases registration would be beneficial and 'invaluable, in cases of foreign manufacturers whose trade mark may not be known in the English market; and in the case of comparatively new manufactures': Joseph Travers Smith, 1862 *Select Committee on Trade Marks* 121 (Q. 2655).

[37] As a result of a treaty of commerce and navigation between Britain and Russia, the UK was said to be under an obligation to alter its law of trade marks. 'It was understood that [article 20 of the treaty] required [the UK] to alter our law and make it more effective than it was at that time for the protection of trade marks': evidence given by T. Gibson, 1862 *Select Committee on Trade Marks* 151 (Q. 3119).

[38] John Jobson Smith (reading from the minutes of the Sheffield Chamber of Commerce Annual Meeting, 1860), 1862 *Select Committee on Trade Marks* 54 (Q. 1132).

[39] An Act to Amend the Law Relating to the Fraudulent marking of Merchandise 25 & 26 Vict. c. 88 (1862).

[40] In 1859 Ryland conducted a study of comparative trade marks law (at that time registration existed in France, Russia, Belgium and Prussia) and suggested the establishment of a register: A. Ryland, 'The Fraudulent Imitation of Trade Marks' (1859), 235.

[41] E. Lloyd, 'On the Law of Trade Marks' (11 May 1861) 5 *Solicitors' Journal* 486.

shared professional bodies (patents and trade mark agents),[42] the nature and form of international treaties,[43] and the logic of industrial property made the connection between trade marks and designs and patents an obvious choice.[44] Indeed, as trade mark law was in the process of formulation, patents, designs and copyright law provided an important point of analogy: for the existence of the right;[45] as an aid to interpreting trade mark doctrine;[46] for the shape the system of registration should take;[47] and the language and structure to be used in trade mark legislation. Another point of connection which existed between trade marks and copyright and design was that they dealt with similar subject matter. At its most extreme it was suggested that a trade mark, like a work subject to copyright and design right, embodied the personality of its creator. As John Smith reported to the 1862 Select Committee on Trade Marks, 'I consider a trade mark to be equivalent to a man's signature to a letter. There may be hundreds of John Smiths, but there would be such an individuality in each man's signature, that you could identify the whole. I consider that when a man puts a mark upon any article he produces to identify it as his production, that it is equivalent to his name.'[48]

[42] James Wann, of an 'advertising agency', gave evidence that he did both trade mark and patent work. They were akin because 'they are dealt with in the same Act; the Patents, Designs and Trade Marks act, and the two professions are constantly overlapping': J. Wann, 1894 *Special Report from the Select Committee on the Patent Agents' Bill* 247 (Q. 2221). 'The consolidation of the Act has had this effect in the minds of the public, that they are not able quite to distinguish the difference between a patent agent and a trade mark agent': *ibid.* See also the evidence of Lack, the Comptroller-General for Patents: *ibid.*, 142 (Q. 2515). On the link between professional ties and registration see J. Bougon, *The Inventor's Vade Mecum: Memorandum on the Laws Effecting the Patents of every Country* (London: Reeves and Turner, 1870), 27.

[43] In the international bilateral agreements, or treaties of commerce, it was commonplace to link marks, designs and models. See, for example, Foreign Office, *Treaty Stipulation between Great Britain and Foreign Powers on the Subject of Trade Marks* (London: Harrison and Sons, 1872), C 633. Most foreign laws treated designs and trade marks distinctly. One exception was the *Portuguese Law of 10 Dec. 1852*, which dealt with trade marks (Art. 296–7) and also with designs and models (Art. 298). On this see Foreign Office, *Reports Relating to the Foreign Countries on the Subject of Trade Marks* (London: Harrison and Sons, 1872), C 596, 57.

[44] H. Trueman Wood, 'The Registration of Trade Marks' (26 Nov. 1875) 24 *Journal of the Society of Arts* 17–18.

[45] A. Ryland, 1862 *Select Committee on Trade Marks* 36 (Q. 745–6).

[46] L. Edmunds, *The Law of Copyright in Designs* (1895), 11. See also C. Drewry, *The Law of Trade Marks* (London: Knight and Co., 1878), 35.

[47] The Designs Register and the Acts which regulated it were used as the model for trade mark registration. See, e.g., 1862 *Select Committee on Trade Marks* 38 (Q. 787–9).

[48] J. J. Smith, 1862 *Select Committee on Trade Marks* 58 (Q. 1210). A trade mark is the 'commercial substitute for one's autograph': *Leidersdorf* v *Flint* (1878) F Cas 260, quoted in H. Toulmin, 'Protection of Industrial Property: Monopolies Granted by Governments' (1915) 3 *Virginia Law Review* 172.

Another practice which helped to reinforce the association between trade marks and intellectual property law arose from the pragmatic actions of trade mark proprietors who, in the absence of a specific, tailor-made register for marks, utilised the pre-existing arrangements for copyright and designs. As well as the quasi-official registration of newspaper titles and labels as books at the Stationers' Company,[49] manufacturers also made use of the Design Register to gain protection for their marks as designs by, for example, registering labels as designs.[50] The association between trade marks and copyright was reinforced by the fact that the pictorial nature of the trade mark also suggested a link with artistic copyright.[51]

While there were many points shared in common between trade marks and the then existing categories of intellectual property law, there were a number of objections to trade marks being accepted as a part of intellectual property law. Indeed, two primary reasons were given as to why trade marks should not be and for a while were not included within the remit of intellectual property law.

The first objection to treating trade marks as a species of intellectual property turned on the issue of creativity.[52] While the rights granted by design, patents and copyright could be excused (and justified) because they were only granted for new creations (and as such nothing was therefore being taken away from the public), this was not the case with

[49] See *Maxwell* v *Hogg* (1867) 2 Ch App 307; *Kelly* v *Hutton* (1868) LR 3 Ch 708; *Chappell* v *Sheard* (1855) 69 ER 717; *Chappell* v *Davidson* (1855) 69 ER 719; C. Drewry, *The Law of Trade Marks* (1878); R. Bartlet, 1862 *Select Committee on Trade Marks* 48 (Q. 1037). A large number of proprietors of trade marks sought to protect their marks by their quasi-official registration at Stationers' Hall 'as artistic designs or as printed matter, according to the predominance of the pictorial or literary element': H. Trueman Wood, 'The Registration of Trade Marks' (1875) , 21–2. Wood reported that since the passing of the 1862 Trade Marks Act the authorities of the Stationers' Company had refused to register anything ostensibly a trade mark.

[50] On the registration of labels as designs see section 9, 1843 Utility Designs Act. For examples of registration of labels as designs under the 1839 Act see Reg. nos. 455, 577, 607, 645, 682, 686, 700, 706.

[51] Early Trade Mark Bills contained provisions to prevent the forging, imitation and false application of the names or marks of artists with intent to defraud. See, e.g., cl. 7, 1862 Merchandise Marks Act.

[52] British commentators were aware of the American decision of *Leidersdorf* v *Flint* (1878) (15 F Cas 260) which held that the constitution of the US did not authorise legislation by Congress on trade marks (except as had been used in commerce with foreign nations or with Indian tribes), basically because of the non-creative nature of trade marks. As Bugbee said in relation to this decision, 'it is therefore necessary that the subjects of patents and copyright involve originality of a higher and more creative order than that associated with trademarks, and that they confer on the public greater benefits than the mere identification of the origin of a commercial product': B. Bugbee, *The Genesis of American Patent and Copyright Law* (Washington, D.C.: Public Affairs Press, 1967), 6. It seems that this was not an impetus so much as support for the idea that trade marks fell outside the remit of intellectual property law in the United Kingdom.

trade marks which in many cases dealt with pre-existing subject matter.[53] Hindmarch, who drafted the Government Bill in 1862, and who was consistently opposed both to allowing assignment of marks separately from goodwill and to treating trade marks as property, captured the tone of these arguments when he said:

> I have heard persons refer to the law of patents, and the law of design, as parallel cases; but there is nothing parallel there. A man who comes and takes a patent gives a consideration for the grant he obtains, and so with a man who comes and registers a design, he acquires a copyright of a limited character, never exceeding three years; he also gives some consideration; there is something new, which the world knows nothing about, and in consideration of that the copyright is given; but in this case, in which it is proposed to give a copyright in a trade mark, there is no consideration ... it would be to create a ... monopoly totally and entirely unknown to law ... and, as I conceive, contrary to the spirit of the great statute against monopolies.[54]

The upshot of this was, as Hindmarch said in another context, that 'copyright in books and designs is a totally different thing [from that of trade marks] because there is a property created'. With trade marks, however, 'we create nothing new, but provide only a new mode of defending the right that we acknowledge'.[55]

The second reason why trade marks were considered to fall outside the intellectual property rubric was that whereas copyright, patents and designs were primarily concerned with the creation and protection of property, trade marks were more concerned with forgery or fraud.[56] While there were arguments to the contrary,[57] the consensus of opinion

---

[53] H. Dircks, *Statistics of Inventions Illustrating the Policy of a Patent Law* (London: E. and F. Spon, 1869), 16.

[54] W. Hindmarch, 1862 *Select Committee on Trade Marks* 129 (Q. 2772).

[55] Question from M. Gibson to Hindmarch, 1862 *Select Committee on Trade Marks* 142 (Q. 2984). A trade mark 'although partaking to some extent of the nature of the monopoly, differs essentially from copyright. Copyright refers to and is intended to protect the *substance* of a production, whether of a literary or artistic nature, while a trade mark protects the *identification* of an article, and of itself in no way affects the production or sale of a similar article by a third person': J. Slater, *The Law Relating to Copyright* (1884), 230; L. Sebastian, *The Law of Trade Marks and their Registration, and Matters Connected therewith* (London: Stevens and Sons, 1878), 10–11.

[56] See, e.g., A. Ryland, 'The Fraudulent Imitation of Trade Marks' (1859), 229; J. Travers Smith, 1862 *Select Committee on Trade Marks* 126 (Q. 2727). See also *Chappell* v *Sheard* (1855) 2 69 ER 717; *Chappell* v *Davidson* (1855) 69 ER 719. In 1860 trade marks were incorporated in A Bill Intituled an Act to Consolidate and Amend the Statute Law of England and Ireland Relating to Indictable Offences by Forgery. On this see 'Forgery of Trade Marks' (11 May 1860) 158 *Hansard* col. 1086.

[57] Kerly said that *Millington* v *Fox* (1838) 40 ER 956 (which held that an injunction could be obtained to restrain infringement of a trade mark) led to the 'obvious deduction, to the establishment of a right of property in trade-marks': D. Kerly, *The Law of Trade-Marks, Trade Names, and Merchandise Marks* (2nd edn) (London: Sweet and Maxwell, 1901), 4. See also J. Smith, 1862 *Select Committee on Trade Marks* 56 (Q. 1156).

was that in 'the existing state of the law a trade mark is clearly no property at all'.[58] Rather, as Macfie said, the object of trade mark legislation 'is to prevent the criminal use of a name or distinguishing indication, in fact to counteract falsification or forgery, which would not only deprive traders of a reputation they have laboured for, but would mislead the public'.[59] Campin was clearer as to the distinction when he said, 'it should be remembered that there was this important difference between patents and trade marks, that copying or infringing the latter was really analogous to forgery, while the infringement of a patent was merely interfering with a private right of property'.[60] Combined together, the facts that trade marks dealt with pre-existing subject matter rather than the creation of new material and that they were more concerned with regulating fraud than property, meant that trade marks were said to fall outside the scope of intellectual property law.

[58] 'In the case of patents and copyright there is a species of property defined by a statutory limitation; but in the case of trade-marks such a definition is to be sought only in the decisions of our courts of law and equity, and there is some difficulty in reconciling the various propositions that have from time to time been laid down in these courts, with the recognition by them of a common principle of interference': E. Lloyd, 'On the Law of Trade Marks' (11 May 1861), 486. See also Joseph Travers Smith, 1862 *Select Committee on Trade Marks* 122 (Q. 2655).

[59] R. Macfie (ed.), *Copyright and Patents for Inventions*, vol. II (1883), 52. 'When you confer a power upon any person to bring an action against another for libel there is hardly a right given; it is a remedy rather': W. Hindmarch, 1862 *Select Committee on Trade Marks* 129 (Q. 2987).

[60] Campin, in discussion on the paper delivered by H. Trueman Wood, 'The Registration of Trade Marks' (1875), 28. 'The origin and nature of the legal right to protection in the use of a trade-mark is to be ascertained from the species of remedy given for its violation. This remedy is an action on the case for deceit, so that the unauthorised use of a trade-mark is obviously deemed to be a fraud': E. Lloyd, 'On the Law of Trade Marks' (11 May 1861), 486. See also L. Sebastian, *The Law of Trade Marks and their Registration and Matters Connected therewith* (2nd edn) (London: Stevens and Sons, 1884), 15.

9   From creation to object

As we have seen at various stages in this work, one of the defining features of intellectual property law in the eighteenth and the first half of the nineteenth century was its concern with mental labour and creativity. While the juridical categories operated in a middle ground that oscillated between action and thing, nonetheless the primary focus of the law remained upon the process of creativity. One of the key features of pre-modern intellectual property law was that it assumed that authors, inventors or designers were the bearers of an innate, autonomous will which was somehow pre-social and pre-legal. It was this will, or mental labour, that the law set out to protect and promote. As well as shaping the way the categories were organised and the boundaries drawn, mental (or creative) labour also influenced the duration, scope and nature of the property. It is not too far from the truth to suggest that mental labour was the most influential organising principle of pre-modern intellectual property law.

Despite the prominent role played by mental labour in pre-modern intellectual property law, by the later part of the nineteenth century the law had shifted its attention away from mental labour and creativity to concentrate more upon the object itself. As the move away from creativity which first began in patent law in the 1860s gradually made its way into and dominated all areas of intellectual property law, the types of arguments which had circulated in the eighteenth and nineteenth centuries began to be discredited. Rather than concentrating on the mental labour embodied in say a work or an invention, the focus of the law fell on works or inventions as entities in their own right. More specifically, instead of concentrating upon the quality of the knowledge embodied within the object or, as was the case earlier, the amount of labour contained within the object, the law came to focus more upon the subject matter as a closed and secure entity. That is, the law moved its focus away from the labour used to create, for example, a book or a machine, to focus, instead, on the book or machine itself. More accurately, the law turned its attention away from the value of the labour

173

embodied in the protected subject matter, to the value of the object itself: to the contribution that the particular object made to the reading public, the economy and so on.

While, in its dealing with intangible property, pre-modern intellectual property law utilised the language of classical jurisprudence, modern intellectual property law tended to rely more on using the language and concepts of political economy and utilitarianism.[1] Therefore, instead of attempting to recreate (or locate) the traces of creativity located in the work, the law came to focus on the trace that the work itself left behind.[2] In these circumstances, what became important was not the labour or creativity embodied within a work but the contribution, typically judged in economic or quasi-economic terms, that the work made.[3] That is, rather than valuing the labour embodied within a particular object, the law came to focus on the macro-economic value of the object; on the contribution it made to learning and progress or, as we would now say, GNP or productivity. Sir James Fitzjames Stephen went so far as to suggest to the 1878 Royal Commission on Copyright that the market should be used to determine whether intangible property ought to be recognised at all. In situations where an original work had a sensible market value (such as with a picture, a statue or a building) he suggested that it should not attract copyright protection. Where the single original work had no market value (as with a book), however, he argued that it should have copyright.[4] As economic arguments became more prominent and as commentators increasingly spoke of intellectual property as a mode of rewarding inventors, as a way of exciting ingenuity and encouraging individuals to exert their talents, the now familiar investment theory began to dominate discussions of intellectual property law.

The nature of these changes was highlighted by Thomas Scrutton in the introduction to his classic work on copyright law written in 1883. Speaking of the period up until the middle of the nineteenth century, he said that any attempt to 'reduce to principle the laws dealing with Copyright, or the similar laws of Patents and Trade-marks ... would naturally commence with an investigation of the nature of the property'.

[1] Lord Belper summed up the nature of the change when he argued that 'an inventor possessed no natural or original right to a monopoly of his invention, and ... the existence of patents could be defended only on the ground of public utility': 'Patents for Inventions Bill' (26 Feb. 1875) 122 *Hansard* col. 926.

[2] Cf. S. Dentith, 'Political Economy, Fiction and the Language of Practical Ideology in Nineteenth-century England' (1983) 8 *Social History* 186.

[3] This was most notable in the increased attention given to the question of the compulsory working of patents (particularly those taken out by foreigners) which dominated debate in the later part of the nineteenth century.

[4] 1878 *Report of the Royal Commissioners on Copyright of 1878* vii–lvii. See also T. Farrer, 'The Principle of Copyright' (1878) 851.

Such an inquiry would 'at once lead the student into what has been called the "realm of legal metaphysics"'. Although this mode of inquiry had once been virtually obligatory, questioning the nature of intangible property in terms of the mental labour it embodied was now said to be 'as fruitful in controversy and as fruitless in proportionate results as that other realm where ignorant armies clash by night: over the debatable fields in Phaenomena and Noumena, destiny and Free Will'.[5] While the nature of the intangible, and the mental labour it embodied, had long played a central role in intellectual property law, like so many others at the time Scrutton felt excused from these forms of inquiry: he was hinting here that what had once been of central importance to intellectual property law (viz., the nature of intangible property) was now regarded as vague, tiresome and irrelevant.[6]

Scrutton also highlighted the related belief, which was increasingly widespread, that the status of intangible property had been clarified and that the law had resolved the types of problems that the opponents of literary property had identified in granting property status to the intangible. As he said, 'Fortunately, however, the necessity for this general preliminary investigation is obviated by the fact that practical agreement prevails amongst modern jurists as to the answer to be obtained'.[7] By deferring to the authority of political economy and utilitarianism,[8] which were 'almost universally accepted not only as the test of legislation but also as offering a scientific foundation for the art of legislation', it was no longer necessary to engage in metaphysical inquiries into the meaning and nature of intangible property.

With the closure of the subject matter in the latter part of the nineteenth century, intangible property was re-conceptualised so that it became detached from naturalistic explanations, from matters of nature,

---

[5] T. Scrutton, *The Laws of Copyright* (1883), 2–3.

[6] In a similar vein, Farrer suggested that *Millar* v *Taylor*, *Donaldson* v *Becket* and *Jefferys* v *Boosey* were 'purely historical', 'far-fetched legal analogies': T. Farrer, 'The Principle of Copyright' (1878), 842–3.

[7] T. Scrutton, *The Laws of Copyright* (1883), 2–3. Lord Granville was even clearer as to the nature of the change, the closure of property, when he said that 'Mr Bramwell, the ablest defender of patent right, although he does not distinctly abandon the ground of property, entirely lays it aside in his argument': 'Patents for Inventions Bill' (26 Feb. 1875) 122 *Hansard* col. 916.

[8] Citing Maine to the effect that the principle of utility might be the only clear rule of reform, Scrutton said that 'Utilitarian formulae are almost universally accepted not only as the test of legislation, but also as offering a scientific foundation for the art of legislation.' Utilitarianism was also said to provided the 'groundwork of the science and art of legislation and ... therefore the justification of any particular law, the reason by which it justifies its enactment': T. Scrutton, *The Laws of Copyright* (1883), 3–4. In this context it is interesting to note Bentham's comments on the literary property debate (which was conducted without the benefit of utilitarianism). See above, p. 9, note 2.

divinity and metaphysics.[9] As the language of classical jurisprudence was replaced by the language of political economy and utilitarianism, mental labour, so important in conceptualising intangible property over the previous century or so, disappeared from view (although, as we shall argue, not in the way some claim).[10] Creations – the work, design and the invention – were thus not only radically detached from their creators, they also acquired a degree of juridical autonomy they had not previously experienced.[11] As mental labour and creativity disappeared from the law's horizon, one of the last remaining traits of the *ancien régime* was swept away: intellectual property law moved one step closer towards its modern form.

As well as being reinforced by the moves towards legal science and positivism that took place at the time,[12] the closure of intangible property and the associated shift away from mental labour and creativity which took place over the course of the second half of the nineteenth century was influenced by two specific factors: the growing fear of judgment and the spread of the modern registration system. We will now consider each of these in turn.

A fear of judgment

The changing fate of intangible property was in part a product of the shifts which took place in law over the course of the nineteenth century towards the nature of judgment. While in its pre-modern guise the law had been more than willing to differentiate between different works on the basis of their quality, and to exclude what it regarded as trivial or

---

[9] A. Pottage, 'Autonomy of Property' (1991), 14.

[10] Cf. B. Edelman, 'Une loi substantiellement internationale. La Loi du 3 juillet sur les droits d'auteur et droits voisins' (1987) 114 *Journal de droit international* 567–8; J. Bergeron, 'From Property to Contract: Political Economy and the Transformation of Value in English Common Law' (1993) 2 *Social and Legal Studies* 13.

[11] Coryton, when explaining the way in which his treatise on patent law was organised, said that while the inventor had played a central role in patent law in the past, in his present work the 'person of the Patentee becomes in comparison with [the invention] a subordinate idea': J. Coryton, *A Treatise on the Law of Letters-Patent* (1855), iv. Coryton's work included selected remarks from leading writers on Political Economy, which he said led to a change in conviction as to the principles on which legislation should be based. The move from creator to creation was not only reflected in what was taken to be problematic and therefore in need of reform, but also had a direct impact on substantive law. For example, in reflection of the shift from 'men of ingenuity' to the 'men of capital', the 1883 Patents, Designs and Trade Marks Act allowed not only inventors but also investors to be patentees. See W. Lawson, *Patents, Designs and Trade Marks Practice* (London: Butterworths, 1884), ix.

[12] Scrutton explicitly drew upon the work of Austin to argue that all rights 'in the strict sense of the word, result from the command of the Sovereign, and have no existence prior to such command': T. Scrutton, *The Laws of Copyright* (1883), 4.

undeserving, over time the law grew wary of such evaluative processes. If we take the case of patents, there were many situations in the eighteenth and first half of the nineteenth centuries where the law explicitly passed judgment as to the quality of inventions and where it tried to exclude from its ambit what were seen as non-deserving creations such as the kaleidoscope. For example, in order for the duration of a patent to be extended, under the Privy Council Rules it was necessary for an applicant to show that the invention was meritorious but unrewarded.[13] Concern with the quality of the inventions protected as patents perhaps reached its peak with the introduction of the requirement that before a patent could be granted, applicants had to be able to produce a declaration that the invention was 'of great public Utility'.[14] In turn, much of the discussion about the reform of patent law at the time attempted to ensure that only inventions of appropriate quality were patented. While present-day commentators tend to be obsessed with the number of patents (design or trade marks) registered, during much of the nineteenth century it was the quality of what was registered that mattered most. Indeed, the multiplication of patents was seen as an evil that needed to be avoided.[15] To this end, attention was given to increasing the cost of registration[16] and to the introduction of an examination system as ways of ensuring that inventions of a trivial or

[13] Prior to 1835, patents were prolonged only as a result of special Acts of Parliament. After Lord Brougham's Act of 1835, however, this process was taken away from Parliament and conducted on the basis of Privy Council Rules: John Waggett, *The Law and Practice Relating to the Prolongation of the Terms of Letters Patent for Inventions* (London: Butterworths, 1887).

[14] See, e.g., Schedule of 1852 Patent Law Amendment Act. On the use of a test of utility as a way of ensuring that useful rather than absurd or trifling inventions were protected by patent law, see Attorney-General (5 Aug. 1851) 118 *Hansard* col. 1876. More generally see G. Armstrong, 'From the Fetishism of Commodities to the Regulated Market: The Rise and Decline of Property' (1987) 82 *Northwestern University Law Review* 79.

[15] The evil arising from the multiplication of patents (not inventions) was said to be twofold. First, 'that of the existence of a number of Patents for alleged inventions of a trivial nature; and in the second place, that of the granting of Patents for inventions which are either old or practically useless, and are employed by the patentees only to embarrass rival manufactures': 1864 *Report on Letters Patent for Inventions* i.

[16] 'The granting of letters-patent ought to be accompanied with conditions strict enough to discourage worthless and impracticable schemes ... It cannot be expected that the law-officers of the Crown, whose time is fully occupied with professional and official duties, can make a searching investigation into the originality or utility of any invention. [Without] the moderate charges now imposed on patentees, amounting altogether, where the patent is held for the full period of fourteen years, to between £150 and £200, the country would be deluged with sham inventions, more mischievous to the interests of the people than if all exclusive proprietary rights in inventions were taken away': Society for Promoting Amendment of the Law: *Annual Report 1860–1* (1861), 8–9. As Webster said, 'the high cost of patenting acted as a check upon the multiplication of patents': T. Webster, 1851 *Select Committee on Patents* 23. See also

undeserving nature were not patented.[17] A similar number of examples of the law engaging in such qualitative evaluations took place with copyright and designs.

Despite the willingness of the law to evaluate the protected subject matter, questions began to be asked during the middle part of the nineteenth century as to whether it was appropriate for the law to engage in such speculative activities. What began as doubts about the appropriateness of these activities grew over time into a fear of judgment and a fear about making qualitative decisions more generally. Rather than attempting to decide whether a pattern was aesthetically pleasing or a particular invention valuable, as the law had so willingly done in the past, it was argued that the law should defer from making decisions of this sort completely. Intellectual property law thus came to echo modernism's fear of being tainted by politics, morality and judgment.[18]

In pre-modern intellectual property law, the wisdom and experience that were regarded as an integral part of the common law mind had equipped judges and lawyers with the faith to evaluate and pass judgment on the protected subject matter.[19] Over the course of the second half of the nineteenth century, however, a crisis of faith developed as to law's ability to engage in such modes of inquiry. The Master of the Rolls, Lord Langdale, summed up these changes when he said in 1851,

I cannot imagine any way in which you can distinguish good inventions from bad ones; I have heard of so many inventions which had been looked on as perfectly wild and ridiculous, which have turned out afterwards to be most advantageous to the public; and on the contrary I have known many which have looked as if they were going to do very great wonders and would be of the greatest public service, which have turned out to be empty bubbles; so that I really think it would be almost impossible for any tribunal to distinguish a good invention from a bad one.[20]

1864 *Report on Letters Patent for Inventions* v; W. Fairburn, 1851 *Select Committee on Patents* 433.

[17] See T. Webster, *ibid.*, 23.

[18] A. Huyssen, *After the Great Divide* (Bloomington: Indiana University Press, 1986), vii. The fear of contamination has remained an important feature of contemporary intellectual property law. For example see Australian Law Reform Commission, *Designs: Issues Paper 11* (Sydney: ALRC, 1993), 35.

[19] This also impacted on the way duration was evaluated. 'A sound copyright law will grant a term which is adequate for the protection of the best works of all classes; only the best need be considered, for no others will survive the shortest term of copyright ... On the other hand it should not differentiate between the various classes; for who would be so bold as to arbitrate upon the relative merits of art, literature and the drama ?': 'Copyright Law Reform' (1910), 489–90.

[20] Question asked of Lord Longdale, Master of the Rolls and Solicitor-General, 1851 *Select Committee on Patents* 655. This fear of judgment was one of the reasons why examination was not taken seriously until early in the twentieth century when the

One of the reasons for this change in attitude was the growing belief that the law was ill equipped to engage in subjective and qualitative decision-making. A particular difficulty that the law faced was that it was not in position to judge in advance the worth or value of say a book, a machine or an ornament, at least when these objects were judged in terms of their quality.[21] These problems were bolstered by *laissez-faire* arguments which attacked the idea that lay behind qualitative judgment: namely, that the law should intervene in and attempt to regulate behaviour.[22] In a period in which the law was under attack from the likes of Macaulay and Dickens, all was done to ensure that it was not brought into further disrepute.

Given that the only secure means by which the value of a book or a machine could be judged was retrospectively,[23] an option usually not open to the law, the law's response was to avoid such modes of questioning in the first place. That is, rather than leaving itself open to the charge of having rejected a work on the basis that it was non-meritorious, and later being proved wrong, the law responded to these envisaged difficulties by attempting to distance itself from judgment. In short, it opted for a form of aesthetic and technical agnosticism. More-over instead of the law passing judgment on the quality of particular subject matter, such evaluative decisions were left to entities such as the public and the market.[24]

expert-examiner was considered competent to decide upon the nature of the invention, design or mark. See J. Greene (4 Aug. 1851) 118 *Hansard* cols. 1848–50.

[21] These problems were exacerbated by the fact that it was impossible for 'even the most penetrating minds to foresee in the early stages of an invention, what will be its qualities and boundaries when ultimately brought into a state of practical utility': C. Drewry, *Observations on Points Relating to the Amendment of the Law of Letters Patent* (London: John Richards and Co., 1839), 7. As Kenrick noted long before , 'If I do not mistake, no less than seven and twenty years passed before Sir Isaac Newton's *Principia* came to a second edition: and ... that when Lord Bacon published his Philosophical Treaties, they were so little understood that they were deemed literary lumber': W. Kenrick, *An Address* (1774), 8–9. If the quality of such works were not recognised when they were first published, what hope did the law have ?

[22] The law's earlier attempts – based on the principles of *laissez-faire*, recently championed by the political economists – to regulate taste, morality, industry, honesty and public opinion were the subject of mockery: J. Coryton, *A Treatise on the Law of Letters-Patent* (1855), 17.

[23] '[N]othing but subsequent experience can afford an adequate test of the utility or inutility of an invention': Lord Overstone, 1864 *Report on Letters Patent for Inventions* 85.

[24] 'The spirit of our institutions is to leave the public the utmost latitude for judging itself upon the questions of merit; and it may, therefore, be concluded that there are no sufficient reasons for making the questions of merit any ground to refuse acknowl-edgment of the rights of invention ... upon the intrinsic merits of an invention the public at large are the best and only judges': Society of Arts: Extracts from the First Report on the Rights of Inventors, 1851 *Select Committee on Patents* Appendix C.

These calls for the subject matter of intellectual property law to be presented in a more stable and closed manner were reinforced by the growing demands for intellectual property to be placed in a form so that it could be rendered calculable. The problem with this, however, was that labour and creation were not readily susceptible to quantification. The particular difficulty which the law faced in rendering pre-modern intangible property calculable was that as the work of a lifetime could be concentrated into a page of mathematical symbols, there was no measure of the amount of labour.[25] With the move away from the labour embodied in the creation towards the object itself, however, these difficulties were resolved: while it was difficult to place labour in a form for it to be calculated, the closed work and the contribution that it made to the economy could be calculated.[26]

Registration and the closure of intangible property

One of the most important explanations for the move away from creativity and mental labour towards a closed subject matter can be traced to the gradual expansion of the modern system of registration to all forms of intellectual property: a process which not only led to the closure of the intangible property and the related exclusion of creativity from the law's immediate concern, but also played a positive role in influencing the shape that intangible property took. It is important to note that while registration played a less consistent role in relation to the subject matter of copyright law than it did with designs, trade marks and patents, nonetheless in one capacity or another registration existed as a prerequisite for full protection for most forms of copyright.[27] Moreover there was widespread and consistent support for making registration a prerequisite for the protection of all forms of copyright[28] – at least until 1911 when formalities were abolished.

---

[25] T. Turner, *On Copyright in Design* (1849), 32.

[26] See J. Waggett, *Law and Practice Relating to the Prolongation* (1887).

[27] This situation was summed up thus: 'other singular distinctions exist as to the law relating to registration of copyrights. No system of registration is provided for dramatic copyright, or for copyright in lectures or engravings. Such a system is provided for copyright in books and paintings, but its effect varies. Registration must in either case precede the taking of legal proceedings for an infringement of copyright, but after registration the owner of copyright in any book may, while the owner of a copyright in a painting may not, sue the persons who infringed his copyright': 1878 *Report of the Royal Commissioners on Copyright*, para. 11.

[28] The Committee of the Jurisprudence Department of the Social Science Association reported that 'registration of copyright in works of all classes published in the United Kingdom, and in dramatic or musical works first performed in the UK ... should be compulsory'. The Committee also recommended that registration be effected at a government office: 'Copyright' (25 March 1881) 29 *Journal of the Society of Arts* 418.

As the system of registration spread to new areas, it took with it many of the main features of bureaucratic property identified earlier.[29] For example, facilitated by improvements in post and transport and the trend towards centralisation of government, there was a move away from locating offices in regional centres towards centralised registries based in London.[30] This was particularly evident in the case of patents which saw the move away from local registers such as those at Edinburgh and Dublin[31] to a single Registry located in London. Another feature shared by the new systems of registration was the manner and circumstances in which proof was manufactured. In the same way in which the production of proof shifted from calico printers to the Design Office, over the second half of the nineteenth century there was a growing expectation that proof, and bureaucratic property more generally, ought to be a matter for public rather than private control. As a result, there was a shift away from private, guild-style modes of regulating evidential issues – such as existed at the Stationers' Hall[32] and the Cutlers' Company at Sheffield – towards institutions which were publicly funded and organised.

The modern system of registration which took shape over the second half of the nineteenth century played an important role in the closure of intangible property and the related move away from creativity in law: one of the features of the expanded registration system was that it ensured that intangible property was placed in a format which was stable yet indefinitely repeatable. Added to this was the fact that registration, particularly as it was refined and rationalised, led to more defined patterns of standardisation, and thereby ensured that the docu-

---

[29] See ch. 2.

[30] In relation to the question as to whether the registrars and courts should be centrally located it was said 'it would be a great deal better for the metropolis ... if every particular trade should have [a registrar or] Board something like that of the Cutlers' Company in Sheffield; I think they would be better able to decide upon marks than a general registrar': G. Wilkinson, 1862 *Select Committee on Trade Marks* 85 (Q. 1769).

[31] There were however a number of exceptions. For example, as well as the London-based Registry, a second Designs Registry, which was supervised by the Keeper of Cotton Marks, was established at Manchester in 1907: Section 62 (4) 1907 Patents and Designs Act, Rules 80–8, Design Rules. On this see the *25th Report of the Comptroller-General of Patents, Designs and Trade Marks for the year 1907* (1908) 25 *PP* 13.

[32] On the status of the Registrar as a public official see A. Moffat, 'The Copyright Bill' (1898) 10 *Juridical Review*, 166. The 1898 Copyright Bill proposed, as did the Commissioners of Copyright in 1878, to set up new Registration Offices (the Stationers' Company was however considered sufficient for the Bill). The gradual adoption of a centralised registration process marked an important change in trade marks. In particular it saw a shift from protection of specific industries (or areas) to protection of more abstract legal categories.

ments which it produced could be trusted and relied upon.[33] Once it was settled that the registration system, its agents and, most importantly, the documents that it produced could be trusted, it was no longer necessary to look beyond the surface of the document: the paper inscription became an end in itself. As the patent specification, the trade mark and the design document came to be treated as ends in themselves, the invention, the trade mark and the design were decontextualised from the environment in which they were produced. The mental labour that played such an important role in the production of the artefact was thus sidelined. By introducing what was in effect a *de facto* form of indefeasibility, registration radically changed the nature of the way the law dealt with intangible property. In so doing it played an important role in the move away from a concern with creativity and mental labour towards a new-found concern with the property as registered.[34] At the same time, the reduction of the intangible property to a paper inscription, which was at the basis of the so-called representative registration,[35] helped to overcome the difficulties of space (which were created by the size of the buildings occupied by the Registry)[36] and distance (generated by the centralisation of the Registers).

Managing the intangible

The expanded and refined systems of registration not only led to the closure of the intangible property: they also played an important role in managing and shaping the limits of that property. The modern system of

---

[33] The benefits of a closed registration process were summed up by Land Registrar Brickdale's comment: 'if you look at the face [of a watch] you can see the time at a glance. If you open the back and look at the machinery, it would puzzle a clever man to guess how it operated, and he would turn with a sigh of relief to an hour glass': Registrar Brickdale, quoted in A. Pottage, 'The Originality of Registration' (1995) 15 *Oxford Journal of Legal Studies* 378.

[34] For example it was said that there 'may be a design, the beauty and utility of which are inseparable, and which may be registered under the Useful or under the Ornamental Designs Acts, but when the registration has been effected and the right in the design is questioned in a suit, the Court can look only at the Act under which the design has been registered': Sir J. Romilly MR, *Windover* v *Smith* (1863) 11 WR 324, quoted in C. Phillips, *The Law of Copyright in Works of Art and in the Application of Designs* (London: Stevens and Haynes, 1863), 238.

[35] Our use of this term differs from the way in which it was used in relation to trade marks where representative registration was introduced to allow manufacturers who used many different, but similar, types of marks to register a representative mark of the class as a whole. On this see *In re Burrows* (1877) 36 LT NS 780; 5 Ch Div 364; 'The Government Patents Bill in its Relation to Trade Marks' (7 April 1883) 74 *The Law Times* 405.

[36] The problem of storage at the Registry was one of the most powerful and consistent arguments used against the supply of models as a prerequisite for protection.

registration thus played a key role in resolving many of the problems the law had experienced in granting property status to the intangible: problems which the opponents of literary property had highlighted in the literary debate nearly a century previously.

In order to appreciate the positive role played by the modern system of registration in shaping intangible property, we need to turn to consider in more detail the raw material with which the expanded system registration worked. While there were some notable exceptions, instead of focusing on the physical object – the machines and fabrics – in which the intangible property was embodied, intellectual property law increasingly came to rely upon written or pictorial representations of the intangible property embodied in those objects.[37] That is, instead of interpreting, for example, a piece of cloth with a design embossed on it (as was necessary under the Calico Printers' Act), applicants were encouraged (and in some situations required) to supply either a written or a pictorial depiction of the object and, in turn, the property claimed.

While registration was a prerequisite for protection for nearly all forms of intellectual property, copyright works were treated differently from the subject matter of other areas of intellectual property. The reason for this was the belief that it was not possible to reduce the subject matter of copyright law beyond the material form in which it existed.[38] More specifically, the non-reductive nature of the copyright

---

[37] There was some confusion in relation to designs. For example, while section 11 of the 1850 Designs Act enabled applicants to furnish drawings or prints representing the design, Hindmarch gives the example of a case in which he was involved where a design had been registered 'and it would have been impossible to have done it by any pictorial representation; and so much has that been found in the case of registered designs, that it was necessary to pass an Act of Parliament ... to get rid of the difficulty; that was the 21 & 22 Vict. c. 70, s. 5 [1858 Copyright of Designs Amendment Act]. Since the passing of that Act, a person may go to the registration office and deposit a piece of cloth or a shawl, and that is to be the registration, and that all arose from the circumstances I have just mentioned. In registration, as originally directed by the Statute, there was nothing but a pictorial description of what the intended design was. Very often the effect of a design has to be produced by a combination of colours in a peculiar way, which could hardly be represented by any drawing, and it is extremely difficult to do it': W. Hindmarch, 1862 *Select Committee on Trade Marks* 143 (Q. 2997). The 1883 Patents, Designs and Trade Marks Act allowed the owner of an original design to leave at the office not 'as now required, an exact copy of the design, but a representation of it sufficient to identify it': Chamberlain (16 April 1883) 278 *Hansard* col. 350.

[38] There were other problems with registration. For example, in relation to musical works Lord Thring, said 'I have omitted the clauses relating to registration. Compulsory registration seems to me to be impossible. One of the great music sellers informed me that he had 20,000 copyrights, and it is obvious that many books especially sheets of music, which are not included under the definition of a book, are of so little value as to make registration of the copyright out of the question': quoted by Lord Monkswell (24 April 1899) 70 *Hansard* col. 359.

work meant that it was not possible to represent the intangible property or to reduce it from the physical format in which it was manifest. Given the belief that it was only ever possible to reproduce the intangible in its complete physical manifestation, this meant that unlike the situation with patents, designs and trade marks where applicants had to describe what it was that they were claiming, in the case of copyright it was the object *itself*, the libretto, the score, or the book, rather than a representation of it, which was deposited at Stationers' Hall.[39]

Despite the widespread nature of these changes, the move towards representative registration and the impact that it had on intellectual property law tended to be ignored. In part this was because intellectual property law drew upon a model of representation that encouraged a form of naturalism: that led participants to conclude, for example, that the representation of a design *was* the design. Moreover, following the lead established earlier, registration tended to be seen primarily as a means of establishing proof of ownership.[40] The preoccupation with the evidential nature of registration can be seen in the context of the 1862 Fine Art Copyright Bill which, as well as introducing copyright protection for the fine arts, also set out to dispense with registration before an action could be brought. In place of registration it proposed 'to invest the author of a work of fine art with the Copyright thereof, upon the simple condition of his *signing* it with his name or monogram.'[41] It is clear that by seeing signature as the equivalent of registration, the drafters of the 1862 Bill considered registration solely in terms of the role it played in manufacturing proof and authenticity: all that registration did was to enable the artist to say, 'Yes, that is my work.'[42]

---

[39] However, section 4 of the 1862 Fine Art Copyright Act required in the case of artworks the 'giving of a short description of the nature and subject of the work'. For discussion of what this involved see *Beal; ex Parte* (1868) 3 QB 387.

[40] 'A registration [of copyright works] is to be nothing more than a record of ownership': 1878 *Report of the Royal Commissioners on Copyright* xxvi, para. 157. See also W. Smith, 1862 *Select Committee on Trade Marks* 26 (Q. 592).

[41] 1861 Bill for Amending Law Relating to Copyright in Works of Fine Art (1861) 1 *PP* 519; 1862 Bill for Amending Law Relating to Copyright in Works of Fine Art (1862) 1 *PP* 485; 1862 Bill for Amending Law Relating to Copyright in Works of Fine Art (as Amended in Select Committee) 1 *PP* 493, sections 5 and 6. See D. Robertson Blaine, *Suggestions on the Copyright (Works of Art) Bill* (London: Robert Hardwicke, 1861), 6.

[42] In his typically astute fashion, Hindmarch was one of the few commentators of the nineteenth century who recognised the changes which were taking place as a result of the move to representative registration. Speaking of the registration of trade marks he said the 'only thing that you could register, or put upon the register, would be a pictorial representation of the intended trade mark; not the trade mark itself, because in nine cases out of ten, the trade mark would be a *materially different* thing from that pictorial representation. A great many marks are embossed, countersunk, or stamped . . . they are produced in hundreds of different ways; and you must, in every case, then reduce the intended trade mark to the shape of a picture.' The consequence of this was

If we turn our attention away from the role registration played in establishing proof of ownership to the means by which registration was carried out, we are led in another, and in many senses a more fruitful, direction: we come to appreciate that, at least in relation to patents, trade marks and designs, registration not only led to the closure of the intangible property, it was also the forum in which what we described earlier as the problems of intangible property came to be played out. In this sense the changes which took place in intellectual property law at the time follow Foucault's observation that judicial institutions have over time been increasingly incorporated into a continuum of apparatuses (medical, administrative and so on) whose functions are for the most part regulatory.[43]

The modern system of registration which took shape over the course of the nineteenth century also played an important role in resolving some of the difficulties that had confronted the law in establishing the *identity* of intangible property. More specifically, as registration offered a process which would produce 'a most valuable record, at any distance of time, of the identity of the work pirated, the time and place of its first publication, and the name of the author',[44] it played a central role in resolving the continuing problem of how the creator and also, and more problematically, the boundaries of the property were to be determined.[45] It did this by shifting the focus of attention and the associated modes of inquiry away from the essence of the property towards the surface of the document.[46] This is because rather than being considered as a poor imitation of the 'true' property – one which was twice removed from the essence of the intangible property – the representation as registered became an end in itself. In the vast bulk of cases, the inscriptions contained in the patent claim, the design document and the trade mark application were all that there was or needed to be. Moreover, it mattered not that they were representations of something else or that they were immensely less than the things they described. As a result

that 'instead of making the right more definite, registration ... would make it less definite or not more definite': W. Hindmarch, 1862 *Select Committee on Trade Marks* 143 (Q. 2997) (emphasis added). While Hindmarch appreciated the impact that representative registration had on intangible property, to see this – as he did – in negative terms is to overlook the positive role it played in intellectual property law.

[43] M. Foucault, *History of Sexuality*, vol. I (tr. R. Hurley) (New York: Pantheon, 1978), 144.
[44] D. Robertson Blaine, *Suggestions on the Copyright (Works of Art) Bill* (1861), 17.
[45] 'Another difficulty, almost peculiar to [property in intellectual labour], is that of identification. The incorporeal, or immaterial element, so to speak, of the manufacture, the book, or the picture, has to be identified under a different form of corporeal or material element in settling the question of differences from two others': T. Webster, 'On the Protection of Property in Intellectual Labour'(1859) *TNAPSS* 238–9.
[46] See I. Brunel, 1851 *Select Committee on Patents* 510.

of the shift towards registration as an end in itself, which prompted and reinforced the closure of the intangible property, there was no fictitious founding entitlement to be retraced or essence to be relocated. In turn this meant that while in granting property status to the intangible the law had long grappled with ways of capturing the essence of the property, suddenly such exercises seemed much less important. The task of identifying the essence of the property and where its boundaries lay, which had proven so problematic in the past, were simply no longer problems that the law had to deal with: they were now resolved bureaucratically. Instead what mattered was the way patent, design and trade mark documents were interpreted. Indeed as Webster reported to the 1851 Select Committee on Patents, nine-tenths of the intellectual property cases at the time turned upon the composition of specifications or written instruments.[47]

By shifting the focus of attention away from the shadowy world of the essence of intangible property, and from creativity and mental labour towards the way in which documents were interpreted, registration also provided, at least in comparison with what had previously been the case, a stable reference point against which the identity of the intangible could be more readily ascertained. Moreover, the fact that the owner had to be named in the application made the task of identifying the owner of the property a relatively straightforward one.

The system of representative registration which developed over the second half of the nineteenth century not only led to the closure of intangible property and the related exclusion of creativity, it also functioned to identify the scope and owner of the property as well as playing an important role in establishing the shape that the intangible property took. In so doing it produced an important change in intellectual property law: as the creativity which had previously been exercised juridically was usurped by the registration process, the mimetic dimension of intellectual property law, namely the positive role that the law played in 'creating' the intangible property, now took place nearly exclusively at the level of administration: in the way documents were drafted, registered and interpreted.

In addition to the direct or indirect control over those who were in a position to draft claims,[48] there was also close monitoring of the content

---

[47] T. Webster, *ibid.*, 23. Consequently, more and more attention was placed on the way the specification should be interpreted. This was particularly the case with the law of patents. In cases involving designs and trade marks, the courts occasionally still looked not just at the representations but also at the design or mark applied to the goods in trade.

[48] The professionalisation of patent agents, which led to the introduction of rules of conduct and educational standards, helped to police the drafting of patent specifica-

of what went into the document to be registered. While there was virtually no stage in the life of a patent claim, a design or a trade mark that was not managed, the extent of regulation differed depending on the subject matter in question. There was for example not the same nicety and accuracy required with a design specification or a trade mark as was required in the specification of a patent.[49] The fact that different areas required different degrees of management corresponded to the complexity of the subject matter in question, with many patents requiring more detailed descriptions than was the case with trade marks and designs. Another explanation for the different degrees of regulation was the distance which existed between the representation and the represented object. While ornamental design was said to be as much the product of genius and the result of composition as the lines of the poet, designs were regarded (at least in this context) as the purest form of intellectual property: with patents and non-ornamental designs there was a gap between the document and the intangible property, whereas with designs (as with pictorial illustrations) 'their form' was said to be 'their essence, and their object the production of pleasure in their contemplation. This is their final end.'[50]

As well as the introduction of requirements that there should only be one creation per application and that specifications ought to define clearly what was claimed, greater controls were placed on the role played by the title to particular applications (which were often used as a shorthand for the creation itself).[51] Moreover, attention was also given to the way applications were drafted – to, if you like, their intelligibility. In the case of patents, for example, the rules developed in 1852 stated that the 'specification ought to define the invention intended to be comprised in a Patent so as to enable any person of ordinary skill and intelligence upon reading it to ascertain without difficulty the nature and extent of the right conferred by the Patent'.[52]

---

tions and in turn the nature of patent property. See F. Campin, 1851 *Select Committee on Patents* 379; W. Spence, *ibid.*, 400.

[49] See Lord Cranworth, *Holdsworth v McCrea* (1867) LR 2 HL 385.

[50] *Baker v Selden* (1879) 101 US 103–4. It seems that the further we get away from the eye as arbiter, the more rules are needed.

[51] See, e.g., section 8, 1852 Patent Law Amendment Act. The title of the invention was to 'point out distinctly and specifically the nature and object of the invention': Rules I–II, third set of rules under Act of 15 & 16 Vict. c. 83, 12 Dec. 1853. It was claimed that one of the earliest situations where titles were used was in 1829 where a person made an affidavit that they had given the patent in question a title: 'It is an improved paddle-wheel': B. Rotch, 1829 *Select Committee on Patents* 116. The title would then act as the basis from which the patent was indexed and interpreted.

[52] While the idea that the specification should only contain one invention was introduced in 1852, it was apparently not enforced by law officers, a situation which was said to have changed under the 1883 Act. See 'New Patents Act' (4 Jan. 1884) 32 *Journal of*

The intangible property recognised as a part of intellectual property law was also constrained by a series of detailed rules which focused upon the minutiae of the documents lodged for registration. For example, the rules enacted by the Commissioners of Patents on 17 May 1876 under the 1852 Patent Law Amendment Act stated that

the drawings to be provided must be on white paper. All lines of the drawing must be absolutely black, Indian ink of the best quality to be used, and the same strength or colour of the ink must be maintained throughout the drawing. Any shading must be in lines, clearly and distinctly drawn, and as open as is consistent with the required effect. Section lines should not be too closely drawn. No colour must be used for any purpose upon this drawing. All letters and figures of reference must be bold and distinct. The border line of the drawing to be one fine line only.

. . . and so on.

By exercising greater control over the way claims were drafted, and by controlling the size of the paper, the margin, and the style, size and scale of the drawings,[53] the law restricted the way the creation was represented and in so doing the scope of the intangible property that was protected.[54] Complaints voiced by applicants at the time attest to the impact these restrictions had on the way claims were drafted.[55]

Another way in which the intangible was constrained came about as a result of the applicants' being placed under an obligation to specify what it was they were claiming.[56] Previously the law had assumed the difficult

---

the *Society of Arts* 121; W. Hindmarch, 1864 *Report on Letters Patent for Inventions* x. In design law, rules developed which required that each specification must be limited to a design and not a multiplicity of designs. See, e.g., *Holdsworth* v *McCrea* (1867) LR 2 HL 381.

[53] For example, the 1843 Utility Designs Act required that the proprietor of the design provide two exactly similar drawing or prints of such design 'on a proper geometric scale' on paper not more than 24″ by 15″ with such description in writing as may be necessary to render the same intelligible and setting forth the parts of the design which were not new or original. See generally M. Rudwick, 'The Emergence of a Visual Language for Geological Sciences: 1760–1840' (1976) 14 *History of Science* 148.

[54] On the need for greater strictness in drawing the specification and claim of the patentees see 1864 *Report on Letters Patent for Inventions* vii.

[55] 'According to the instructions issued by the [Designs] office we are only allowed to show two views of an article. Now I will take this inkstand for instance. Every side of the inkstand might have an ornament on it, or a different design. How can I show that design if I am limited to two views. If I show it in perspective you know that to a certain extent it distorts an object. The part of the inkstand which is further away from me would be smaller than that which is in the foreground': E. de Pass, Fellow of the Institute of Patent Agents, 1888 *Patent Office Inquiry* 81 (Q. 1375). While the problem could have been met by allowing the designer to represent more than two figures, there was still the problem that designers were 'very much limited to space. We sometimes have to draw designs very small, because it is only foolscap size that we are allowed': *ibid.* (Q. 1378).

[56] For example, the 1883 Patents, Designs and Trade Marks Act introduced requirements that no registration was valid unless the application contained a statement as to the

task of having to distil the nature of the intangible property; now, with
the onus placed on applicants to outline what it was they were claiming,
the law's role in identifying the scope and limits of the intangible
property was greatly simplified. Carpmael went so far as to suggest to
the 1851 Select Committee on Patents that 'the law requires that the
patentee shall define to what boundary his invention extends, otherwise
the patent could not have a construction put upon it by judges'.[57] In
case applicants or their agents hoped to use this freedom as an opportunity to extend the scope of their property, the law built into the
registration process a number of self-regulatory devices which further
restricted the scope of what was registered. Whether it was design law
specifying that applicants needed to outline what it was that a design
protected (pattern, shape or configuration)[58] and in turn the purpose
which the shape or configuration was to perform, or patent law requiring
patentees to clearly state the particular purpose or utility that the
invention was to perform, these requirements restricted the scope of the
property. The self-regulatory controls placed upon applicants were
reinforced by the fact that increasingly examiners played a more prominent role in policing applications.[59]

Intangible property was further restricted by the fact that when
applications made their way to the relevant register, they had to be
lodged within a particular class or category. While the impact that the
classes of registration had upon the scope of the property varied as
between different forms of intellectual property (they were more important in design and trade marks than was the case with patents), nonetheless in many cases the ambit of the property was restricted by the
class in which it was registered.[60] This meant that if a design was
registered within the category of designs for glass, for example, it could
be copied in earthenware. While in many ways the classes of registration
employed in the new registries replicated the organisational structures of

---

nature of the design. 'In practice the Patent Office officials do not interfere with claims,
but leave the applicant to make them as he pleases and at his own risk':
H. Cunynghame, *English Patent Practice* (1894), 195. See also J. Imray, 'Claims'
(1887–8), 6 *Proceedings of the Institute of Patent Agents* 203.

[57] 1851 *Select Committee on Patents* 312.

[58] 1883 *First Report of the Comptroller-General of Patents, Designs and Trade Marks* 28 PP 33
(1883 *Design Rules*), no. 9. The consequence of this was that it was left to the applicant
to determine the purpose or object for which the design was to be registered and in so
doing limit the nature of the intangible property.

[59] See, e.g., W. Carpmael, 1864 *Report on Letters Patent for Inventions* 6 (Q. 168).

[60] The 1883 Patents, Designs and Trade Marks Act stated in section 58 that infringement
was to be considered with reference to the particular class or classes in which the design
was registered. The rules on classification established by the Board of Trade under the
Act are to be found in 1883 *First Report of the Comptroller General of Patents, Designs and
Trade Marks* 28 PP, Appendix B, 33 ff.

the industries,[61] we should recognise that a great deal of effort went into the construction of the classificatory schemes and that they played a role in shaping the limits of intangible property.[62]

The registration system also impacted on intangible property in unexpected ways. For example, the decision to exclude colour from the scope of what could be registered as a mark was the result not of principled argument but arose from the practical difficulties in the way trade marks were registered.[63] While the 1875 Trade Marks Act[64] made no mention of colour in relation to registration, the rules were interpreted in such a way that colour was excluded from the remit of what was protectable as a trade mark. The reason for this was that the 8th rule of registration required applicants to supply the Registrar with a description of their trade mark in writing, accompanied where practical by a representation of the trade mark in duplicate. This was then advertised in the *Trade Marks Journal*. However, as was explained by the Master of the Rolls in *In re Robinson*,[65] as applicants were required to furnish the printer with a wood-block or electrotype of the trade-mark, 'the difficulty of advertising was so great, and the difficulty of getting the shade of colour with chromo-lithography was so great, that colour was abandoned simply for practical purposes'.[66]

The controls exercised over the intangible property continued once a

---

[61] While the legal categories shifted from the particular to the abstract, the specific demands of various industries were retained in the registries. The function which had previously been performed by specialised registries (that is of dealing with particular types of marks and designs) was incorporated into the categories of registration.

[62] The way in which the classes were organised impacted on different groups in different ways. For example, the classes used at the Designs Registry tended to favour manufacturers at the expense of designers, because of the practice whereby designers often provided manufacturers with a number of different designs, while manufacturers tended to choose one design for a particular category of goods. Whereas registration of that design for that category would suit the needs of the manufacturer it was often unsatisfactory from the point of view of the designer. For the designer the design was an abstract entity which could be applied to many varieties of goods; registration for one specific category was too limited. See H. Trueman Wood, 'The Registration of Trade Marks' (1875), 25; and 'Trade Marks: Classification' (30 Sept. 1913) 24 (9) *The Manchester Chamber of Commerce Monthly Record* 253.

[63] This was particularly important in relation to cotton marks, the 'whole distinctiveness of which consisted in the colour in which they were represented, [so that] registration in colour was essential ... with respect to such marks it is easy to see that registration by any other mode than by deposit would be futile, as the whole essence of the trade-mark consists in colour': 'Registration of Trade Marks in Colour: Part I' (5 Feb. 1881) 25 *Solicitors' Journal* 255.

[64] 1875 An Act to Establish a Register of Trade Marks 38 & 39 Vict. c. 91 (1875 Trade Marks Act).

[65] (1880) 29 WR 31. Note also *Drewhurst's Application for a Trademark* (1896) 2 Ch 137, 13 RPC 288 (words and pictures); *In re Worthington & Co's Trademark* (1880) 14 Ch D 8; *Hanson* (1887) 37 Ch D 112.

[66] 'Registration of Trade Marks in Colour: Part I' (1881), 255.

claim had successfully made its way through the registration process. As well as being constrained by the rules of procedure as set out in the 1852 Common Law Procedure Act,[67] the way in which the claims were interpreted also played a role in determining the shape that intangible property took. While more expansive readings of the claims would have broadened the scope of what was protected, the courts attempted, at least as a starting point, to restrain the property to the surface of the document as registered. In patents this was done by attempting to confine the patent to the literal wording rather than the equity of the specification.[68] What was protected as a design was restricted by the fact that designs were always interpreted by the unerring judge, the eye,[69] and not by any of the other senses. With trademarks, however, as with musical works in copyright, account was taken of resemblances in sound as well as visual resemblances.[70]

Although representative registration played an important role in shaping intangible property which was protected by patents, designs,

[67] 1852 An Act to Amend the Process, Practice and Mode of Pleading in the Superior Courts of Common Law at Westminster and in the Superior Courts of the Counties Palatine of Lancaster and Durham 15 & 16 Vict. c. 76 (1852). This Act provided that no forms or cause of action need be mentioned by the plaintiff in the writ by which the action was started. The Judicature Act of 1873 (An Act for the Constitution of a Supreme Court and for Other Purposes Relating to the Better Administration of Justice in England and to Authorise the Transfer to the Appellate Division of such Supreme Court of the Jurisdiction of the Judicial Committee of Her Majesty's PC 36 & 37 Vict. c. 66 (1873)) provided that pleadings should contain a statement in summary form of the material facts on which the party pleading relied. The requirement that the plaintiff specify the cause of action in this manner constrained the limits of the property. On this see W. Carpmael, *Report on Letters Patent for Inventions* 16 (Q. 364).

[68] Commentators had difficulties in achieving this end. For example, Frost said that 'there used to be an idea that it was possible to infringe upon the equity of a statute. If it were not possible to show that the words of the statute had been infringed, it was contended that the equity had been invaded; and similarly by a confusion of ideas a notion was prevalent that there might be an infringement of the equity of patent. There is, however, no sound principle of this kind in patent law; that which is protected is that which is specified.' While Frost attempted to limit the property interest to the surface of the specification, typically he fails. As he said, 'that which is held to be an infringement must be an infringement of that which is specified, though it may not be the less of an infringement because it has been coloured or disguised by additions or subtractions': R. Frost, *Patent Law and Practice* (1891), 401.

[69] As Lord Westbury said, 'in the case of those things as to which the merit of the invention lies in the drawing, or in forms that can be copied, the appeal is to the eye, and the eye alone is the judge of the identity of the two things. Whether, therefore, there be piracy or not is referred at once to an unerring judge, namely, the eye, which takes the one figure and the other figure, and ascertains whether they are or are not the same': *Holdsworth v McCrea* (1867) LR 2 HL 381.

[70] See, e.g., *Ouvah Ceylon Estates v Uva Ceylon Rubber Estates* (1910) 27 RPC 645; (1910) RPC 753 *Pianost's Application* (1906) 23 RPC 777. As well as shaping the scope of the property, the expectation that documents were to be interpreted in a particular way also influenced the way the claims were drafted in the first place.

and trade marks law, the same cannot be said about copyright. The reason for this is that while, when dealing with patents, designs and trade marks the law was presented with a representation of the protected object, in the case of copyright the law was confronted with the object itself rather than a representation of that object. The upshot of this was that, unlike the situation with patents, designs and trade marks, where the scope and identity of the intangible property were largely determined through representative registration, when the law came to consider matters to do with copyright it found itself having to grapple with metaphysical problems concerning the nature and limits of intangible property, similar to those which had been discussed in the literary property debate. These were questions which were said to be 'unworthy of a legislature and should be left to administration'.[71] Once the few options available at the bureaucratic level were exhausted[72] the difficult task of formulating techniques that would enable the copyright work to be identified fell to the legislature and the courts.[73] As well as the development of detailed rules as a way of determining what a work was and how it could be transformed,[74] there were also attempts to demarcate the copyright work through the exercise of legal protocols and aphoristic reasoning. Despite the effort that went into establishing these techniques, they were only of limited assistance. As a result, when dealing with the subject matter of copyright the law still often finds itself in the uncomfortable situation where it must first distil the nature of the intangible property: to this extent, unlike the other areas of intellectual property law, copyright law remains pre-modern. To recognise this not only highlights an important point of difference between the legal categories, it also helps us to understand aspects of present-day copyright law. In part the pre-modern nature of copyright law (which is not

[71] T. Turner, *Remarks on the Amendment of the Law of Patents* (1851), 16.
[72] In the case of literary works deposited at the Stationers' Hall the person depositing the book also had to sign a witnessed form which, if wrongly signed, attracted specific penalties. See C. Rivington (Clerk to the Stationers' Company and Registering Officer under the Copyright Act), 1898 *Report from the Select Committee of the House of Lords on the Copyright Bill (HL) and the Copyright Amendment Bill (HL)* 194 ff.
[73] In 1928, it was said that as 'copyright is inherent and independent of formalities, and as all disputes as to copyright are settled not by administrative machinery but by the Courts, the current work thrown on the Industrial Property Department [of the Board of Trade] was comparatively small': Sir H. Llewellyn Smity, *The Board of Trade* (London: Puttnams, 1928), 207–8.
[74] For example from two- to three-dimensional. The 1881 Copyright Bill proposed that in the case of a book which was a work of fiction, it was an infringement of copyright to take the dialogue, plot, or incidents related therein in the book, and use them for or convert them into or adapt them for a dramatic work (cl. 56); that copyright in a picture of a scene did not prevent other pictures being made (cl. 59); and that copying a copyright work as a part of a scene was not an infringement of copyright (cl. 61). Similar provisions also existed for musical compositions and paintings. See also 1911 Copyright Act.

intended to be read pejoratively) can help to explain why it is that copyright law has acquired the justifiable reputation for convoluted reasoning and its lengthy and often unwieldy statutes. Moreover, to recognise that one of the central tasks that confronts copyright law remains that of identifying and demarcating the scope of the property helps us better to understand the problem that the law has experienced in dealing with subject matter such as digital technology and multimedia.[75] It also explains why it is that copyright law, much more so than any of the other areas of intellectual property law, is so consistently caught out by new forms of subject matter.

[75] On this see *Sega Enterprises* v *Galaxy Electronics* (1996) 35 *Intellectual Property Reports* 161. This case, which drew upon *Millar* v *Taylor* and *Jefferys* v *Boosey*, considered the nature of material form in relation to digitised works.

10   Closure and its consequences

While the changes which led to intangible property being presented as a unitary, closed object, and the related displacement of mental labour, can be seen as a further stage in the reification of creativity which had long been a feature of intellectual property law and, if you like, a shift from natural law to positive law, it would be a mistake to see them solely in these terms: the shift from action to thing or from labour to work that came with the closure of intangible property in the second half of the nineteenth century marked an important change in the logic of intellectual property law.

The closure of the subject matter of intellectual property law brought with it a shift away from what had been called the metaphysics, or what we would now call the doctrine, of intellectual property law towards questions of political economy and policy. The move from creation to product also had a profound effect on what we described earlier as the creative or mimetic faculty of law. While we return to this in more detail later, it is enough to note here that the closure of intangible property played an important role in the (apparent) disappearance of creativity from intellectual property law.

The changing nature of intangible property also impacted on the categories of intellectual property law. On one level, the changes served to reopen the boundary between patents and utility models (or non-ornamental designs): previously the willingness of the law to pass judgment as to the inherent nature of an invention or a mechanical device meant that the law had a standpoint from which it could decide what properly belonged in patent law and what did not. In so doing, it provided a useful way of managing the boundary between the two categories. With the shift away from what were expressly regarded as qualitative decisions, the policing role that they played was also lost.[1]

---

[1] In 1912, Temple Franks, then Comptroller-General of Patents, wrote, 'we do not reject upon the patent side any device, however small or insignificant, provided it is unanticipated, and may be said to form a '"new manner of manufacture"'. Thus, 'designs for the ornamentation of Christmas cards, toys, the shapes of window fasteners,

The shift away from mental labour also impacted on the way the categories were explained. While designs, patents and copyright had previously been distinguished in terms of the quantity and later the quality of the labour embodied in the work in question, with the disappearance of mental labour from the law's horizon this was no longer possible. In a move which reaffirmed the pivotal role played by intangible property in organising the categories of intellectual property law, the categories were still differentiated in terms of their relative 'value'. The main difference was that value now tended to mean the macro-economic value of the property rather than, as had been the case previously, the quantity of the mental labour embodied in the property in question. With this change what became important was not the labour or creativity contained within the work but the (external) contribution (typically judged in economic or quasi-economic terms) that the subject matter made. That is, the differences between the categories of intellectual property law were explained in terms of the contribution that the respective property interests made. Similar rationales were used to explain why certain attributes (such as duration) differed between, and also occasionally within, classes of intellectual property.

As with the other factors which operated to distinguish designs, copyright and patents, the value placed upon the archetypical object fluctuated over time. Moreover, the way in which the equation was determined – what was chosen as being representative of a particular area of law; how the contribution that the object made was determined and how that particular contribution was valued – was influenced by broader concerns. Nonetheless, it is clear that the relative contributions provided by the respective categories played a central role in explaining the shape of modern intellectual property law.[2] This can be seen in the second half of the nineteenth century when it came to be believed that while patents and copyright both contributed in their own way to the common good, to what was taken to be the welfare and advancement of society, they were distinguished from each other in terms of the relative

---

etc. have all been allowed as subject-matter of patents. It should be noted that this is not the case in Germany, where insignificant or unimportant matters are not allowed patent rights, but are only protected as utility models ... [there is in] Germany no great probability of this system [of utility models] conflicting with their practice in regard to patents, insomuch as the benefits of the patent law are restricted to the more important classes of inventions. In this country, however ... it has been the practice to extend patent rights to every class of invention, large or small, and the utility and importance of the invention are, generally speaking, no way considered. It follows, therefore, that if a system of *Gebrauchsmustern* is set side by side with our patent system as it exists, there would, of necessity, be no clear dividing line': W. Temple Franks, 1 Oct. 1912, BT/209/480, 2.

[2] M. Leverson, *Copyright and Patents; or, Property in Thought* (1854), 9.

bearing they had on the 'public interest'.[3] More specifically, while copyright served to promote learning and knowledge, patents were useful, important and necessary for the growth of industry. A similar approach was also used to distinguish design law from patents and copyright. This can be seen, for example, in the open letter written in 1840 by James Thomson (Fellow of the Royal Society) to the Vice President of the Board of Trade on the subject of design law. After characterising the contribution made by copyright and patents, Thomson turned to focus on the nature of the contribution offered by designs. To this end he argued:

> If a pattern were an ending thing, like an engine or a book, a reversionary interest in it for the public would be desirable and just; but patterns are for the most part like soap-bubbles blown in the sunshine; glittering and incandescent, they burst almost at the moment of their birth, and leave not a trace behind. Novelty, the handmaid of Fashion and some times of Taste, enjoys but a short and fleeting existence – it is of its very essence quickly to fade and pass away. Some exceptions do not affect the general truth of this statement.[4]

While Thomson's argument in favour of longer protection for designs ultimately failed, it exemplifies the basis on which design law was distinguished from patents and copyright: while the subject matter protected by patents and copyright both provided a valuable reversionary interest, designs were seen to leave less of an imprint or trace.

The third situation in which the changing status of intangible property impacted on the categories of intellectual property law was in terms of the status of trade marks as a form of intellectual property. As the law of trade marks came to adopt a modern rather than pre-modern form, it was generally accepted that it did not belong within the remit of intellectual property law, despite the many points shared in common with patents, designs and copyright. This was because, firstly, while intellectual property dealt with creations, trade marks law was concerned with pre-existing entities and, secondly, while intellectual property law was concerned with matters of property, trade marks law was not. Despite these difficulties, in 1876 Daniel was able to write that the law of trade marks resembled or belonged to the same class or family as copyright, patents and designs.[5] While in some ways Daniel's comments

---

[3] L. Playfair, 'On Patents and the New Patents Bill' (1877), 318.

[4] J. Thomson, *A Letter to the Vice President of the Board of Trade on Protection to Original Designs and Patterns, Printed upon Woven Fabrics* (2nd edn) (Clitheroe: H. Whalley, 1840), 18–20.

[5] E. Daniel, *The Trade Marks Registration Act 1875* (London: Stevens and Haynes, 1876), 3. 'It is important for the clear apprehension of the subject to distinguish between property in invention or patents, in trade marks, and in copyright. These are all distinct in substance and in principle': Daniel, *A Complete Treatise upon the New Law of Patents, Designs and Trade Marks* (London: Stevens, 1884), 75.

were premature, he was right to suggest that the objections which had
been raised against the incorporation of trade marks in intellectual
property were starting to be overcome.[6]

The first objection brought against the inclusion of trade marks law as
a sub-category of intellectual property law was overcome as a result of
changes not so much in trade marks as in intellectual property law itself.
As we saw earlier, one of the reasons why it was argued that the category
of trade marks fell outside the remit of intellectual property law was that
it was not concerned with the regulation of creativity. With the change
in intellectual property law, which saw the disappearance of creativity in
favour of the closed work, this stumbling block was removed. Given that
modern intellectual property law was no longer directly concerned with
creativity (or mental labour) but with intangible property as an object in
its own right, it could no longer be argued that the non-creative nature
of trade marks meant that trade marks law did not belong within the
remit of intellectual property law.

Although the claim that trade marks did not belong within intellectual
property law because they were non-creative was diverted by changes in
intellectual property law itself, the problems which stemmed from the
status of trade marks as a species of property were overcome as a result
of changes in the way trade marks were perceived. More specifically,
these problems were circumvented by the fact that gradually trade
marks came to be seen as a form of property.[7] As Edward Lloyd argued
in 1861, while 'it may, no doubt, be urged that in the case of trade
marks there is no property', on the basis of recent decisions[8] it had
however become clear that

by the use of such a name or mark injuriously affecting the rights of any person
who has established his claim to use it to distinguish articles to his manufacture
... there is an injury done to property. Having therefore once fixed the notion of
this species of property, the analogy between [copyright and patents] and ...
trade-marks, more properly so called, is, to my mind, no longer far fetched or
illusory.[9]

[6] Although it is difficult to date this change precisely, it is clear that by the 1880s the law
of trade marks was accepted as a fully paid-up member of intellectual property law.

[7] See E. Daniel, *The Trade Marks Registration Act 1875* (1876), 1; C. Drewry, *The Law of
Trade Marks* (1878); *Chappell* v *Sheard* (1855) 69 ER 717; *Chappell* v *Davidson* (1855)
69 ER 719.

[8] In 1862, Lord Westbury said that the true ground for the court's jurisdiction was
property: *Hall* v *Burrows* (1863) 46 ER 719.

[9] E. Lloyd, 'On the Law of Trade Marks: No. VIII' (27 July 1861) 5 *Solicitors' Journal*
666. The judicial recognition of trade marks as a form of property was also prompted by
the fact that in the second half of the nineteenth century it was critically important to
establish that such marks were property, in order to enable the judiciary to grant
injunctions preventing imitation. As Fredrick Pollock pointed out, 'the protection of
trade marks and trade names was originally undertaken by the courts on the ground of

While judicial recognition of property in trade marks played an important role in conferring property status on trade marks, equally important was the decision to introduce a registration system for trade marks in 1875:[10] the registration of trade marks, which was designed to simplify issues of proof,[11] was 'in truth the official recognition of ownership'.[12] Registration provided *prima facie*, rather than an unchallengeable, proof of priority:[13] unlike the common law position, where trade marks conferred a remedy, the act of registration conferred a right on the applicant.[14] Importantly, this was taken to mean that if the mark was registered it was 'taken for granted, on the production of the certificate of the registrar, to be the property of the person in whose name it is'.[15] With the recognition that registration established a form of bureaucratic property in trade marks, the second obstacle to the inclusion of trade marks within the rubric of intellectual property law was overcome.

While trade mark law was now seen as exhibiting the requisite characteristics for it to fall within the family of intellectual property law, and the debt owed by trade marks to copyright, designs and patents was widely acknowledged,[16] nonetheless it was still treated as a separate

preventing fraud. The right to a trade mark, after being more and more assimilated to proprietary rights, has become a statutory franchise analogous to patent rights and copyright': F. Pollock, *On Torts* (12th edn) (London: Stevens and Sons, 1923), 312–3.

[10] See M. Gibson (18 Feb. 1862) 165 *Hansard* col. 415. Calls were made for the introduction of a modern specialised register for trade marks rather 'than the heterogeneous one of the Stationers' Hall, where book-titles, newspapers, and trade marks were jumbled together without system, illustration or classification, and utterly inaccessible for reference, comparison, or even legal proof': discussion following paper by W. Wybrow Robertson, 'On Trade Marks' (1869), 420. The fact that the Government Bill introduced in 1862 failed to provide for a system of registration meant that trade marks could not have 'individual property about it', that it left them with 'no property to fall back on': John Jobson Smith, 1862 *Select Committee on Trade Marks* 54 (Q. 1136).

[11] E. Potter, *ibid.*, 99 (Q. 2181).

[12] 'Trade Marks' (31 July 1912) *Manchester Chamber of Commerce Monthly Record* 198.

[13] Registration moved the onus of proof upon the defendant to disprove ownership (which is a very different thing from having to prove ownership). See W. Wybrow Robertson, 'On Trade Marks' (1869), 414.

[14] While common law trade marks only provided applicants with remedies, it was said that, under the proposed Trade Marks Bill, a person was given a right to use a particular trade mark: W. Hindmarch (and Roebuck), 1862 *Select Committee on Trade Marks* 142 (Q. 2987 ff).

[15] R. Jackson, 1862 *Select Committee on Trade Marks* 3 (Q. 38).

[16] As with other forms of intellectual property, this created other problems such as scope of protection (similar to idea/expression in copyright). 'It is manifest that no one ought to be granted the exclusive use of a word descriptive of the quality or character of any goods. Such words of descriptions are the property of all mankind, and it would not be right to allow any individual to monopolise them and exclude others from their use': 1888 *Patent Office Inquiry* xi. 'The details of the systems to be applied in treating and recording grants of patents, and registration of designs and trade marks are almost identical ... To ensure an efficient administration for the new Trade Marks Registration

category of intellectual property law rather than as a subsidiary of one of the existing categories, as was sometimes suggested. Drawing upon the definition of property then in circulation, trade mark law was distinguished from the other categories of intellectual property law in a similar manner as was used to differentiate designs, patents and copyright.[17] If we take the case of trade marks and designs, for example, these two categories were distinguished in terms of the social, economic and commercial benefits they provided and the manner in which their value was acquired. More specifically, while trade marks and designs shared many features in common, they were distinguished in terms of the different purposes which they served: trade marks signified the source or origin of goods, whereas designs, which beautified objects, were aesthetically pleasing in themselves. Another difference was that while designs attracted the greater part of their value from their novelty, trade marks acquired their value through time. Reiterating the second-rate status of designs, it was said that 'a design is an ephemeral thing; a mere creature of fashion. It is in vogue today, but next year it will be completely consigned to oblivion ... there is a constant succession of new designs and patterns coming out which have to be registered.' This was in marked contrast to the value of trade marks 'which only comes with time and the longer that trade mark exists: the longer the excellence of the article which has always been symbolised by that trade mark is maintained - the more valuable it becomes as time rolls on'.[18]

The return of creativity and essence

One of the notable features of modern intellectual property law as it developed over the course of the nineteenth century was that it saw the closure of intangible property and the consequential exclusion of creativity and mental labour from the law's immediate horizon. During the course of the second half of the nineteenth century the law's focus on

Office, it will merely be necessary to take the Patent Office as a model and adopt it': H. Trueman Wood, 'The Registration of Trade Marks' (1875), 18.

[17] In relation to the protection given to trade marks it was said, 'as with the other monopolies just mentioned [viz. patents and copyright], it is only the consideration of a general advantage that can justify a special privilege ... We believe that the protection of inventions fosters and encourages industry, therefore we grant to the inventor a patent-right in his ideas; we argue that the protection of literary and artistic property aids in the development of our literature and the arts, therefore we grant the writer or the artist copyright in his works; so experience teaches us that by giving the trader every possible assistance in the prosecution of his business he has established, we promote the growth of commerce': H. Trueman Wood, 'The Registration of Trade Marks' (1875), 18–19.

[18] W. Smith, 1862 *Select Committee on Trade Marks* 27 (Q. 598).

mental labour and creativity was replaced by a new-found concern with a detached, neutral and closed intangible property, but this process was not as neat or complete as we might appear to have suggested: while there may have been a change of emphasis, this is not to suggest that creativity disappeared from intellectual property law, that there was a complete detachment of, for example, authors from their work, or that the law was now in a position where it no longer needed to worry about the essence of intangible property. The reason for this is that despite all its best efforts, modern intellectual property law has been unable to confine intangible property to the document as registered or, and this is particularly the case with copyright, the immediate physical form in which it is expressed.

While in the modern law creativity may not have played the central role that it once did, instead of being banished from intellectual property law creativity appeared in new guises.[19] In particular, as it migrated from the substantive to the adjectival, creativity reappeared in the form of the requirements of originality and non-obviousness, in which applicants had to show, in effect, that their respective works were creative.[20] In addition, while an important trait of modern intellectual property law has been its aversion to or fear of judging the quality of particular creations, nonetheless it still engages in such activities, albeit in a different manner from that which had hitherto been the case, one that was much more oblique. For example, while the modern law may be unwilling to cast judgment over the quality of particular subject matter it is more than willing to pass judgment about classes of objects: to consider whether, for example, photographs are creative or the art of Indigenous Australians is original. In addition, while questions as to whether a work

[19] For example, in contemporary intellectual property law fine art is often distinguished from industrial design in terms of the relative contribution (and value) of the authors' contribution to the final product. The logic of creation employed by the law – which links creators, creations and users of creations – can still be seen at work in the exclusion of principles from patentable subject matter. Modern patent law does this by requiring the applicant, when pressed, to show technical effect (or physical change): to show the marks or traces of the process of individualisation (which suggests a gap between nature and invention). The non-obviousness and originality examinations of patent and copyright law can be seen as requiring applicants to show that the object for which they are seeking legal protection came about as a result of the logic of creation.

[20] It is not surprising that at the same time as we witness the closure of intangible property we also see the introduction of more formal requirements of novelty and non-obviousness into intellectual property law. One of the earliest situations in which novelty and originality were discussed in a way we would now find meaningful was in 1894 when, in considering the question of novelty, Cunynghame said it was 'formulated by asking (1) is the invention ingenious [i.e. non-obvious] (2) Has it been anticipated? ... Both these branches are embraced in the use of the word "novelty"': H. Cunynghame, *English Patent Practice* (1894), 77. See also Willes J, *Tathham* v *Dania* (1869) Giff 213.

may have been obscene or immoral are generally not permitted to impact upon the primary question of whether property subsists in the work, they are taken into account when the property is exploited.[21]

In addition, while the closure of the intangible property and the spread of representative registration (at least in relation to patents, designs and trade marks) shifted attention away from the essence of the property towards the document registered, this does not mean that the law was no longer required to search for the chimerical essences underlying the intangible. Despite all its best efforts intellectual property law was unable either to limit the intangible interest to the paper inscription or to restrict it to the immediate physical form that the property took. While in many cases it was not necessary to look beyond the object in which the property was embodied, nonetheless (and this was particularly the case with copyright) the law often found itself in a situation where it had to identify (or, as we argued earlier, help create) the essence of the property. Despite the success of the registration system and the more general shift towards the closure of the intangible property, the courts have continually found themselves pushed away from the surface towards the essence of the property. In the same way as it was recognised during the literary property debate that it was not feasible to limit literary property to the printed word, it was acknowledged that for intellectual property to be viable, it was necessary for it to extend beyond the immediate format in which it was manifest. One reason for this was that when the courts considered questions of infringement, it was unusual for the objects under consideration to be identical. Instead, while there was usually a degree of similarity, there was also sufficient difference for the matter to be adjudicated. In relation to patents, for example, a concern to ensure that the property was not undermined by a strict literal reading of the claims led the courts to extend the scope of protection beyond such readings.[22] The upshot of this was, as Coryton said, that patent infringement 'necessarily involves for its determination a knowledge of what constitutes the *essence* of the invention'.[23] Similar changes took place in relation to designs and trade marks.[24]

[21] *Glyn v Weston Feature Film Co* [1916] 2 Ch D 261.

[22] For an examination of patent infringement see R. Frost, *Patent Law and Practice* (1891), 403; R. Wallace and J. Williamson, *The Law and Practice Relating to Letters Patent for Inventions* (London: William Clowes and Sons, 1900), 221 ff; J. Norman, *A Treatise on the Law and Practice Relating to Letters Patent for Inventions* (1853), 133 ff.

[23] J. Coryton, *A Treatise on the Law of Letters-Patent* (1855), 257. 'If the defendant has imitated and adopted the essence of the invention, he will not be allowed to escape because he has not adopted the form or words in which the essence of the invention is cloathed': *Thorn v Worthing Skating Rink Co.* (1876) 6 Ch D 415.

[24] For example, we are told that 'the essence of a design resides, not in the elements individually, nor in the method of arrangement, but in the *tout ensemble* – in that

Whether it is called essence, personality, creativity or mental labour, it is clear that modern law has been unable to suppress the creative or mimetic nature of intellectual property law.[25] Moreover, while by the later part of the nineteenth century there was an appearance that the problems of the type signalled by the opponents of literary property in the law granting property status to the intangible were no longer present, it was only that: an appearance. While the aversion to judgment, the widespread use of representative registration and the closure of the intangible property brought about important changes in the law, nonetheless the mimetic issues that we identified earlier in the law granting property status to the intangible remain a central and in many ways irreconcilable feature of modern intellectual property law. In spite of the law's continued efforts – a reliance on technical effect in determining what is an invention, the reduction of obviousness in patent law to more quantifiable criteria such as commercial success,[26] or the provision of more refined and detailed rules to ascertain when a copyright work has been infringed – the law is still confronted with the types of questions that arose during the literary property debate, albeit now in a more oblique and uncertain manner.

While in its pre-modern guise the law developed a number of sophisticated techniques which enabled it to deal with such questions, the usual response adopted by modern intellectual property law when forced to pursue the essence of intangible property has been less successful. Confronted with what had earlier been described as the metaphysical nature of intangible property, when it has not resorted to the trite and unhelpful comment that it depends on the facts of each case[27] modern

---

indefinable whole that awakens some sensation in the observer's eye ... Impressions thus imparted may be complex or simple .. but whatever the impression, there is attached in the mind of the observer, to the object observed, a sense of impression and character': L. Edmunds and H. Bentwich, *The Law of Copyright in Designs* (1908), 19. Similarly it was said that the extent of rights under utility model protection were not 'defined by the concrete bodily "Model" which in some such way as a drawing accompanies the application, but by the concept, defined in respect of the space lying at the base of the model': H. Hatfield (Comptroller), 23 March 1912, BT/209/479, 5.

[25] S. Stewart, *Crimes of Writing* (1991), 280.

[26] In relation to a question about the difficulties of determining whether an invention was trivial or not, the Attorney-General said, 'I judge of that as I do of any other question of fact; how do a jury judge what damages they may give for a broken leg?': 1871 *Report from the Select Committee on Letters Patent* 624.

[27] For example, one of the few intellectual property treatises from the nineteenth century which remains in publication, Terrell's treatise on patents, says that 'the question as to what amounts to an infringement, like many other points which arise in the law of letters patent, must depend upon the particular facts of each case': T. Terrell, *Law and Practice Relating to Letters Patent for Inventions* (3rd edn) (rev. W. Rylands) (London: Sweet and Maxwell, 1895), 222.

law has been reduced at best to circular reasoning[28] and at worst to silence.[29] The remarks by Thomas Turner are particularly telling in this context. As he said in relation to the frailty of the subject matter of patents, 'while an ordinary chattel can be physically restored to its owner, the [subject matter of a patent] can no more be re-secreted than the genii of Arabian Nights re-inclosed in the jar'.[30] Coryton reiterated these sentiments, although somewhat less poetically, when he explained that the on-going problems in patent law were caused by the lack of clear understanding as to what an invention was which, in turn, could be traced to the 'fact that the idea of "invention" in Law is somewhat metaphysical, being a conventional arrangement to preserve the harmony of the Law and having in some few instances no corresponding expression of fact'.[31]

While modern law remains relatively comfortable with intellectual property as a closed and stable entity, it is much less sanguine when the property is unpackaged: as the law has been unable to close the property, it is often placed in the difficult situation where it must identify the essence of the protected subject matter. The reason why legal commentators, jurists and judges have experienced so many problems when they have been forced to identify the essence of intangible property is that the creative or mimetic skills which this task requires depend upon what are essentially mute forms of knowledge which do not lend themselves to being either formalised or spoken. While many aspects of intellectual property law can be explained in terms of rules and principles, they offer little guidance when it comes to determining the essence of intangible property. As Hutcheson said in his discussion of the difficulty of legal judgment written earlier this century, where he cites as his prime example the infringement of patents, a person hearing

---

[28] 'If you ask me to define an infringement of a patent, I cannot do it. On the cases the judges say, that to infringe a patent you must attain substantially the same result in substantially the same mode; but that is saying no more than you infringe a patent; one direction is nearly as full of information as the other': W. R. Grove, 1871 *Report from the Select Committee on Letters Patent* 632.

[29] In response to the question of whether it was impossible to put on paper a definition of the class of inventions which should be patented and those which should not, Grove said, 'I do not feel able to put on paper a definition of anything; it is what has puzzled the world form Plato's time to the present day': *ibid.*

[30] T. Turner, *Remarks on the Amendment of the Law of Patents* (1851), 23

[31] J. Coryton, *A Treatise on the Law of Letters-Patent* (1855), 65. More recently it was said '"Invention", for patent purposes, has been difficult to define. Efforts to cage the concept in words have proved almost as unsuccessful as attempts verbally to imprison the concept "beautiful" ... To the casual observer, judicial patent decisions are the adventures of judges' souls among inventions. For a decision as to whether or not a thing is an invention is a value judgement': Frank J, *Picard* v *United Aircraft Corporation* (1942) 128 F (2d) 632, 639.

a patent case must exhibit 'the same imaginative response to an idea, something of that flash of genius that there is in the inventor, which all great patent judges have had, that intuitive brilliance of the imagination, that luminous quality of the mind, that can give back, where there is an invention, an answering flash for flash'.[32] As well as highlighting the mimetic faculty of intellectual property law in creating the property interest, Hutcheson also alerts us to the important role played by speculation, intuition and insight in intellectual property law: issues which have been suppressed and sidelined in modern law. By reminding us that speculation, intuition and insight have not only been deprived of a voice by which they can be heard but also of a conceptual framework within which they can operate, Hutcheson highlights the limits of modern analysis. More specifically, he reminds us that while speculation and intuition remain important features of modern intellectual property law, the law is unable to accommodate or deal with these in an appropriate or satisfactory manner, because the resources that it has at its disposal are set up to deal with closed and stable entities.

[32] J. Hutcheson, 'The Judgement Intuitive: The Function of the "Hunch" in Judicial Decision' (1928) 16 *Cornell Law Quarterly* 284.

11   Remembering and forgetting

While gradual, haphazard and in some ways still incomplete, the move from pre-modern to modern intellectual property law marked an important transformation in the law which granted property rights in mental labour. In this chapter we concentrate on the fact that at the same time as modern intellectual property law emerged as a separate and distinct category, the law also began to develop a series of narratives by which this newly formed entity was explained and justified. We hope to highlight the role played by the stories that the law tells about itself in the making and remaking of intellectual property law. In part, the emergence of these explanatory narratives was a consequence of the fact that profound changes in consciousness such as that brought about by the formation of modern intellectual property law 'bring with them characteristic amnesias. Out of such oblivions, in specific historical circumstances spring narratives'.[1] One of most interesting things about the narratives which developed during the second half of the nineteenth century, which played and continue to play such an important role in informing modern intellectual property law, is that in many ways they are at odds with the history that we have outlined here. For example a central theme of the explanatory narratives of modern intellectual property law has been that creativity played at best an ambivalent and at worst an extremely limited role in this area of law: a suggestion which is in marked contrast to the way we have presented pre-modern (and to a

---

[1] B. Anderson, *Imagined Communities* (1983), 204. 'After experiencing the physiological and emotional changes produced by puberty, it is impossible to "remember" the consciousness of childhood ... How strange it is to need another's help to learn that this naked baby in a yellowed photograph ... is you. The photograph, fine child of the age of mechanical reproduction, is only the most pre-emptory of a huge modern accumulation of documentary evidence (birth certificates, diaries, report cards, letters, medical records, and the like) which simultaneously records a certain apparent continuity and emphasises its loss of memory. Out of this estrangement comes a conception of personhood, *identity* (yes, you and that naked baby are identical) which because it cannot be "remembered" must be narrated': *ibid.*, 205.

lesser extent) modern intellectual property law.[2] While the explanatory narratives may often be at odds with the history of intellectual property law we have presented here, this should not be taken as suggesting that these narratives are false and that they therefore ought to be ignored. Similarly, while we wish to question the perceived history of the subject we do not, however, reject such a history. Rather, if we suspend our realist assumptions we see that as 'real fictions' these narratives played an important role in constituting and reinforcing the identity and self-image that the law has of itself. Moreover, we also see that the image that the law has of its past plays an important role in shaping its present and its future.

Although the narratives cover a wide range of topics we wish to focus here on three interrelated groups. The first concerns the story which is told and retold about the origins of intellectual property law: that, for example, copyright began with the 1710 Statute of Anne and patent law with the 1624 Statute of Monopolies. We then go on to explore the narrative which presents British law as indigenous and home-grown. In so doing we highlight the fact that in order to present British law as being pure and unadulterated, it was necessary to ignore the impact that foreign legal systems had on British law. Finally we chart the rise of principle and theory as part of the attempt to explain the shape of modern intellectual property law. We argue that, contrary to what many present-day commentators believe, the way in which property rights arise (whether by registration, publication or creation) or the shape that the right took (absolute monopoly or a right to prevent copying) played little if any part in the historical development of the categories. Similarly we argue that theory, so called, played at best an *ex post facto* role in legitimating the grant of property rights in mental labour.

The origins of intellectual property law

One of the most important ways in which the narratives which took shape in the nineteenth century explained the law was that they provided a history and a biography of intellectual property law. It is important to note that it was not so much that, with the emergence of modern intellectual property law, there was a change in the way the history of the subject was written, as that the official history was written for the first

[2] Interestingly, after the *Feist* decision in the United States (*Feist Publications* v *Rural Telephone* (1991) 111 S Ct 1282), there appears to be a resurgence of interest in creativity in copyright law. As yet similar patterns have not yet developed in the United Kingdom or Australia.

time.[3] A notable feature of the official history which developed in the mid-nineteenth century was that it assumed that the abstract, forward-looking law that emerged at the time already existed in the law (albeit it in a nascent form). This can be seen, for example, in Lord Monkswell's attempt to explain the 'glorious muddle' of nineteenth-century copyright law: a situation which he attributed to the 1710 Statute of Anne.[4] As he said: 'I have said that the muddle began with the Statute of Anne. One would have thought it was not very easy to begin with a muddle, because that was the first Statute passed, but the muddle began in this way.' No matter how counter-factual it may have been, Lord Monkswell's belief in the timeless and evolutionary nature of intellectual property law led him to conclude 'that the Statute of Anne was apparently passed by a Legislature who had evidently not the slightest idea that there was any Law of Copyright in existence at all'.[5]

While intellectual property law was occasionally treated as a timeless, almost essentialist concept, for the most part the official history of intellectual property law that emerged in the second half of the nineteenth century was written evangelically; that is, it was presumed that particular areas of law could be traced back to a single moment or event. Reflecting the increasingly self-referential nature of law and the growing influence of legal positivism,[6] the roots of intellectual property were typically traced back to legal (legislative) sources. More specifically, the 1710 Statute of Anne and the 1624 Statute of Monopolies came to be seen as the genesis or origin of copyright law and patents respectively. It is important to note that this way of thinking about intellectual property law largely took place for the first time in the later part of the nineteenth century; that prior to this the Statute of Monopolies and the Statute of Anne were not regarded as marking the beginnings of either patent or

[3] As Underdown said as a consequence of the passage of the 1862 Fine Art Copyright Act, it was 'now possible to write histories of the law of artistic copyright': E. Underdown, *The Law of Artistic Copyright* (1863), 5. Hindmarch's work on patents was used as basis for the history of patents in the 1849 *Report of the Committee on the Signet and Privy Seal Office* i.

[4] 'Since the first Statute on the subject of copyright was passed in the time of Queen Anne, the Law of Copyright seems to have been the sport of some malignant demon as it were, and we find that at present the Law of Copyright is contained in 18 Acts of Parliament, and in some ill-defined common law principles ... [the law was in] glorious muddle': Lord Monkswell (11 May 1891) 353 *Hansard* col. 438.

[5] Lord Monkswell continued: 'and it so happens that it was more than 60 years before the lawyers could decide whether the Common Law of Copyright was superseded by the Statute of Anne ... But we find that the draftsmen in the time of Queen Victoria show absolutely and precisely the same ignorance as the draftsmen of the time of Queen Anne, and that they fell into precisely the same error as the draftsmen of the former reign': *ibid.*, col. 439.

[6] See, e.g., T. Scrutton, *The Laws of Copyright* (1883), 4. W. Briggs, *The Law of International Copyright* (1906).

copyright law. For example, in its pre-modern guise, the 1710 Statute of Anne (or as it was then known An Act for the Encouragement of Learning by Vesting the Copies of Printed Books in the Authors and Purchasers of such Copies) was considered as a subject-specific statute that provided authors and their assigns with limited rights to copy. With the emergence of modern intellectual property law, however, the Statute of Anne not only changed from a Literary Property Act to become the first Copyright Statute, it also came to be seen as the source of the modern law.[7] Given that, at least according to our reading, there was no (modern) copyright law (as it understood today) until the middle period of the nineteenth century, it is unsurprising that the Statute of Anne was not (and could not have been) seen as the foundation of that which did not yet exist.

The changes which occurred as a result of the formation of these explanatory narratives were even more striking in relation to patents. While the 1624 Statute of Monopolies is now widely accepted as laying down the foundations of patent law,[8] in pre-modern law patents had a different lineage. This can be seen, for example, in the way patents were presented in the Report of the 1829 Select Committee on Patents, which was set up to inquire into the state of the law and practice relevant to the granting of patents for inventions. What is most surprising about this inquiry is that while contemporary commentators regularly present the Statute of Monopolies as having provided the basis of patent law, it was treated very differently by the Select Committee. More specifically, while modern law gives pride of place to the Statute of Monopolies, the 1829 Select Committee slotted it in between, and treated it more or less the same as, An Act Containing the Censure given in Parliament against Sir Francis Mitchell, Francis Viscount Saint Albane Lord Chancellor of England and Edward Flood[9] and An Act to Confirm a Judgement given in Chancery for Annulling Certain Letters Patent Granted to Henry Heron, for the Sole Privilege of Salting, Drying and Packing of Fish within the Counties of Devon and Cornwall.[10] As well as being treated in a similar way as the other Acts (or patents) which had been granted by the Crown, the Statute of Monopolies (or as it was then called An Act concerning Monopolies and Dispensations with Penal Laws and the

---

[7] See, e.g., S. Stewart, *International Copyright and Neighbouring Rights Law and Practice* (London: Butterworths, 1989), 8.

[8] The roots of patent law are also occasionally traced to Venice. A notable exception to this way of thinking is provided by Bugbee, who suggests that the 1852 Patent Act provided the statutory basis to the type of letters patent specifically granted for inventions: B. Bugbee, *The Genesis of American Patent and Copyright Law* (1967), 40.

[9] 18 Jac. I c. 1 of Private Acts (1621).

[10] 21 Jac. I c. 11 (1623).

Forfeitures thereof) was derided by the fact that in those rare instances where it was specifically mentioned, it was said to be 'chiefly declaratory of what had been held to be law by judges'.[11]

What does the lack of prominence given to the 1624 Statute of Monopolies reveal to us? If we were, like Lord Monkswell, insensitive to the object under investigation we could answer that the Select Committee (and also, by implication, the many commentators, judges and treatise writers who shared similar beliefs) simply misunderstood the law: they got it wrong. If we resist the temptation to rewrite history in our own image, it becomes clear that the Statute of Monopolies played, at best, a minimal role in pre-modern patent law. Rather, the foundation or basis for patent law lay in the Royal Charters and Royal Letters Patent of the Crown:[12] and not, as present-day histories often suggest, the Statute of Monopolies.[13] The nature of this change is apparent in the fact that while in 1835 the MP for Lymington William Mackinnon was able to say that there was 'no express statute according to which patents might be granted ... the granting did not rest upon the foundation of statute law',[14] by 1891 Robert Frost was able to say without hesitation in his text on patent law that the Statute of Monopolies was the statutory foundation of modern patent laws.[15]

The adoption of the official history had a number of consequences for

---

[11] The appendix to 1829 *Select Committee on Patents* reads: 'British Law of Patents for Inventions. A list of the various Acts of Parliament, by which the operations of exclusive privileges granted by Royal Charters and Royal Letters Patent, is limited and restrained, and other Acts by which the granting of Royal Letters patent is authorised and regulated.'

[12] The factor that united those Acts which enabled merchant strangers to buy and sell in the UK without disturbance (9 Ed. III s. 1 c. 1 (1335)) and those Acts for encouraging the distilling of brandy and spirits from corn (2 W. & M. c. 9 (1690)) was that they had been granted by the Crown. See L. Playfair, 'On Patents and the New Patents Bill' (1877), 316.

[13] This is not suggest that the 1624 Statute of Monopolies or the 1710 Statute of Anne played no role in the history of intellectual property, for they clearly did. Rather, it is to argue that the way in which these (and related) events were perceived changed, sometimes dramatically, with the emergence of modern intellectual property law.

[14] W. Mackinnon, 'Patent Laws' (14 Feb. 1837) 36 *Hansard* col. 555. This move to highlighting statutory sources rather than the Crown as the basis of patent law echoes broader developments in narratives of the constitution. In the second half of the nineteenth century Whig interpretations of the constitution, articulated by the likes of Dicey and Bagehot, gained widespread currency. The Crown came to be separated from the 'dignified' part of the constitution, Parliament being the source of 'official' power.

[15] R. Frost, *Patent Law and Practice* (1891), 23. 'It is on the basis of the statute of 1624, as interpreted first by the Council and afterwards by the courts, that the modern patent law rests today': W. Holdsworth, *A History of English Law*, vol. XI (1938), 430. Clause 6 of the Statute of Monopolies was elevated to 'all-sacred status ... which no one would have the courage to interfere with': Lord Chancellor, 'Patents for Inventions Bill' (12 Feb. 1875) 222 *Hansard* col. 265.

the way intellectual property law is viewed. One of the consequences of presuming that the abstract, forward-looking law which developed in the mid-nineteenth century already existed, albeit it in a nascent form, was that it was necessary for the law of the eighteenth century to be reinterpreted. In particular with the tendency to trace areas of intellectual property law back to isolated legal events, the history of intellectual property law usually skips from 1624 (the Statute of Monopolies) or 1710 (the Statute of Anne) through to the twentieth century, with the occasional detour along the way. While the literary property debate has now received some attention, for the most part it is as if the late eighteenth and nineteenth centuries simply did not exist. Moreover, in order to write legal history in this manner, it was necessary to ignore the fact that during the eighteenth and nineteenth centuries the image of intellectual property law that came to prominence was only one of a number of ways in which the law could have been organised. For example, in the nineteenth century, patents might have been abolished, reformed on the basis of the design system (which to some extent did occur), or incorporated within a law of arts and manufacture. Equally, the Statute of Anne might have been rendered irrelevant had the decision in *Millar* v *Taylor* not been overturned by *Donaldson* v *Becket*. As well as engendering a sense of certainty and inevitability which is at odds with the open, fluid and contingent history that we have presented here, another consequence of adopting what amounts in effect to an official history of intellectual property law is that while it authorises certain views to be taken seriously, others are marginalised, derided, excluded, even prohibited. Because only those views which confirm and support the official story of intellectual property law are retained, authors such as Thomas Turner and William Kenrick have been read out of that history.[16]

The narratives that took shape with the emergence of modern intellectual property law had a particularly important impact on design law. Although design law was arguably the first modern area of intellectual property law to emerge, the foundational narratives that developed in the later half of the nineteenth century functioned, in effect, to exclude design law from the history of intellectual property law. The reason for this was that while copyright and patents were given a history, and more importantly provided with foundations, design law was provided with no new tradition, no origin from which its heritage could

---

[16] In recognition of the growing kudos attached to philosophy and theory in modern intellectual property law, to the extent that they were replaced it was by the likes of Locke and Hegel. See, e.g., P. Drahos, *A Philosophy of Intellectual Property Law* (Aldershot: Dartmouth, 1996).

be traced. The consequence of this has been that the history of design law has been described at best as obscure[17] and at worst as the product of historical accident.[18]

The status of design law has been further derided by the tendency to prioritise patents and copyright over all other forms of intellectual property. This bipolar model, which is embodied in the Berne and Paris Conventions, shapes both the way contemporary law is understood and the way the history of intellectual property is written.[19] Indeed for some, the ontological reality of intellectual property law is only imaginable through this single, privileged system of representation.[20] When the rootless nature of design law is combined with the growing influence of the patent–copyright dichotomy, it is unsurprising that design law has, depending on the inclination of the commentator in question, either been subsumed within the remit of copyright or patents,[21] or said to

[17] W. Cornish, *Intellectual Property: Patents, Copyright, Trademarks and Allied Rights* (3rd edn) (London: Sweet and Maxwell, 1996), 487, n. 25.

[18] 'There would appear to be no reason for the development or retention of a separate branch of the law dealing with design outside the Copyright Acts other than historical accident and the fact that at the time of passing of the first designs legislation the law of copyright had not developed beyond giving protection to a very narrow range of intellectual works, not at all to be equated at that time with the work of the industrious artisan': J. Lahore, 'Art and Function in the Law of Copyright and Designs' (1971) 4 *Adelaide Law Review* 189.

[19] For example, it was said, 'in all European countries there is a continuing struggle between the two philosophies, the proponents of which are often specialists in either copyright or industrial property': H. Cohen Jehoram, 'Design Laws in Continental Europe and their Relation to Copyright Law' (1981) 8 *EIPR* 235. 'The basic principles of the [Australian] Copyright Act derive from Australia's obligations under the Berne Convention for the Protection of Literary and Artistic Works': Attorney-General's Department, Submission to House of Representative Standing Committee on Aboriginal and Torres Strait Islander Affairs: Culture and Heritage Inquiry (1 May 1995), 26–7.

[20] One of the clearest examples of this is Reichman's examination of the status and place of legal hybrids (such as designs and computer programs) in present-day law. Reichman not only assumes that patents and copyright are opposites, he also assumes that the so-called 'classical model' (which is made up of industrial property on the one hand and literary and artistic copyright on the other) provides the foundation of twentieth-century law: J. Reichman, 'Legal Hybrids between the copyright and patent paradigms' (1992); id, 'Electronic Information Tools – The Outer Edge of World Intellectual Property Law' (1992) 17 *University of Dayton Law Review* 797.

[21] For example it was said in relation to the 1787 Calico Printers' Act that 'the basic question is raised: why should designs and models constitute a separate branch of industrial property at all [?] ... the regime of designs under this Act [are] similar to that of artistic property, but the references to invention and novelty are confusing': J. Lahore, *Intellectual Property Law in Australia: Patent, Designs and Trade Marks Law* (North Ryde: Butterworths, 1996), Service 36, para. 2.1.017. The reason for the 'confusion' is that design law is subjugated to artistic copyright (which was not recognised in law until 1862). In part, design law's diffuse identity can be explained by the fact that it has nearly always been defined in negative terms: in the ways in which it differs from patents and copyright.

flow from the marriage of these two areas:[22] hence the familiar (but historically inaccurate) suggestion that design law is the step-child of patents and copyright.[23]

Indigenous intellectual property law

Another important and enduring characteristic of the explanatory narratives which developed in the second part of the nineteenth century was that for the first time intellectual property law came to be defined *against* other legal systems: 'our' law was different from that in France, America and Russia.[24] The belief that the British style of intellectual property law was naturally and inevitably different from the approach adopted in other jurisdictions (an idea which has matured today as the sterile *copyright* v *droit d'auteur/Urheberrecht* debates) is in marked contrast to the situation in the eighteenth and early nineteenth centuries which saw a lot of cross-fertilisation between different legal cultures. Indeed, in the reports, Select Committees, commentaries, tracts and pamphlets of this period, references were frequently made to other legal systems, to how they protected intellectual property and to whether elements of those systems could be imported into Britain. (The primary source for inspiration was France for copyright and design law, and the United States for patents and trade marks – although this varied over time.)[25] Translations of non-English materials and regular reports from foreign envoys meant that the Board of Trade and Parliament as well as commentators and critics more generally had access to a wide variety of materials ranging from updates on Saxon copyright law, Prussian patent applications and the nature of the Belgian textile industry through to information on the book-buying habits of the residents of St Petersburg

---

[22] 'As the two systems [of patents and copyright] became more specialised and gradually grew apart, it became inevitable that a sort of intellectual property no man's land should separate them. The prime occupants of this no man's land were industrially exploited designs': J. Phillips and A. Firth, *Introduction to Intellectual Property Law* (3rd edn) (London: Butterworths, 1995), 338.

[23] Annette Kur offers a rare exception to this when she speaks of the 'unfortunate but common view that designs must belong either to the patent or the copyright side ... It was exactly this fruitless "patents versus copyright" dilemma which the authors of the [EC] Green Paper [on designs] have tried to escape in choosing a genuine designs approach'. See A. Kur, 'The Green Paper's Design Approach – What's Wrong with it' (1993) 10 *EIPR* 376.

[24] English law now differed 'materially from that of continental nations': W. Briggs, *The Law of International Copyright* (1906), v.

[25] On the impact of American trade marks law in the UK see L. Sebastian, *The Law of Trade Marks* (2nd edition)(1884). The 1911 Copyright Act was said to have closely followed the then existing American law: Sir H. Llewellyn Smith, 12 Dec. 1910, BT/209/477. On the lead offered by France and the United States in the reform of British patent law see T. Turner, *Remarks on the Amendment of the Law of Patents* (1851), 7.

and a translation of Kant's *Was ist ein Buch?*[26] The cross-fertilisation was reinforced by the fact that foreign parties were often involved in petitioning the UK parliament for changes in British law.[27]

In order for the idea of an indigenous, home-grown intellectual property law to be presentable, it had first to be purified. For this to happen it was necessary to ignore the various situations where foreign legal systems impacted on British intellectual property law. In some instances the process of purification was so successful that not only were all traces of foreign influences expunged from the history of British law, British law also came to be seen as the source of foreign intellectual property law. In the case of patents, for example, Gordon proclaimed in a flourish of national chauvinism earlier this century that the 'patent-laws of the world, numerous and various as they are, are all, directly and indirectly, derived from the Patent-law of this country' and that the 'germ of our Patent-law was conveyed with the common law which [countries around the world] inherited from the Motherland'.[28] In a move which reinforced the image of an insular legal regime it was also said that the system of property used in patent law was 'very clearly apprehended and consistently worked out by our own Common lawyers. But early in the history of the transplantation of Patent law to foreign countries, it became obscured by the Philosophising of other legislatures than our own.' That is, patent law, which was the gift of the English to the world, was now being tainted by (ungrateful) foreigners. If the formation of feral intellectual property laws in the colonies was not bad enough, it was even worse that the French, who had (so the argument went) borrowed their patent system from the British, 'substituted the theory of patents as an act of Royal bounty' with the more 'democratic view that an inventor had an inherent right in the ideas which were the creation of his own mind' – to fit within a Republican-

---

[26] Kant's ideas had also entered English-language journals by the 1840s. See L. Cushing, 'An Analysis of Kant's Doctrine of the Rights of Authors' (1840) 22 *American Jurist* 84.

[27] See, e.g., the evidence of Daniel Lee before the Select Committee on Copyright of Designs who was questioned as to the country of origin of the petitioners for reform: 1840 *Select Committee on Designs* 287 (Q. 4966 ff). The cross-fertilisation can be seen in the debates about the abolition of patents. In 1870, the recommendations for the abolition of patents for inventions made by Count von Bismark, the government of Prussia and Mr Flock (the Minister of Interior of the Netherlands) were published in the UK as Parliamentary Paper (1870) 61 *PP* 1. The arguments made before the Dutch parliament included references to the House of Commons debate and quoted Lord Stanley at length (29 May 1870). Later, the fact that the German government decided to reform rather than repeal its patent law was used as a reason for following a similar course in the UK.

[28] J. Gordon, 'Patent Law Reform' (30 Nov. 1906) 55 *Journal of the Society of Arts* 26. See also J. MacDonnell, *A Survey of Political Economy* (Edinburgh: Edmonston and Douglas, 1871), 399; 'British versus Foreign Patent Law' (26 Feb. 1904) 52 *Journal of the Society of Arts* 323.

based legal system. As well as making their way into American law, these ideas 'powerfully affected the patent legislation of the rest of the world' and also 'reacted upon the views and working theory of our own [British] courts'.[29] Similar changes occurred in copyright law where the 1710 Statute of Anne came to be represented not just as the origin of the British law but also as the world's first copyright Act.[30] In the same way to that in which the history of intellectual property law was cleansed of foreign influences, the categories of intellectual property law were also purified. While in the emergence of those categories there was a great deal of cross-fertilisation between *all* areas of intellectual property law, the explanatory narratives promoted the idea of separate and distinct histories for each of the areas of intellectual property law: a belief that there was little if any cross-fertilisation or influence between the different categories.

The image of a closed, insular and vernacular law continues to have an important impact on intellectual property law. While the perceived neutrality of science, trade and commerce makes it easier for patents to escape the confines of local culture,[31] the idea that copyright law (or more accurately the works that it protects) is inextricably linked to the idiosyncratic features of national culture has recently been considered to create a stumbling block to the harmonisation of copyright laws in Europe.[32] The image of an insular, home-grown law has also served to encourage the erroneous belief that many concepts are foreign and as such cannot be transplanted into English law. The image of a vernacular copyright can also be seen, without too much cynicism, to have

---

[29] J. Gordon, 'The Patents and Designs Act, 1907' (May 1910) 356 *The Law Magazine and Review* 289, 297–8. In an address on some possible improvements in British Patent Law before the Society of British Gas Industries, Dugald Clark said, 'to read the writings of one party, it would be imagined that here in England we have the worst patent law possible while the laws of America, Germany, France etc. are immeasurably superior to ours ... it should not be forgotten ... that the British patent laws form the model upon which the whole of the patent laws of the world have been framed ... in my opinion, our British patent laws are superior to those of any other country': BT/ 209/467.

[30] See, e.g., V. de Sanctis, 'The Development and the International Confirmation of Copyright' (1974) 79 *RIDA* 206.

[31] This is because of the belief that patents are more readily translated into a language or form that can cross boundaries.

[32] The European Commission decided to defer harmonising the originality requirement in copyright law because it is a cultural and local matter: 'the harmonisation of the originality criterion [would] prove to be an extremely difficult task, because the different applications of the criterion is based on different legal and not least cultural traditions': European Commission, *EC Green Paper on the Legal Protection of Industrial Designs*, Doc. III/F/5131/91, June 1991, para. 4.2.7. See further M. Moller, 'On the Subject of the Green Paper' (tr. M. Platt) (1989) 141 *RIDA* 22, 40; P. Legrand, 'Comparative Legal Studies and Commitment to Theory' (1995) *Modern Law Review* 269, n. 35.

prompted (or at least to have influenced) recent moves to treat intellectual property as a human right.[33] By simultaneously trading on the pathos and the perceived neutrality and universality of human rights, this approach can be seen as an attempt to escape the confines of local culture. Another technique which has been adopted to this end is to reconfigure copyright in economic terms. This provides both a means to speak to the commercially minded and also a standardised basis from which copyright and moral rights can be translated into different legal cultures.

The organisational narratives

A further notable feature of the post-identity memory which developed in the nineteenth century was that there was a change in the way the law was explained. As we have seen, under pre-modern intellectual property law (and in the formative years of modern intellectual property law) the quantity and later the quality of the mental labour embodied within what was taken as archetypical subject matter was used as the basis for explaining the way the categories were organised. We have also seen that, with the closure of the subject matter and the related exclusion of creativity from the law's immediate horizon, increased attention was given to the contribution made by the archetypical work to the reading public, the economy and so on. Alongside this growing concern with the macro-value of the subject matter, the law began to resort to what we would now term the principles and theory of intellectual property law in order to explain the way intellectual property law was organised – and it did so in a way it had never done before.[34]

Whether it was called theory or principle – the main difference between the two now being that principles are drawn from legal sources whereas theory tends to come from outside of law (usually from political philosophy) – the explanatory narratives presumed that intellectual property law could be reduced to a number of key ideas or concepts.[35] It

---

[33] Cf. the *John Huston* decision (Cour d'appel de Paris, 4 chambre, sect. B, 6 July 1989). On this see B. Edelman, 'Applicable Legislation Regarding Exploitation of Colourised US films in France: The John Huston Case' (1992) *IIC* 629. For an examination of recent attempts to treat intellectual property as a human right see M. Hilf and T. Oppermann, 'International Protection of Intellectual Property: a German Proposal' in (eds.) S. Chowdhury, E. Denters and P. de Waart, *The Right to Development in International Law* (Dordecht: Kluwer, 1992).

[34] 'Patent protection grew out of a practical need; theoretical justifications came later and varied according to times and fashions of thinking': J. Vojacek, *A Survey of the Principal National Patent Systems* (New York: Prentice Hall, 1936), 3.

[35] Patterson and Lindberg argue that there 'are seven interrelated principles of copyright which can be identified with reasonable certainty': L. Patterson and S. Lindberg, *The*

was also presumed that these ideas provided the foundation around which intellectual property law was organised. While the philosophical pedigree of British law is often said to be more humble (and pragmatic) than that of countries such as France and Germany, a notable feature of the explanatory narratives that formed with the emergence of modern intellectual property law was that they tended to prioritise intellectual factors over more mundane pragmatic concerns.

Although the law had long made use of principles as a way of explaining the form that it took,[36] it had never done so to the same degree as occurred in the second half of the nineteenth century. Philosophers and theorists did not attract the same degree of kudos then as they now do, but it is noteworthy that in the late nineteenth century jurists such as John Austin began to appear in textbooks in a way they had never done before.[37]

The belief that intellectual property law could be reduced to a core essence continues to exercise a powerful hold over present-day intellectual property law.[38] Indeed, commentators who are attracted by the prestige which is now attributed to theory regularly debate whether, for example, intellectual property law is based on natural rights or whether it is an artificial right created by legislature.[39] These principles also

Nature of Copyright (1991), 59. It has also been said that there 'are three broad theories that explain why ownership of intangible rights such as those protected by the Copyright Act should be considered private property. Copyright can be considered either (1) a "natural" right; (2) an artificial right created by the legislature and judiciary, or (3) a "personal" right integral to an artist's very identity': L. Lacey, 'Of Bread and Roses and Copyrights' (1989) *Duke Law Journal* 1539.

[36] As we have seen in the context of patents and designs, it was believed that, once identified, principles would be able to explain the shape of the law as well as ensuring that the appropriate subject matter was registered in the correct category.

[37] While in considering the nature of property and the way in which the grant of property was to be justified the odd reference was made to the likes of Puffendorf and Locke, the late nineteenth century was the first occasion in which theory, so called, was used to explain the shape that the law took. To the extent that it is possible to evaluate the claim which is frequently made concerning the impact of philosophy on the development of legal doctrine there is little, if any, evidence of direct cross-fertilisation.

[38] Patterson and Lindberg argue that 'only a unified theory of copyright can ensure that the rules relate to each other and to the whole in a consistent way, which is to say that only a unified theory can provide the needed basis for integrity in the law of copyright': L. Patterson and S. Lindberg, *The Nature of Copyright* (1991), 111. The absence of a unified theory of copyright is said to result in the use of legal fictions 'since an ambivalent theoretical foundation provides leeway for interpretation and therefore leads to a malleable concept subject to opportunistic modification': *ibid.*, 135.

[39] For example, Patterson says that the reason for what he calls the over-extension of copyright can be traced to the 'ambiguous, and therefore infirm, intellectual conception of copyright which is a product of the dispute as to whether copyright is the grant of a limited statutory monopoly or the natural-law property right of the author': L. Ray Patterson, 'Copyright Overextended: A Preliminary Inquiry into the Need for a Federal Statute of Unfair Competition' (1992) 17 *University of Dayton Law Review* 386. While

provide a common language which enables intellectual property law in different jurisdictions to be contrasted, thereby reinforcing the insularity of British law and also flattening out the nuances and subtleties of different legal cultures.[40]

Although the principles of intellectual property law played an important role in ensuring that the law was made more manageable, when it came to distinguishing the categories of intellectual property law a different logic was employed. More specifically, at the same time as intellectual property law came to take its now familiar shape, there was also a move away from attempts to explain the differences between the categories. Instead of focusing on *a priori* factors which were said to have given rise to the particular form that intellectual property took, there was a gradual acceptance of these categories; they were taken as givens. What we see in place of this was an increased reliance on obvious external differences that existed between the categories. Copyright was different from design law in that it arose automatically on creation and was not dependent on registration. Copyright was different from patents in that patents provided an absolute monopoly whereas copyright protection was limited to the copying of the work – and so on. Gradually, these external differences came to be treated as if they were causes for the separate categories. Copyright was different from design law *because* it arose automatically on creation and was not dependent on registration.[41] Copyright was different from patents *because* patents provided an absolute monopoly whereas copyright protection was limited to the copying of the work. In contemporary law, where this mode of analysis has become the primary basis for explaining and distinguishing the different categories of intellectual property,[42] it is

reference had long been made to the language and concepts of natural law, it was only with the shift towards principle and theory that the debate between natural law and positive law took on the position that it now occupies in intellectual property law. It is interesting that when natural law arguments were first explicitly used (at least in the way they are now employed), it was as a part of an attempt to regulate and govern colonial copyright (especially in Canada). For example, it was said that the idea, which was 'confirmed by International agreement, that copyright law involved the protection of literary and artistic property as a natural right of an author to the fruit of his labour', was used to argue that there was an obligation on all members of the Empire (viz. Canada) to recognise the 'natural rights of authors': 'Canadian Copyright' (Oct. 1895) 19 *The Chamber of Commerce Journal* 1.

[40] To this end we often read, for example, that 'the "droit d'auteur" system puts the emphasis on the principles of natural justice, the common law system on the economic argument and socialist system on the social argument': S. Stewart, *International Copyright* (1989), 6.

[41] See, e.g., H. MacQueen, *Copyright, Competition and Industrial Design* (2nd edn) (Edinburgh: Edinburgh University Press, 1995), 32.

[42] For example, in explaining why little progress had been made at the Third Congress of the Industrial Property Treaty in Brussels, it was said there 'are in fact two different

frequently said that there are two main distinguishing features of the various forms of intellectual property: the presence or absence of a registration system[43] and the nature of the protection offered (patent monopoly or copyright style).[44]

If we resist the temptation to rewrite history in this manner,[45] it becomes clear that monopoly and registration played, at best, a minor role in determining the distinctive character of the respective rights. For example, there is little evidence to suggest that the scope of protection granted played any role in influencing the categories: indeed, it was not until late in the nineteenth century that there was any consensus as to the scope of the property. Similarly, given that, at least until 1911, registration existed as a pre-requisite for protection for nearly all forms of intellectual property (including copyright), it is not possible to use this as a way of explaining the shape the law took. Any differences which did exist can be attributed to the nature of the property protected. As such, registration and the scope of property protected are better seen as products of differences, rather than as causes for the difference in the first place.[46]

---

currents of opinion; the first wishing to assimilate the laws protecting designs with the laws concerning the right of reproduction; the second, on the contrary, insisting on the maintenance of a system of deposit': *Industrial Property: Texts Adopted by the Third Congress of the Industrial Property*, Brussels, 21–7 June 1925, 11.

[43] In his taxonomy of intellectual property law, Bainbridge says that 'a practical distinction that can be used to subdivide the various [intellectual property] rights is whether there is a requirement for registration, that is whether the right is dependent upon the completion of formalities, or whether it automatically springs into life at a specified time'. This in turn was influenced by the nature of the right itself: 'the rights subject to formalities are generally monopolistic in nature': D. Bainbridge, *Intellectual Property Law* (3rd edn), (London: Pitman, 1996), 4–5.

[44] See, e.g., J. Lahore, *Intellectual Property Law in Australia* (1996), para. 2.1.005; Lord Bridge, *British Leyland v Armstrong Patents Co.* (1986) 1 All ER 855.

[45] For example, Lahore reads a modern concern with monopoly into the history of design law when he claims that the 1842 Designs Act 'clearly conferred a monopoly on the design proprietor for the first time'. This was 'despite the fact that the Act refers to "copyright" in designs': J. Lahore, *Intellectual Property Law in Australia* (1996), para. 2.1.019.

[46] It was not until the latter part of the nineteenth century that there was any degree of certainty as to what it meant to infringe patents, designs and copyright. Lord Blackburn highlighted this situation in relation to patents when he said, 'I do not think it would be material, in order to support an action for infringement of [the plaintiff's] property, to show it was knowingly infringed; whether it was done knowingly or not it would be equally an infringement of their property': *Nobel's Explosives Co. v Jones, Scott and Co.* (1882) LR Ch D 721, quoted in L. Edmunds, *The Law and Practice of Letters Patent for Inventions* (London: Sweet and Maxwell, 1890), 220.

The need to remember

The image of intellectual property law that developed during the nineteenth century and the narrative of identity which this engendered
played and continue to play an important role in the way we think about
and understand intellectual property law. For example, a number of the
traits associated with the copyright law that were imagined in the
nineteenth century continue to shape contemporary law. The romantic
image of a copyright law which is beyond the remit of trade and
commerce manifests itself, for example, in the discussions about how
applied art should be protected and in terms of the debate as to how the
overlap between copyright and design law should be managed. It also
plays an important role in shaping the arguments which focus on the
question of the proper place for computer programs within intellectual
property law. As the negotiations surrounding GATT/TRIPS have
shown, the notion of the vernacular and localised nature of copyright
works continues to have an important impact. The cultural dimension
of copyright law has also been highlighted in relation to the question of
indigenous intellectual property rights which was raised, for example, as
a consequence of the Australian High Court decision in *Mabo*.[47] If we
turn to consider patent law, the organisational narratives which have
been used to explain the law help to explain why it is that the law has
experienced so many difficulties in accommodating ethical concerns
into the patent process.[48]

The model of intellectual property law that took shape during the
nineteenth century not only plays an important role in influencing the
way we think of intellectual property law, it also restricts the questions
we ask about it. One of the consequences of a narrative which teaches us
that, within a historical context, intellectual property law is timeless,
natural and inevitable, and that it is driven by principle, is that it leads
us away from the changes that occurred over the course of the nineteenth century. Perhaps most importantly of all, the image that we have
of the law also limits what we imagine is possible and consequently what
we demand of the subject. While much energy in this area of law is taken
up with reform and harmonisation and, as such, is constantly concerned
with the future, there are many reasons why time should be taken to
consider the image of intellectual property law that shapes and informs

---

[47] See K. Puri, 'Copyright Protection for Australian Aborigines in the Light of Mabo' in
(eds.) M. Stephenson and S. Ratnapala, *Mabo: A Judicial Revolution: The Aboriginal
Land Rights Decision and Its Impact on Australian Law* (Brisbane: University of
Queensland Press, 1993).

[48] See L. Bently and B. Sherman, 'The Ethics of Patenting: Towards a Transgenic Patent
System' (1995) 3 *Medical Law Review* 275.

those discussions. Moreover, if the law is to achieve what we demand of it, it is not only necessary to recognise the influence that the various narratives in operation have upon the law, it is also important that we set about inventing new narratives. As intellectual property grapples with the issues that flow from its attempts to regulate digital technology and organic computing as well as indigenous artistic and cultural expression, these needs are as urgent and pressing as they ever were.

Bibliography

'A Few Words on International Copyright' (1852) 95 *Edinburgh Review* 148.

A Vindication of the Exclusive Rights of Authors to their own Works: A Subject now under Consideration before the Twelve Judges of England (London: Griffiths, 1762).

Abrams, H. 'The Historic Foundation of American Copyright Law: Exploding the Myth of Common Law Copyright' (1983) 29 *Wayne Law Review* 1120.

Abrams, M. *The Mirror and the Lamp* (New York: Oxford University Press, 1953).

An Enquiry into the Nature and Origin of Literary Property (London: Printed for William Flexney, 1762).

Anderson, B. *Imagined Communities: Reflections on the Origin and Spread of Nationalism* (London: Verso, 1983).

Armstrong, G. 'From the Fetishism of Commodities to the Regulated Market: The Rise and Decline of Property' (1987) 82 *Northwestern University Law Review* 79.

'Art. V: Publications of the Honourable Commissioners of Patents' (Jan. 1859) 105 *Quarterly Review* 136.

'Art. XII: Report from Select Committee on the Law relative to Patents for Inventions' (1835) 22 *The Westminster Review* 172.

Attorney-General's Department, Submission to House of Representative Standing Committee on Aboriginal and Torres Strait Islander Affairs: Culture and Heritage Inquiry (1 May 1995).

Australian Law Reform Commission, *Designs: Issues Paper 11* (Sydney: ALRC, 1993).

Bainbridge, D. *Intellectual Property Law* (3rd edn) (London: Pitman, 1996).

Barthes, R. *Roland Barthes* (tr. R. Howard) (London: Macmillan, 1977).

Bastide, F. 'The Iconography of Scientific Texts: Principles of Analysis' (tr. G. Myers) in (eds.) M. Lynch and S. Woolgar, *Representations in Scientific Practice* (London: MIT Press, 1990), 187.

Batzel, V. 'Legal Monopoly in Liberal England: The Patent Controversy in the Mid-Nineteenth Century' (1980) 22 *Business History* 189.

Becker, L. *Property Rights: Philosophic Foundations* (London: Routledge, 1977).

Bell, Q. *The Schools of Designs* (London: Routledge and Kegan Paul, 1963).

Benjamin, W. 'The Work of Art in the Age of Mechanical Reproductions' (tr. H. Zohn) in (ed.) H. Arendt, *Illuminations* (New York: Harcourt, Brace and World, 1968).

Bentham, J. *Manual of Political Economy* (ed. W. Stark) (London: George Allen and Unwin, 1952).

Bently L. and B. Sherman, 'The Ethics of Patenting: Towards a Transgenic Patent System' (1995) 3 *Medical Law Review* 275.

Bergeron, J. 'From Property to Contract: Political Economy and the Transformation of Value in English Common Law' (1993) 2 *Social and Legal Studies* 5.

Billing, S. and A. Prince, *The Law and Practice of Patents and Registration of Designs with the Pleadings and all the Necessary Forms* (London: Benning, 1845).

Birrell, A. *Seven Essays on the Law and History of Copyright in Books* (London: Cassel and Co., 1899).

Bismark, V. 'Patents for Inventions' (1870) 61 *PP* 1.

Blackstone, W. *Commentaries on the Laws of England* (London: A. Strahan, 1809).

Blagden, C. *The Stationers' Company: A History, 1403–1959* (London: Allen and Unwin, 1960).

Blaine, D. Robertson *Suggestions on the Copyright (Works of Art) Bill* (London: Robert Hardwicke, 1861).

Bougon J. *The Inventor's Vade Mecum: Memorandum on the Laws Effecting the Patents of Every Country* (London: Reeves and Turner, 1870).

Bourdieu, P. 'Codification' in *In Other Words: Essays Towards a Reflexive Sociology* (tr. M. Adamson) (Cambridge: Polity Press, 1990), 76.

Bowen, J. 'Notice Issued by the Registrar: Copyright of Designs for Articles of Utility' (1843) 2 *Repertory of Patent Inventions* 251.

Brace, G. *Observations on Extension of Protection of Copyright of Design, with a View to the Improvement of British Taste* (London: Smith, Elder and Co., 1842).

Brewer, J. *Three Sinews of Power: War, Money and the English State, 1688–1783* (London: Century Hutchinson, 1988).

Bridge Adams, W. 'Patent Laws' (21 Jan. 1871) 19 *Journal of the Society of Arts* 186.

'Proposed Bill for the Protection of Mental Property' (21 Oct. 1870) 18 *Journal of the Society of Arts* 186.

Briggs, W. *The Law of International Copyright (with Special Sections on the Colonies and the USA)* (London: Stevens and Haynes, 1906).

'British versus Foreign Patent Law' (26 Feb. 1904) 52 *Journal of the Society of Arts* 323.

Brown, L. 'The Board of Trade and the Tariff Problem, 1840–2' (1953) *English Historical Review* 394.

Bugbee, B. *The Genesis of American Patent and Copyright Law* (Washington, D.C.: Public Affairs Press, 1967).

Bulajic, M. 'International Protection of Intellectual Property in the Context of the Right to Development: Comment on the German Proposal' in (eds.) S. Chowdhury, E. Denters and P. de Waart, *The Right to Development in International Law* (Dordecht: Kluwer, 1992).

Burrow, J. *The Question Concerning Literary Property by the Court of Kings Bench on 20th April 1769, in the Case between Andrew Millar and Robert Taylor* (London: W. Strahan and M. Woodfall, 1773).

Campin, F. *Law of Patents for Inventions with Explanatory Notes on the Law as to the Protection of Designs and Trade Marks* (London: Virtue and Co., 1869).

'Canadian Copyright' (Oct. 1895) 19 *The Chamber of Commerce Journal* 1.

Carpmael, W. 'Copyright of Designs' (1843) 2 *Repertory of Patent Inventions* 250.

'Introductory Observations on the Law of Patents for Inventions' (1835) 3 *Repertory of Patent Inventions* 67.

'Registration of Designs' (1842) 17 *Repertory of Patent Inventions* 37.

'The Law of Patents for Inventions: Part III' (1835) 3 *Repertory of Patent Inventions* 242.

Law Reports of Patent Cases (London: MacIntosh, 1843).

Registration of Designs in order to Secure Copyright (3rd edn) (London: MacIntosh, 1846).

The Law of Patents for Inventions Familiarly Explained for the Use of Inventors and Patentees (6th edn) (London: Stephens, 1860).

Chapman, S. *The Cotton Industry in the Industrial Revolution* (London: Macmillan, 1972).

Chapman, S. and S. Chassagne, *European Textile Printers in the Eighteenth Century: a Study of Peel and Oberkamps* (London: Heinemann Educational, 1981).

Chartier, R. 'Figures of the Author' in (eds.) B. Sherman and A. Strowel, *Of Authors and Origins: Essays on Copyright Law* (Oxford: Clarendon Press, 1994), 7.

Clay, J. 'The Copyright of Designs, as Applicable to Articles of Textile Manufacture' (1859) *TNAPSS* 244.

Cliffe Leslie, T. 'The Law of Patents' (April 1865) 121 *Edinburgh Review* 578.

Cohen, E. *The Growth of the British Civil Service: 1780–1939* (London: Allen and Unwin, 1941).

Collier, J. *An Essay on the Law of Patents for New Inventions* (London: A. Wilson, 1803).

'Considerations [by the late Dr Johnson] on the Case of Dr. Trapp's Sermons, Abridged by Mr Cave' (July 1787) 57 *Gentleman's Magazine* 555.

Considerations on the Nature and Origin of Literary Property (Edinburgh: Alexander Donaldson, 1767) (attributed to J. MacLaurin, Lord Dreghorn).

Coombe, R. 'Challenging Paternity: Histories of Copyright' (1994) 6 *Yale Journal of Law and the Humanities* 397.

Copinger on Copyright (5th edn) (ed. J. Easton) (London: Stevens, 1915).

Copinger, W. *The Law of Copyright in Works of Literature and Art, including that of Drama, Music, Engraving, Sculpture, Painting, Photography and Ornamental and Useful Design* (London: William Clowes and Sons, 1870).

'Copyright' (25 March 1881) 29 *Journal of Society of Arts* 418.

Copyright Convergence Group, *Highways to Change: Copyright in the New Communications Environment* (Canberra: Microdata, 1994).

'Copyright Law Reform' (1910) 216 *Quarterly Review* 483.

Cornish, W. *Intellectual Property: Patents, Copyright, Trade Marks and Allied Rights* (3rd edn) (London: Sweet and Maxwell, 1996).

Coryton, J. *A Treatise on the Law of Letters-Patent for the Sole Use of Inventions in the United Kingdom of England and Ireland: To which is Added a Summary of the Patent Laws in Force in the Principal Foreign States* (London: H. Sweet, 1855).

Coulter, M. *Property in Ideas: The Patent Question in Mid-Victorian Britain* (Kirksville, Mo.: Thomas Jefferson University Press, 1991).

Craig, A. *Patents, Trade Marks and Designs* (London: Bazaar Office, 1879).

Cunynghame, H. *English Patent Practice* (London: William Clowes and Sons, 1894).

L. Cushing, 'An Analysis of Kant's Doctrine of the Rights of Authors' (1840) 22 *American Jurist* 84.

Daniel, E. *A Complete Treatise upon the New Law of Patents, Designs and Trade Marks* (London: Stevens, 1884).

Daniel, E. *The Trade Marks Registration Act 1875* (London: Stevens and Haynes, 1876).

Davies, J. *A Collection of the Most Important Cases Respecting Patents of Inventions* (London: W. Reed, 1816).

A Pamphlet on Patents (London: Weale, Simpkin and Co, 1850).

Davison L. and T. Keirn, 'The Reactive State: English Governance and Society 1688–1750' in (eds.) L. Davison, T. Hitchcock and R. Shoemaker, *Stilling the Grumbling Hive: The Response to Social and Economic Problems in England, 1688–1750* (Stroud, Glos. and New York: Alan Sutton and St Martins Press, 1992).

Dentith, S. 'Political Economy, Fiction and the Language of Practical Ideology in Nineteenth-century England' (1983) 8 *Social History* 183.

Derrida, J. 'Psyche: Inventions of the Other' in (eds.) Lindsay Waters and Wlad Godzich, *Reading de Man Reading* (Minneapolis: University of Minnesota Press, 1989), 25.

Dieckmann, H. 'Diderot's Conception of Genius' (1941) 11 *Journal of the History of Ideas* 151.

Dircks, H. *Statistics of Inventions Illustrating the Policy of a Patent Law* (London: E. and F. Spon, 1869).

Drahos, P. *A Philosophy of Intellectual Property Law* (Aldershot: Dartmouth, 1996).

Drewry C. *Observations on the Defects of the Law of Patents* (London: V. and R. Stephens and Sons, 1863).

The Patent Law Amendment Act (London: John Richards and Co., 1838).

Observations on Points Relating to the Amendment of the Law of Letters Patent (London: John Richards and Co, 1839).

The Law of Trade Marks (London: Knight and Co, 1878).

Dutton, H. *The Patent System and Inventive Activity during the Industrial Revolution 1750–1852* (Manchester: Manchester University Press, 1984).

Dworkin, G. 'Why are Registered Designs so Unpopular?' (Feb. 1993) *Intellectual Property Newsletter: Special Report No. 8* 1.

Edelman, B. 'Applicable Legislation Regarding Exploitation of Colourised US Films in France: The John Huston Case' (1992) *IIC* 629.

'Une loi substantiellement internationale. La Loi du 3 juillet sur les droits d'auteur et droits voisins' (1987) 114 *Journal de droit international* 567.

Ownership of the Image (tr. E. Kingdom) (London: Routledge and Kegan Paul, 1979).

Edmunds, L. *The Law and Practice of Letters Patent for Inventions* (London: Sweet and Maxwell, 1890).

The Law of Copyright in Designs (London: Sweet and Maxwell, 1895).

Edmunds, L. and H. Bentwich, *The Law of Copyright in Designs* (London: Sweet and Maxwell, 1908).

Eisenstein, E. *The Printing Press as an Agent of Change* (New York: Cambridge University Press, 1979).

Enfield, W. *Observations on Literary Property* (London: Johnson, 1774).

European Commission, *EC Green Paper on the Legal Protection of Industrial Designs*, Doc. III/F/5131/91, June 1991.

Evans, J. 'Change in the Doctrine of Precedent during the Nineteenth Century' in (ed.) L. Goldstein, *Precedent in Law* (Oxford: Clarendon, 1991).

Farrer, T. 'The Principle of Copyright' (1878) 24 *Fortnightly Review* 836.

Feather, J. 'The Publishers and the Pirates: British Copyright Law in Theory and Practice, 1710–1775' (1987) 22 *Publishing History* 5.

A History of British Publishing (London: Croom Helm, 1988).

Foreign Office, *Reports Relating to the Foreign Countries on the Subject of Trade Marks* (C 596) (London: Harrison and Sons, 1872).

Treaty Stipulation between Great Britain and Foreign Powers on the Subject of Trade Marks (C 633) (London: Harrison and Sons, 1872).

Foucault, M. *History of Sexuality*, vol. I (tr. R. Hurley) (New York: Pantheon, 1978).

Fraser, J. *Handy-Book of Patent and Copyright Law* (London: Sampson and Co., 1860).

Frost, R. *Patent Law and Practice* (London: Stevens and Haynes, 1891).

Gebauer, G. and C. Wulf, *Mimesis: Culture, Art, Society* (tr. D. Reneau) (Berkeley, Calif.: University of California Press, 1993).

Geller, P. 'Legal Transplants in International Copyright: Some Problems of Method' (1994) 13 *University of California at Los Angeles Pacific Basin Law Journal* 200.

'General Notes: Patent Office' (27 May 1887) 35 *Journal of the Society of Arts* 435.

Ginsburg, J. 'Creation and Commercial Value: Copyright Protection for Works of Information' (1990) 90 *Columbia Law Review* 1865.

Ginzburg, C. 'Clues: Roots of an Evidential Paradigm' in *Clues, Myths and the Historical Method* (tr. J. and A. Tedeschi) (Baltimore, Md.: Johns Hopkins University Press, 1989), 96.

Godson, R. 'Law of Patents' (19 Feb. 1833) 15 *Hansard* col. 974.

A Practical Treatise on the Law of Patents for Inventions and of Copyright (London: J. Butterworth, 1840).

A Practical Treatise on the Law of Patents for Inventions and of Copyright with an Introductory Book of Monopolies (London: Joseph Butterworth, 1823).

A Practical Treatise on the Law of Patents for Invention and of Copyright: Supplement (London: Benning and Co., 1844).

A Practical Treatise on the Law of Patents for Invention and of Copyright: Supplement (ed. P. Burke) (London: Benning and Co, 1851).

A Practical Treatise on the Law of Patents: A Supplement (London: J. Butterworth, 1832).

Goodman, D. 'Epistolary Property: Michel de Servan and the Plight of Letters on the Eve of the French Revolution' in (eds.) J. Brewer and S. Staves, *Early Modern Conceptions of Property* (London: Routledge, 1995), 339.

Gordon, J. 'Patent Law Reform' (30 Nov. 1906) 55 *Journal of the Society of Arts* 26.

'The Patents and Designs Act, 1907' (May 1910) 356 *The Law Magazine and Review* 289.

Gordon, R. 'Paradoxical Property' in (eds.) J. Brewer and S. Staves, *Early Modern Conceptions of Property* (London: Routledge, 1995), 95.

Greysmith, D. 'Patterns, Piracy and Protection in the Textile Printing Industry, 1787–1850' (1983) 14 *Textile History* 165.

Hancox, J. *The Queens Chameleon: The Life of John Byrom* (London: Jonathan Cape, 1994).

Hands, W. *The Law and Practice of Patents for Inventions* (London: W. Clarke, 1808).

Hargrave, F. *An Argument in Defence of Literary Property* (London: Otridge, 1774).

Harrison, J. 'Some Patent Practitioners Associated with the Society of Arts, *c.* 1790–1840' (July 1982) *Journal of the Royal Society of Arts* 494.

Hawes, W. 'On the Economical Effects of the Patent Laws' (1863) *TNAPSS* 830.

Hennessy, P. *Whitehall* (London: Secker and Warburg, 1989).

Hewish, J. *The Indefatigable Mr Woodcroft: The Legacy of Invention* (London: British Library, 1983).

Hilf M. and T. Oppermann, 'International Protection of Intellectual Property: a German Proposal' in (eds.) S. Chowdhury, E. Denters and P. de Waart, *The Right to Development in International Law* (Dordecht: Kluwer, 1992).

Hindmarch, W. *Observations on the Defects of the Patents Laws of this Country: With Suggestions for the Reform of them* (London: W. M. Benning and Co, 1851).

A Treatise on the Law Relating to Patent Privileges (London: Stevens, 1846).

Law and Practice of Letters Patent for Inventions (London: Stevens, 1848).

Hinton v Donaldson (1773) in *The Decision of the Court of Session upon the Question of Literary Property in the Cause of John Hinton, London Bookseller, against Alexander Donaldson, Bookseller in Edinburgh* (Edinburgh: Boswell, 1774).

HMSO, *Subject List of Works on the Laws of Industrial Property (Patents, Design and Trademarks) and Copyright* (London: Darling and Son, 1900).

Holdsworth, W. *A History of English Law*, vol. XI (London: Sweet and Maxwell, 1938).

Hoppitt, J. 'Patterns of Parliamentary Legislation, 1660–1880' (1996) 39 *History Journal* 109.

Hugenholtz, P. 'Protection of Compilations of Facts in Germany and the Netherlands' in (eds.) E. Dommering and P. Hugenholtz, *Protecting Works of Fact: Copyright, Freedom of Expression and Information Law* (Deventer: Kluwer, 1991), 59.

Hulme, E. 'Privy Council Law and Practice of Letters Patent for Inventions from the Restoration to 1794' (1917) 33 *LQR* 180.

Hunter, D. 'Copyright Protection for Engravings and Maps in Eighteenth Century England' (1987) 8 *Library* 128.

Hutcheson, J. 'The Judgement Intuitive: The Function of the "Hunch" in Judicial Decision' (1928) 16 *Cornell Law Quarterly* 274.

Huyssen, A. *After the Great Divide* (Bloomington: Indiana University Press, 1986).

Imray, J. 'Claims' (1887–8) 6 *Proceedings of the Institute of Patent Agents* 203.

Industrial Property: Texts Adopted by the Third Congress of the Industrial Property Treaty, Brussels, 21–7 June 1925.

Information for John Mackenzie of Delvin, Writer of the Signet, and others, Trustees appointed by Mrs Anne Smith, Widow of Mr Thomas Ruddiman, Late Keeper of the Advocates' Library, Pursuers against John Robertson, Printer in Edinburgh, Defender (30 Nov. 1771), *Lord Monboddo Reporter.*

Information for John Robertson, Printer in Edinburgh (Defender) against John Mackenzie of Delvin (10 Dec. 1771), *Lord Monboddo Reporter.*

Inlow, E. Burke, *The Patent Grant* (Baltimore, Md.: The Johns Hopkins Press, 1950).

Innes, J. 'Parliament and the Shaping of Eighteenth-century English Social Policy' (1990) 5th series 40 *Transactions of the Royal Historical Society* 63.

'Is Copyright Perpetual? An Examination of the Origin and Nature of Literary Property' (1875–6) 10 *American Law Review* 16.

Iselin, J. 'The Protection of Industrial Property' (18 Feb. 1898) 46 *Journal of the Society of Arts* 293.

Jackson, E. 'The Law of Trade Marks' (19 May 1899) 47 *Journal of the Society of Arts* 563.

Jehoram, H. C. 'Design Laws in Continental Europe and their Relation to Copyright Law' (1981) 8 *EIPR* 235.

'The EC Green Paper on the Legal Protection of Industrial Design. Halfway down the Right Track – A View from the Benelux' (1992) 3 *EIPR* 75.

Johnson, E. 'The Mercantilist Concept of "Art" and "Ingenious Labour"' (1931) 6 *Economic History* 234.

Johnson, S. *A Dictionary of the English Language* (1755) (London: Times Books, 1983)

Jones, R. 'The Myth of the Idea/Expression Dichotomy in Copyright Law' (1990) *Pace Law Review* 551.

Kaufman, P. 'Heralds of Original Genius' in *Essays in Memory of Barrett Wendell* (Cambridge, Mass.: Harvard University Press, 1926).

Kellett, J. 'The Breakdown of Guild and Corporation Control over the Handicraft and Retail Trade in London' (1957–8) 10 *Economic History Review* 381.

Kenrick, W. *An Address to the Artists and Manufacturers of Great Britain: Respecting an Application to Parliament for the Further Encouragement of New Discoveries and Invention in the Useful Arts* (London: Domville, 1774).

Kerly, D. *The Law of Trade-Marks, Trade Name, and Merchandise Marks* (2nd edn) (London: Sweet and Maxwell, 1901).

Kohler, J. *Autorrecht, eine zivilistische Abhandlung* (1880). Quoted in P. Bernt Hugenholtz, 'Protection of Compilations of Facts in Germany and the Netherlands' in (eds.) E. Dommering and P. Hugenholtz, *Protecting Works of Fact: Copyright, Freedom of Expression and Information Law* (Deventer: Kluwer, 1991), 59.

Kur, A. 'The Green Paper's Design Approach – What's Wrong With It' (1993) 10 *EIPR* 374.

Kusamitsu, T. 'The Industrial Revolution and Design' (PhD Thesis, Sheffield University, 1982).

Lacey, L. 'Of Bread and Roses and Copyrights' (1989) *Duke Law Journal* 1539

Ladas, S. *Patents, Trademarks, and Related Rights: National and International Protection*, vols. I–II (Cambridge, Mass.: Harvard University Press, 1975).

Lahore, J. 'Art and Function in the Law of Copyright and Designs' (1971) 4 *Adelaide Law Review* 182.

Intellectual Property Law in Australia: Patent, Designs and Trade Marks Law (North Ryde: Butterworths, 1996) Service 36.

Latour, B. 'Drawing Things Together' in (eds.) M. Lynch and S. Woolgar, *Representation in Scientific Practice* (London: MIT Press, 1990), 19.

Law, J. 'On the Methods of Long-distance Control: Vessels, Navigation and the Portuguese Route to India' in (ed.) J. Law, *Power, Action, and Belief* (London: Routledge, 1986).

'Law of Literary Property and Patents' (1829) 10 *Westminster Review* 444.

Lawson, W. *Patents, Designs and Trade Marks Practice* (London: Butterworths, 1884).

Legrand, P. 'Comparative Legal Studies and Commitment to Theory' (1995) 158 *Modern Law Review* 262.

'Letters Patent' (27 Oct. 1871) 19 *Journal of the Society of Arts* 846.

Leverson, M. *Copyright and Patents; or, Property in Thought, Being an Investigation of the Principles of Legal Science Applicable to Property in Thought* (London: Wildy and Sons, 1854).

Lloyd Wise, W. 'Patent Law' (19 Nov. 1880) 29 *Journal of the Society of Arts* 17.

Lloyd, E. 'Consolidation of the Law of Copyright' (28 June 1862) 6 *The Solicitors' Journal and Reporter* 626.

'On the Law of Trade Marks' (11 May 1861) 5 *Solicitors' Journal* 486.

'On the Law of Trade Marks: No. VIII' (27 July 1861) 5 *The Solicitors' Journal* 665.

Locke, J. *Two Treatises of Government* (1690) (ed. P. Laslett) (Cambridge: Cambridge University Press, 1967).

Longfield, A. 'William Kilburn and the Earliest Copyright Acts for Cotton Printing Designs' (1953) 45 *Burlington Magazine* 230.

'Lord John Manners's Copyright Bill for Consolidating and Amending the Law Relating to Copyright 1879' (22 Aug. 1879) 27 *Journal of the Society of Arts* 879.

Ludlow, H. and H. Jenkins, *A Treatise on the Law of Trade-Marks and Trade Names* (London: William Maxwell and Son, 1877).

Lukes, S. *Individualism* (Oxford: Basil Blackwell, 1985).

Macaulay, C. *A Modest Plea for the Property of Copy Right* (London: Printed by R. Cruttwell in Bath for E. and C. Dilly, 1774).

MacDonnell, J. *A Survey of Political Economy* (Edinburgh: Edmonston and Douglas, 1871).

Macfie, R. 'Miscellaneous' (1865) *TNAPSS* 261.

'The Law of Patents for Inventions' (1858) *TNAPSS* 147.

'The Patent Question' (1863) *TNAPSS* 818.

The Patent Question under Free Trade: A Solution of Difficulties by Abolishing or Shortening the Invention Monopoly and Instituting National Recompense (2nd edn) (London: W. J. Johnson, 1863).

Macfie, R. (ed.) *Copyright and Patents for Inventions: Pleas and Plans*, vols. I and II (Edinburgh: T. and T. Clark, 1879–83).

Machlup, F. and E. Penrose, 'The Patent Controversy in the Nineteenth Century' (1950) 10 *Journal of Economic History* 1.

Macleod, C. 'The Paradoxes of Patenting: Invention and its Diffusion in 18th- and 19th-Century Britain, France and North America' (1991) *Technology and Culture* 885.

Inventing the Industrial Revolution: The English Patent System 1660–1800 (Cambridge: Cambridge University Press, 1988).

MacQueen, H. *Copyright, Competition and Industrial Design* (2nd edn) (Edinburgh: Edinburgh University Press, 1995).

Maine, H. *Ancient Law* (London: Dent, 1917).

McKendrick, N. 'Josiah Wedgewood and Factory Discipline' (1961) *Historical Journal* 30.

Memorial for the Booksellers of Edinburgh and Glasgow Relating to the Process against them by Some of the London Booksellers (1774); reprint *The Literary Property Debate* (ed. S. Parks) (New York: Garland, 1974).

Memorial for the Booksellers of Edinburgh and Glasgow. The Decision of the Court of Session upon the Question of Literary Property in the Cause John Hinton against Alexander Donaldson per Lord Auchinleck (1774); reprint *The Literary Property Debate* (ed. S. Parks) (New York: Garland, 1974).

Memorial from Manufacturers of Norwich to Board of Trade (2 March 1838) BT/1/338 25G.

Miller, D. 'Into the Valley of Darkness: Reflections on the Royal Society in the Eighteenth Century' (1989) 27 *History of Science* 155.

Minute Book of the Law Society.

Moffatt, A. 'The Copyright Bill' (1898) 10 *Juridical Review* 161.

'What is an Author?' (1900) 12 *Juridical Review* 217.

Moller, M. 'On the Subject of the Green Paper' (tr. M. Platt) (1989) 141 *RIDA* 22.

Morrell J. and A. Thackray, *Gentlemen of Science: Early Years of the British Association for the Advancement of Science* (Oxford: Clarendon Press, 1981).

'Mr Mackinnon's New Patent Law Bill' (1839) 32 *Mechanics' Magazine* 351.

Murdoch, H. *Information respecting British and Foreign Patents, and the Registration of Designs* (2nd edn) (London: G. Briggs, 1867).

'New Patents Act' (4 Jan. 1884) 32 *Journal of the Society of Arts* 120.

'New Textiles Designs Committee' (1910) 21 (19) *The Manchester Chamber of Commerce Monthly Record* 265.

Newton, W. 'Copyright of Designs' (1840) 16 *The London Journal of Arts and Sciences* 95.

Norman, J. *A Treatise on the Law and Practice Relating to Letters Patent for Invention* (London: Butterworths, 1853).

Nowell-Smith, S. *International Copyright Law and the Publisher in the Reign of Queen Victoria* (Oxford: Clarendon Press, 1968).

O'Brien, C. *The British Manufacturers' Companion and Calico Printers' Assistant; Being a Treatise on Callico Printing, in all its Branches, Theoretical and Practical; with an Essay on Genius, Invention and Designing* (London: Printed for the Author and Sold by Hamilton and Co., 1795) (first published in 1789 as *The Calico Printers' Assistant from the First Operation of Designing Patterns, to the Delivery of Works for Sale* (London: Charles O'Brien, 1789).

Ong, W. *Orality and Literacy: The Technologizing of the Word* (London: Methuen and Co., 1988).

Oyama, S. *The Ontogeny of Information: Developmental Systems and Evolution* (Cambridge: Cambridge University Press, 1985).

Palmer, J. (11 Dec. 1874) 23 *Journal of the Society of Arts* 76.

Panofsky, E. *Idea: A Concept in Art Theory* (tr. J. Peake) (Columbia, S.C.: University of South Carolina Press, 1968).

'Patent Laws' (17 Nov. 1876) 25 *Journal of the Society of Arts* 11.

'Patents' (Jan. 1859) 105 *Quarterly Review* 136.

'Patents, Designs and Trade Marks' (June 1898) *The Chamber of Commerce Journal* 125.

Patterson, L. *Copyright in Historical Perspective* (Nashville, Tenn.: Vanderbilt University Press, 1968).

  'Copyright Overextended: A Preliminary Inquiry into the Need for a Federal Statute of Unfair Competition' (1992) 17 *University of Dayton Law Review* 385.

Patterson, L. and S. Lindberg, *The Nature of Copyright: A Law of Users' Rights* (Athens, Ga.: University of Georgia Press, 1991).

Pearsall Smith, L. 'Four Romantic Words' in *Words and Idioms: Studies on the English Language* (London: Constable and Co., 1925).

Peters, J. 'The Bank, the Press and the "Return of Nature": On Currency, Credit, and Literary Property in the 1690s' in (eds.) J. Brewer and S. Staves, *Early Modern Conceptions of Property* (London: Routledge, 1995), 365.

Phillips, C. *The Law of Copyright in Works of Art and in the Application of Designs* (London: Stevens and Haynes, 1863).

Phillips, J. and A. Firth, *Introduction to Intellectual Property Law* (3rd edn) (London: Butterworths, 1995).

Playfair, L. 'On Patents and the New Patents Bill' (1877) 1 *The Nineteenth Century* 315.

Pocock, J. *Virtue, Commerce and History* (Cambridge: Cambridge University Press, 1985).

Pollock, F. *On Torts* (12th edn) (London: Stevens and Sons, 1923).

Pottage, A. 'Autonomy of Property', paper presented to Hart Workshop, London, 1991.

  'The Originality of Registration' (1995) 15 *Oxford Journal of Legal Studies* 371.

Potter, E. *A Letter to Mark Phillips Esq MP in Reply to his Speech in the House of Commons, Feb. 9th 1841, on the Designs Copyright Bill* (Manchester: T. Forrest, 1841).

'Proposed Bills for the Protection of Mental Property' (21 October 1870) *Journal of Society of Arts* 186.

Prosser, R. 'Use of the Word "Patent"' (1840) 32 *Mechanics' Magazine* 740.

Puri, K. 'Copyright Protection for Australian Aborigines in the Light of Mabo' in (eds.) M. Stephenson and S. Ratnapala, *Mabo: A Judicial Revolution: The Aboriginal Land Rights Decision and Its Impact on Australian Law* (Brisbane: University of Queensland Press, 1993).

Rae, D. *Information for Mess. John Hinton and Attorney against Mess. Alexander Donaldson and Others* (2 Jan. 1773), *Lord Coalston Reporter.*

'Registration of Trade Marks in Colour: Part I' (5 Feb. 1881) *The Solicitors' Journal* 254.

Reichman, J. 'Electronic Information Tools – The Outer Edge of World Intellectual Property Law' (1992) 17 *University of Dayton Law Review* 797.

'Legal Hybrids between the Patent and Copyright Paradigms' in (eds.) W. Korthals *et al.*, *Information law Towards the 21st Century* (Deventer, Boston: Kluwer, 1992).

Remarkable Decisions of the Court of Session (1730–1752) (Edinburgh: A. Kincaid and J. Bell, 1766).

Report of Registrar of Designs to the Board of Trade Respecting the Origin, Nature and Tendency of the Designs Copyright Act (3 Nov. 1841), *Letters to the Board of Trade* BT/1/379.

'Review of Charles Babbage, *Reflexions on the Decline of Science in England, and on Some of its Causes*' (1830) 43 *Quarterly Review* 304.

Reynolds, J. *Discourses on Art* (1771) (ed. R. Wark) (New Haven: Yale University Press, 1959).

Rifkin, A. 'Success Disavowed: The Schools of Design in Mid-Nineteenth Century Britain' (1988) 1 *Design History* 89.

Riley M. 'Trade Marks' (31 July 1912) 23 *Manchester Chamber of Commerce Monthly Record* 198.

Robertson, J. 'Law Report of Registration' (1845) 5 *Repertory of Patent Inventions* 262.

(1839–40) 32 *Mechanics' Magazine* 221.

Robertson, G. *The Law of Copyright* (Oxford: Clarendon, 1912).

Robertson, W. Wybrow, 'On Trade Marks' (23 April 1869) 17 *Journal of the Society of Arts* 414.

Robinson, A. 'The Evolution of Copyright, 1476–1776' (1991) *Cambrian Law Review*, 67.

Robinson, E. 'James Watt and the Law of Patents' (1971) 12 *Technology and Culture* 115.

'The Early Diffusion of Steam Power' (1972) 34 *Journal of Economic History* 91.

Robinson, E. and A. Musson, *James Watt and the Steam Revolution: A Documentary History* (New York: A. M. Kelley, 1969).

Rogers, J. 'On the Rationale and Working of the Patent Laws' (1863) 26 (2) *Journal of the Statistics Society* 125.

Rose, M. 'The Author as Proprietor: *Donaldson v Becket* and the Genealogy of Modern Authorship' in (eds.) B. Sherman and A. Strowel, *Of Authors and Origins: Essays on Copyright Law* (Oxford: Clarendon Press, 1994), 23.

'The Author in Court: *Pope v Curll* (1741)' (1992) 10 *Cardozo Arts and Entertainment Law Review* 475.

Authors and Owners: The Invention of Copyright (Cambridge, Mass.: Harvard University Press, 1993).

'Authority and Authenticity: Scribbling Authors and the Genius of Print in Eighteenth-Century England' (1992) 10 *Cardozo Arts and Entertainment Law Journal* 495.

Ross, T. 'Copyright and the Invention of Tradition' (1992) 26 *Eighteenth Century Studies* 1.

Rudwick, M. 'The Emergence of a Visual Language for Geological Sciences: 1760–1840' (1976) 14 *History of Science* 148.

Ryan, A. *Property and Political Theory* (Oxford: Basil Blackwell, 1984).

Ryland, A. 'The Fraudulent Imitation of Trade Marks' (1859) *TNAPSS* 229.

Sanctis, V. de, 'The Development and the International Confirmation of Copyright' (1974) 79 *RIDA* 206.

Saunders, D. *Authorship and Copyright* (London: Routledge, 1992).

Schechter, F. *The Historical Foundations of the Law Relating to Trade Marks* (New York: Columbia University Press, 1925).

Schroder, J. 'Observations on Mr Mackinnon's Bill' (1837) 10 *The London Journal of Arts and Sciences* 108.

Scrutton, T. *The Law of Copyright* (3rd edn) (London: William Clowes and Sons, 1896).

The Laws of Copyright: An Examination of the Principles which Regulate Literary and Artistic Property in England and Other Countries (London: John Murray, 1883).

Sebastian, L. *The Law of Trade Marks and their Registration, and Matters Connected therewith* (London: Stevens and Sons, 1878).

The Law of Trade Marks and their Registration, and Matters Connected therewith (2nd edn) (London: Stevens and Sons, 1884).

Seville, C. 'Principle or Pragmatism ? The Framing of the 1842 Copyright Act' (PhD Thesis, University of Cambridge, 1996).

Sherman, S. 'Printing the Mind: The Economics of Authorship in *Areopagitica*' (1993) 60 *English Literary History* 323.

Shortt, J. *The Law Relating to the Works of Literature and Art* (London: Horace Cox, 1871).

Simpson, A. 'The Rise and Fall of the Legal Treatise: Legal Principles and the Forms of Legal Literature' in *Legal Theory and Legal History: Essays on the Common Law* (London: The Hambeldon Press, 1987), 273.

Slater, J. *The Law Relating to Copyright and Trade Marks Treated more Particularly with Reference to Infringement* (London: Stevens and Sons, 1884).

Smith, A. *The Wealth of Nations* (1776) (ed. Edwin Cannan) (London: Grant Richards, 1904).

Smity, H. Llewellyn, *The Board of Trade* (London: Puttnams, 1928).

Society for Promoting Amendment of the Law, *Annual Report 1860–1* (London: McCorquodale and Co, 1861).

Speakman, W. 'Copyright Act: Designs' (31 May 1912) 23 (5) *Manchester Chamber of Commerce Monthly Record* 141.

Spectator, 'The Unanswered Charges of Piracy Against Mr S. Hutchinson – The State of English Patent Law' (1839–40) 32 *Mechanics' Magazine* 390.

Spence, W. 'Patents as Channels of Industry' (1868) *TNAPSS* 256.

A Treatise on the Principles Relating to a Specification of a Patent for Inventions (London: Stevens, 1847).

Copyright of Designs as Distinguished from Patentable Inventions (London: Stevens and Norton, 1847).

The Public Policy of a Patent Law (London: Printed for the Author and sold at 8 Quality Court, 1869).

Stearns, L. 'Copy Wrong: Plagiarism, Process, Property, and the Law' (1992) 80 *California Law Review* 513.

Stewart, S. *Crimes of Writing: Problems in the Containment of Representation* (New York: Oxford University Press, 1991).

International Copyright and Neighbouring Rights Law and Practice (London: Butterworths, 1989).

Symonds, [no initial], 'Summary of Proceedings of the Trade and International Law Department: Patent Law' (1862) *TNAPSS* 884.

Temple Franks W. 'The Protection Afforded to Artistic Designs' (30 June 1910) 21 *The Manchester Chamber of Commerce Monthly Record* 165.

Terrell, T. *Law and Practice Relating to Letters Patent for Inventions* (3rd edn) (rev. W. Rylands) (London: Sweet and Maxwell, 1895).

'The Benefit of a Patent-Law' (13 July 1877) 25 *Journal of the Society of Arts* 818.

'The Bill for Amending the Patent Laws' (1833) 19 *Mechanics' Magazine* 302.

The Cases of Appellants and Respondents in the Cause of Literary Property before the House of Lords (London: Printed for J. Bew, 1774).

'The Copyright Bill' (30 Sept. 1911) 22 (9) *The Manchester Chamber of Commerce Monthly Record* 259.

'The Copyright Question' (1841–2) 49 *Quarterly Review* 186.

'The Government Patents Bill in its Relation to Trade Marks' (7 April 1883) 74 *The Law Times* 404.

'The Law of Copyright and Designs' (31 Jan. 1911) 22 (1) *The Manchester Chamber of Commerce Monthly Record* 4.

'The Law of Trade Marks' (18 Jan. 1879) 2 *The Legal News* 25.

'The Proposed Legislation as to Designs and Trade Marks: Part III' (12 May 1883) 27 *Solicitors' Journal* 464.

'The Protection Afforded to Artistic Designs' (30 June 1910) *The Manchester Chamber of Commerce Monthly Record* 165.

Thomson, J. *A Letter to the Right Honourable Sir Robert Peel, on Copyright in Original Designs and Patterns for Printing* (London: Smith, Elder and Co, 1840).

A Letter to the Vice President of the Board of Trade on Protection to Original Designs and Patterns, Printed upon Woven Fabrics (2nd edn) (Clitheroe: H. Whalley, 1840).

'Title to Sue for the Protection of Industrial Property' (1892) 36 *Solicitors' Journal* 213.

Tompson, R. 'Scottish Judges and the Birth of British Copyright' (1992) *Juridical Review* 18.

Toulmin, H. 'Protection of Industrial Property: Monopolies Granted by Governments' (1915) 3 *Virginia Law Review* 163.

'Trade Marks' (31 July 1912) *Manchester Chamber of Commerce Monthly Record* 198.

'Trade Marks: Classification' (30 Sept. 1913) 24 (9) *The Manchester Chamber of Commerce Monthly Record* 253.

Trueman Wood, H. 'The Patents for Inventions Bill, 1877' (9 March 1877) 25 *Journal of the Society of Arts* 339.

'The Registration of Trade Marks' (26 Nov. 1875) 24 *Journal of the Society of Arts* 17.

Turner, T. *Counsel to Inventors of Improvements in the Useful Arts* (London: Elsworth, 1850).

On Copyright in Design in Art and Manufactures (London: Elsworth, 1849).

Remarks on the Amendment of the Law of Patents for Inventions (London: Elsworth, 1851) .

Underdown, E. *The Law of Artistic Copyright: The Engraving, Sculpture and Designs Acts, the International Copyright Act and the Artistic Copyright Act 1862* (London: John Crockford, 1863).

'Unreasonableness of Judge-made Law in Setting Aside Patents' (1835) 22 *Westminster Review* 447.

Unwin, G. *The Guilds and Companies of London* (4th edn) (London: Frank Cass and Co, 1963).

Van Zyl Smit, D. 'Professional Patent Agents and the Development of the English Patent System' (1985) 13 *International Journal of the Sociology of Law* 79.

'The Social Creation of a Legal Reality: A Study of the Emergence and Acceptance of the British Patent System as a Legal Instrument for the Control of New Technology' (PhD Thesis, University of Edinburgh, 1980).

Vojacek, J. *A Survey of the Principal National Patent Systems* (New York: Prentice Hall, 1936).

Waggett, J. *The Law and Practice Relating to the Prolongation of the Term of Letters Patent for Invention* (London: Butterworths, 1887).

Wallace, R. and J. Williamson, *The Law and Practice Relating to Letters Patent for Inventions* (London: William Clowes and Sons, 1900).

Wallace, W. 'Protection for Designs in the United Kingdom' (1975) 22 *Bulletin of the Copyright Society of the USA* 437.

Warburton, W. *A Letter from an Author to a Member of Parliament concerning Literary Property* (London: John and Paul Knapton, 1747).

Webster, T. 'On the Protection of Property in Intellectual Labour as Embodied in Inventions, Books, Designs and Pictures, by the Amendment of the Laws of Patent-right and Copyright' (1859) *TNAPSS* 237.

Webster, T. *On the Subject Matter, Title and Specification of Letters Patent for Inventions and Copyright of Designs for Articles of Manufacture* (London: Elsworth, 1848).

Webster, T. *Counsel to Inventors of Improvements in the Useful Arts* (London: Elsworth, 1850).

Webster, T. in (ed.) H. Dircks, *Statistics of Inventions Illustrating a Patent Law* (London: E. and F. Spon, 1869), 45.

On Property in Designs and Inventions in the Arts and Manufactures (London: Chapman and Hall, 1853).

The Law and Practice for Letters Patent for Inventions (London: Crofts and Blenkman, 1841).

The Subject Matter of Letters Patent for Inventions and the Registration of Designs (3rd edn) (London: Elsworth, 1851).

Whicher, J. 'The Ghost of *Donaldson* v *Beckett*' (1962) 9 *Bulletin of the Copyright Society of USA* 102.

Wittkower, R. 'Imitation, Eclecticism and Genius' in (ed.) E. Wasserman, *Aspects of the Eighteenth Century* (Baltimore, Md.: Johns Hopkins University Press, 1965), 143.

Woodmansee, M. 'The Genius and the Copyright: Economic and Legal Conditions of the Emergence of the "Author"' (1984) 17 *Eighteenth-Century Studies* 425.

Yeo, R. 'Ephraim Chambers' *Cyclopedia* (1728) and the Tradition of Commonplaces' (March 1996) *Journal of the History of Ideas* 157.
'Reading Encyclopaedia: Science and the Organisation of Knowledge in British Dictionaries of Arts and Sciences, 1730–1850' (1991) 82 *ISIS* 24.

Zionkowski, L. 'Aesthetics, Copyright and the Goods of the Mind' (1992) 15 *British Journal for Eighteenth Century Studies* 167.

SELECT COMMITTEES

Abbreviated titles and Command Paper numbers, where appropriate, are given in parentheses.

1829 *Report from the Select Committee Appointed to Inquire into the Present State of the Law and Practice Relative to the Granting of Patents for Inventions* 3 *PP* (332) (1829 *Select Committee on Patents*).

1831 *Minutes of Evidence Before Select Committee on Manufactures, Commerce and Shipping* 6 *PP* 240 (690).

1831 *Report from the Select Committee on Dramatic Literature* 7 *PP* 1 (679).

1836 *Report of the Select Committee on Arts and their Connexion with Manufactures* 9 *PP* 18 (568) (1836 *Select Committee on Arts and Manufactures*).

1840 *Report from the Select Committee on Copyright of Designs* 6 *PP* (442) (1840 *Select Committee on Designs*).

1849 *Report of the Committee Appointed by the Lords of the Treasury on the Signet and Privy Seal Office* 22 *PP* (1099) (1849 *Report of the Committee on the Signet and Privy Seal Office*)

1851 *Select Committee of the House of Lords Appointed to Consider the Bills for the Amendment of the Law Touching Letters Patent for Inventions* 18 *PP* (486) (1851 *Select Committee on Patents*).

1862 *Report from the Select Committee on Trade Marks Bill, and Merchandise Marks Bill: Together with the Proceedings of the Committee, Minutes of Evidence* 12 *PP* (212). (1862 *Select Committee on Trade Marks*).

1864 *Report of the Commissioners Appointed to Inquire into the Working of the Law Relating to Letters Patent for Inventions* 29 *PP* (5974) (1864 *Report on Letters Patent for Inventions*).

1864 *Report from the Select Committee on the Copyright (No. 2) Bill* 9 *PP* (441) .

1871 *Report from the Select Committee on Letters Patent* 10 *PP* (3681).

1872 *Report from the Select Committee on Letters Patent* 11 *PP* (193).

1878 *Report of the Royal Commissioners on Copyright of 1878* 24 *PP* (C 2036).

1887 *Report of the Committee Appointed by the Board of Trade to Inquire into the Duties, Organisation and Arrangements of the Patent Office under the Patents, Designs and Trade Marks Act 1883 Having Special Regard to the System of Examination of the Specifications which Accompany Applications for Patents now in Force under the Act* 66 PP (C 4968).

1888 *Report of the Committee Appointed by the Board of Trade to Inquire into the Duties, Organisation and Arrangements of the Patent Office under the Patents, Designs and Trade Marks Act, 1883, so far as Relates to Trade Marks and Designs* 81 PP (C 5350) (1888 *Patent Office Inquiry*).

1894 *Special Report from the Select Committee on the Patent Agents' Bill* 14 PP (235).

1897 *Report from the Select Committee on Merchandise Marks* 11 PP (346).

1898 *Report from the Select Committee of the House of Lords on the Copyright Bill (HL) and the Copyright Amendment Bill (HL)* 9 PP (393).

1899 *Report from the Select Committee of the House of Lords on the Copyright Bill (HL) and the Copyright (Artistic) Bill (HL)* 8 PP (362).

1900 *Report from the Select Committee of the House of Lords on the Copyright Bill (HL) and the Copyright (Artistic) Bill (HL)* 6 PP (377).

1910 *Report of the Committee on the Law of Copyright (1909) (Cd 4976) with Minutes of Evidence (1910)* 21 PP (Cd 5051) (1910 *Gorrell Report*)

1910 *Report of the Committee on the Law of Copyright Cd 4976; Minutes of Evidence taken before the Law of Copyright Committee. Sessional Papers* 21 PP (241).

Index

abridgements, 55
aesthetics of law, *see* law, form of
Arts and Manufacture: Select Committee
    on Arts and Manufactures (1836),
    104
Austin, John, 216
Australia, 127, 206, 211
author
  as individual, 35
  collaborative nature of authorship,
    37–8
  detachment from work, 200
  invention of, 36
autopoesis, 57

Babbage, Charles, 102
Baines, Edward, 104, 105
Barlow, John Perry, 1, 5
Bastide, F., 49
Bentham, Jeremy, 9
Berne Convention (1886), 124, 162
Blackstone William, 21, 53 n. 34, 147 n. 24
book trade, 12, 36, 39, 118 n. 83
  regulation of, 11
Boulton and Watt v *Bull* (1795), 46, 108
  Buller, Justice, 46
Brougham, Lord Chancellor, 103
bureaucratic property, 71
  see also registration

calico printers, 67–73
  of London, 63
  see also design
Carpmeal, William, 189
categories of intellectual property law, see
  intellectual property law
codification, 62, 121, 135
Collier, J., 107
colonies and dominions, 112, 136
  feral laws, 136
  Imperial Copyright Conference, 136
commodification, 50
common law copyright, 13

Common Law Procedure Act (1852), 191
common property, 28
copies, 55
compilations, 55
Comptroller-General of Patents, 51, 162,
  166
copies, 55
Copinger, W., 53
copyright law
  Artistic Copyright, 127
  attempts at reform, 136–7
  automatic protection 164
  codification, 135
  compared with patent law, 153–7
  crystallisation of, 111–28
  cultural nature of 125
  emergence of, 111–28
    role of text book, 111
    role of legislative reform, 111
    role of bilateral treaties, 111–28
  entrenchment of, 128, 137–40
  for art and not trade, 161, 163
  glorious muddle, 135, 217
  images of, 119–25
  non-commercial nature of, 124–5
  overlap with design, 123–4, 163–5, 166
  pre-modern nature of, 192–3
  see also literary property
copyright legislation
  Copyright Act (1911), 128, 129, 135,
    137
  Copyright Amendment Act (1842), 116
  Copyright of Designs Act (1839), 64, 65,
    70
  Fine Arts Copyright Act (1862), 127
  Fine Arts Copyright Bill (1862), 184
  International Copyright Act (1838), 114,
    115, 116, 117
  International Copyright Act (1844), 114,
    115, 116
  Literary Property Act, 208
  Statute of Anne (1710), 12, 36, 40, 74,
    135, 207, 208, 210, 214

Printed in the United Kingdom
by Lightning Source UK Ltd.
104008UKS00001B/58